MW00680014

Chinatown, Europe

Is Chinatown a ghetto, an area of exotic sensations or a business venture? What makes a European Chinese, Chinese?

The histories of Chinese communities in Europe are diverse, spanning (amongst others) Teochiu-speaking migrants from French Indochina to France, and Hakka- and Cantonese-speaking migrants from Hong Kong to Britain. This book explores how such a wide range of people tends to be – indiscriminately – regarded as 'Chinese'.

Christiansen explains Chinese communities in Europe in terms of the interaction between the migrants, the European 'host' societies and the Chinese 'home' where the migrants claim their origin. He sees these interactions as addressing several issues: citizenship, political culture, labour market exclusion, generational shifts and the influences of colonialism and communism, all of which create opportunities for fashioning a new ethnic identity. *Chinatown, Europe* examines how many sub-groups among the Chinese in Europe have developed in recent years and discusses many institutions that shape and contribute ethnic meaning to Chinese communities in Europe.

Chinese identity is not a mere practical utility or a shallow business emblem. For many, China remains a unifying force while local and national bonds in each European state are of equal importance in giving shape to Chinese communities. Based on in-depth interviews with overseas Chinese in many European cities, *Chinatown, Europe* provides a complex yet enthralling investigation into many Chinese communities in Europe.

Flemming Christiansen teaches Chinese Studies at the University of Leeds.

Chinese Worlds

Chinese Worlds publishes high-quality scholarship, research monographs, and source collections on Chinese history and society. 'Worlds' signals the diversity of China, the cycles of unity and division through which China's modern history has passed, and recent research trends toward regional studies and local issues. It also signals that Chineseness is not contained within borders – ethnic migrant communities overseas are also 'Chinese worlds'.

The series editors are Gregor Benton, Flemming Christiansen, Delia Davin, Terence Gomez and Frank Pieke.

The Literary Fields of Twentieth-Century China
Edited by Michel Hockx

Chinese Business in Malaysia
Accumulation, ascendance, accommodation
Edmund Terence Gomez

Internal and International Migration
Chinese perspectives
Edited by Frank N. Pieke and Hein Mallee

Village Inc.
Chinese rural society in the 1990s
Edited by Flemming Christiansen and Zhang Junzuo

Chen Duxiu's Last Articles and Letters, 1937–1942
Edited and translated by Gregor Benton

Encyclopedia of the Chinese Overseas
Edited by Lynn Pan

New Fourth Army
Communist resistance along the Yangtze and the Huai, 1938–1941
Gregor Benton

A Road is Made
Communism in Shanghai 1920–1927
Steve Smith

The Bolsheviks and the Chinese Revolution 1919–1927
Alexander Pantsov

Chinas Unlimited
Gregory Lee

Friend of China – The Myth of Rewi Alley
Anne-Marie Brady

Birth Control in China 1949–2000
Population policy and demographic development
Thomas Scharping

Chinatown, Europe
An exploration of overseas Chinese identity in the 1990s
Flemming Christiansen

Financing China's Rural Enterprises
Jun Li

Confucian Capitalism
Souchou Yao

Chinese Business in the Making of a Malay State, 1882–1941
Kedah and Penang
Wu Xiao An

Chinatown, Europe

An exploration of overseas Chinese identity in the 1990s

Flemming Christiansen

RoutledgeCurzon
Taylor & Francis Group

LONDON AND NEW YORK

First published 2003
by RoutledgeCurzon, an imprint of Taylor & Francis
11 New Fetter Lane, London EC4P 4EE

Simultaneously published in the USA and Canada
by RoutledgeCurzon
29 West 35th Street, New York, NY 10001

RoutledgeCurzon is an imprint of the Taylor & Francis Group

Typeset in Baskerville by
HWA Text and Data Management Ltd, Tunbridge Wells
Printed and bound in Great Britain by
Antony Rowe Ltd, Chippenham, Wiltshire

British Library Cataloguing in Publication Data
A catalogue record for this book is available from the British Library

Library of Congress Cataloging in Publication Data
Christiansen, Flemming, 1954–
   Chinatown, Europe : an exploration of overseas Chinese identity in
   the 1990s / Flemming Christiansen.
      p. cm.
   Includes bibliographical references and index.
      1. Chinese–Europe–Social conditions. 2. Chinese–Europe–Ethnic
   identity. 3. Europe–Ethnic relations. I. Title.

   D1056.2.C55C49 2003
   305.895'104'09049–dc21   2002037047

ISBN 0–7007–1072–8

Contents

Preface

This book seeks to understand how the identity of the overseas Chinese in Europe is structured and changes over time, by examining the main factors that may influence it. It also asks whether there exists a pan-European Chinese identity. This question is, in a sense, frivolous and naive, for one can hardly expect a sensible answer to it. But in another sense it is a central and relevant question with which to begin an examination of how overseas Chinese in European countries fare. They live in countries that treat their ethnic minorities, immigrants, resident 'foreigners' or 'strangers' differently. At the same time the European member states converge into a European super-polity that provides new rights for ethnic groups. China's strengthening in the 1980s and 1990s has inspired the increasing integration of overseas Chinese communities across borders, both within Europe and beyond. One notion that underlies most of this book is that overseas Chinese communities in Europe interact across borders and other lines of division.

The main viewpoint of the research is that *major social actors create ethnic identity in interaction among groups whose rights or access to political, social and economic resources are determined by their ethnic background*. The focus is thus on *interaction* between and within ethnic groups (Barth 1969), the *competition* for economic, social and symbolic resources (Bourdieu 1977), and the *construction* of ethnic identity as a collective response to forces in the economic and political environment.

The book draws on 65 detailed interviews with overseas Chinese in different European countries. These interviews were taken in 1996 by Liang Xiujing, sometimes alone, and sometimes with my participation. They were taken in Mandarin or Cantonese, and transcribed into Chinese text. I used the software package NVivo 1.0 from QSR to extract meaning from the interviews. I have anonymised references to and quotations from the interviews, and do not list them lest somebody attribute statements to individual interviewees.[1] The overseas Chinese community is focused on the initiative and creativity of individuals, and many of the interviewees were keen to be cited without restriction and with full attribution. However, others talked in confidence; interviewees may also find that their words said in the context of an interview in 1996 do not reflect their thinking today. No person interviewed or providing information for this book can in any way be made morally, politically or otherwise responsible for any statement made or conclusion drawn in this book.

The research for this book was conducted under the Pacific Asia Programme of the Economic and Social Research Council.[2] The research project was carried out jointly with Professor Gregor Benton, who was my colleague at Leeds and later moved to the University of Wales at Cardiff. Gregor Benton was involved in designing and discussing topics related to the research, and he has given advice on and made corrections to the manuscript. After his involvement with the manuscript, I have changed so much that it is more than a matter of form to say that I am solely responsible for any shortcomings in any part of the book. His support and knowledge have been invaluable for the project.

Liang Xiujing carried out all the interviews and was instrumental in operationalising the research in its early phases. She has laid most of the empirical basis for the research. Without her help, the book would never have been written.

More than one hundred overseas Chinese in all parts of Europe have contributed material used in this book, in the form of interviews, pieces of information, advice, clippings, and written accounts. Without their ready and cordial cooperation this research would not have come true. I am also grateful to officials in the Overseas Chinese Affairs Office under the State Council of the People's Republic of China for informal discussions, to officials of the Overseas Chinese Affairs Commission in Taibei for materials and information, and to Peter Ma of the Hong Kong Representative Office in London who agreed to an interview on the eve of closing down his function and leaving for Hong Kong.

Writing the book I have profited from a six months' leave spent as Visiting Professor at the School for Postgraduate Interdisciplinary Research on Interculturalism and Transnationality (SPIRIT) at Aalborg University, and from a year spent at the Department of East Asian Studies at Aarhus University. Most important for my work, however, has been the fertile and creative intellectual environment of the Department of East Asian Studies at the University of Leeds.

In this book, the Hanyu Pinyin transcription is generally used for transliterating Chinese terms. Chinese expressions that have general currency in Europeanised forms have been retained in those forms, because their use is semantically divorced from the Chinese. For example, Cantonese, Teochiu, Hakka and Hokkien in the European form signify both a dialect group as well as a person speaking the dialect or belonging to a community of such speakers. Names of overseas Chinese are given in the western form (where known), with the Hanyu Pinyin transcription (where known) on the first appearance. Names of Taiwanese and Hong Kong persons are given in Hanyu Pinyin with the westernised form (where known) on the first apperance. The names Sun Yat-sen (Sun Zhongshan, Sun Yixian) and Chiang Kai-shek (Jiang Jieshi) are given only in the western versions, which are based on local pronunciation in China. Chinese geographical names are in Hanyu Pinyin, except Hong Kong (Xianggang) and Macau (Aomen). Names of overseas Chinese and Hong Kong organisations are given in the European form (where known), with the Chinese name in Hanyu Pinyin transcription on the first occurrence. Names of overseas Chinese newspapers often have hybrid titles in characters and the local European language; these titles are retained, transliterating characters into Hanyu Pinyin, where the European name does not include a different trans-literation of the characters (e.g. *Ouzhou Shibao – Nouvelles d'Europe*, but *Sing Tao Daily*). Names of official bodies in China are translated throughout.

Introduction

I have lived in Sweden for 17 years, and I am together with Swedes most of the time. Although I am born in Sweden, my mother is Chinese, and my appearance is yellow skin and black hair. Because of mother, I have gradually developed an interest in Chinese. At home I speak Cantonese and Shanghainese, but when I began to study Chinese, it was Mandarin. So studying Chinese meant that I was studying another 'language' from scratch.

There are not that many Chinese in Sweden, and there are no Chinese in my school, so my contact with Chinese language is small. I can speak Chinese, but I am not good at writing or reading it.

Although I have gone to China several times, the time there was so limited that there was no time to learn Chinese characters. I am very fond of Chinese history, but not knowing Chinese, how can I read Chinese books? Two years ago, I found a Chinese school and began to learn eagerly, and made great strides. Knowledge on China is like an ocean, so rich! It is simply a treasure trove of knowledge, and Chinese is my key to open that treasure trove. I want to learn Chinese, because I want to enter this ocean of knowledge.

Chen Hui (17 years)[1]

The question of Chinese identity permeates Chen Hui's life. But is identity determined by belonging to the Chinese race ('yellow skin and black hair'), speaking a Chinese dialect (Cantonese and Shanghainese), mastering China's national language (Mandarin), having knowledge of Chinese history, or being able to acquire knowledge through the medium of the Chinese language? Chen Hui does not distinguish between these aspects of being Chinese. Readers of the overseas edition of the *People's Daily* that published the letter recognise in it a typical problem faced by a second-generation teenager. The editors who selected it for publication did not see its contents as inept or as problematic. In their context, Chen Hui's feelings about identity are normal and coherent, and we can relate to them emotionally. However, if we analyse their meaning, we are likely to discover its many conflicting dimensions and especially the contradiction between identity as genetic or acquired through learning.

When we change the perspective from the individual to the social context, the issue of identity takes a different form. We move away from the individual emotions of 'being' or 'not being' Chinese or 'belonging' or 'not belonging' to the Chinese ethnic group towards generalised statements about 'what constitutes the ethnic group' and 'how one can determine membership of the ethnic group'.

This book regards Chinese identity in Europe as a social process. It is only marginally concerned with the individual's emotional or existential identifications and instead seeks to explore the Chinese ethnic identity in Europe in the 1980s and 1990s as a dynamic force shaping and transforming communities. Individual ethnic identification, of course, informs this study in important ways, most importantly as the raw material (in the form of interviews) for our understanding of the social dimensions of ethnic identity. Individual affection is an important expression of ethnicity; the anecdote or the individual case contributes to constructing shared feelings. There is a fine line between the existential experience of belonging and the instrumental use of ethnic stereotypes to represent group interest. The effort of this book is not to reduce individual feelings of belonging to calculating utility, but to find out the rich and complex collective processes that bring forth ethnic communities.

There is only now an emerging literature on overseas Chinese in Europe.[2] Benton and Pieke's (1998) is the first book to include all of Europe, albeit in individual country studies. Campani, Carchedi and Tassinari's book (1994) is mainly on Italy, but also includes parts on overseas Chinese in Paris and Spain. It makes sense to juxtapose overseas Chinese in European countries, but it has rarely been done, probably because the material is scattered in different countries and often in many languages.

The present book ventures into a research area that in most respects is uncharted. Juxtaposing developments in European countries, looking at interaction across borders and identifying causalities and dynamics of ethnic identity-building are at the core.

The book relies on interviews as a major source. Of the total 67 interviews we made, we transcribed and used 65 during the work on the book. In addition, we had a number of informal conversations and telephone contacts that provided background information and clarified details. The interviews had a dual function. They corroborated factual information and provided new empirical data. They also furnished data on feelings and attitudes of the interviewees on their ethnic identity and their situation. Both aspects were needed, for much of the existing published material did not provide the types of information needed for our research. Overseas Chinese media provide detailed information, but its significance only becomes clear when related to information obtained in interviews. The interviews were made with the intention of exploring the forces that create and maintain ethnic identification among overseas Chinese in a number of European countries. Their distribution does not constitute a representative sample in a statistical sense. They were made in 25 different cities in Britain, Denmark, Germany, the Netherlands, Belgium, France and Italy, and also included interviews with a Hungarian (by telephone) and a Spanish overseas Chinese (in Italy). An effort was made to ensure a spread over typologies; of the 65 interviews, 17 were with Taiwan-leaning overseas Chinese. The distribution included people from all the most important places of immigration origin (New Territories, Southern Zhejiang, Shanghai, French Indochina, Guangdong, Chaozhou, Taiwan and so on). The interviewees included people in catering, commerce and services, top people in voluntary organisations and academics. The analysis does not make any presumptions about representativeness and does not extract quantitative values from the sample. The analysis aimed at understanding the formation of ethnic identity by examining how the interviewees talked about it and which factors stood out as pertinent in the interviews.

Background

The Chinese have arrived in Europe on a certain scale since the 1880s, but only in significant numbers after the Second World War, and with great intensity only since the early 1980s. As a result, their communities have not had the opportunity to mature and integrate, but are constantly upset by new waves of immigrants. They have arrived from many different places in China, Asia, and other parts of the world, and many different dialects are current among them. They live in more than 20 different European states, the largest communities being in France, Britain and the Netherlands. National rules for dealing with communities of non-native residents differ widely in different European countries. Can one claim that they form a community? Is it possible to talk about a shared ethnic identity among Chinese in Europe?

The interaction among those who claim or are claimed to belong to the 'overseas Chinese' enables us to understand the meaning of Chinese identity. The category overseas Chinese is not defined by hard external criteria, it is understood through an analysis of their social practice. Who does and does not belong to the group, is an issue of group behaviour and social practice. The main perspective of this book is on how the Chinese manifest themselves as a group by asserting their belonging to the group, socially, politically and culturally.

Mette Thunø (1998, 175–6) has described how Chinese in Denmark in a certain period were dispersed and assimilated (partly due to marriage with Danes), and so became invisible as an ethnic group. By not interacting socially, they did not form a community, and their ethnic identity was not an issue of social interest (although it may be important as a personal psychological attribute). Some people display assimilation with the host society (or the 'mainstream', zhuliu, as many Chinese call it) in some situations, and emphasise their Chineseness in other contexts. Other people may totally negate their status as Chinese and yet be perceived as overseas Chinese by their environment. Teenage Chinese children sometimes turn their back on their parents and rebel against anything Chinese; yet the racial and ethnic expectations of their classmates and other non-Chinese peers force them to consider their ethnic identity. The pressure from peers may take many forms, ranging from racist exclusion to affirmative emphasis on diversity in specific social settings.

Ethnic identity of the Chinese in Europe takes many forms, and changes over time. For many Chinese, descent in the bloodline from Chinese forefathers is a strong criterion for deciding who is and who is not a Chinese. Yet those who make this claim readily acknowledge that it fails as a criterion in their own experience. Several interviewees made a distinction between overseas Chinese who know Chinese and Chinese culture, and Chinese who have lost their Chinese identity and language through assimilation.

The norms for group membership are interpreted by the members of the group themselves during their social interaction. Individuals use them to claim their birthright, or to cast doubt on other individuals' claim to a status within the group. Governments use them to bestow differential rights on people. Membership of the group is constantly reconstructed by its members through their participation in the activities that constitute the group. *This book, accordingly, does not subscribe to the idea that membership of the ethnic group is fixed or is defined by fixed attributes of its members, and does not define the ethnic group in opposition to other ethnic groups.* It rejects the idea that there is a fixed historical, religious, cultural, linguistic or genetic core that defines the ethnic group. History, religion, culture, language and heritage are all interpreted in social interaction, are manipulated collectively by members of the ethnic group, and their meaning, content and significance shift over time and are reflected in a multitude of different situations.

Ethnic identity reflects the quest by members of the ethnic group to achieve social safety and status and benefit by interacting with each other and with people outside the ethnic group. The main tools for this social interaction are shared cultural stereotypes, behavioural assumptions, moral values, references to customs and history, and use of language. Power and status are embedded in a cultural value system that is constantly recreated. The cultural value system, and its behavioural manifestations, do not have an objective ontology; they do not exist as a reality independent of the collective minds of the participants in the ethnic interaction; their relevance is entirely situational, and their power instrumental. They do not exist prior to social relations, but are used by the participants to conduct them; they do not guide the behaviour of the ethnic group, they provide props and backdrops for acting out the ethnic drama, actively moved around and changed by the cast.

How can one assert that the Chinese in Europe share an ethnic identity, given the great differences that exist among them? It is obvious that the large majority of Chinese in European countries form communities and interact socially, using cultural values and symbols distinct from those of other ethnic groups. Why have they not been assimilated and become invisible? It is also obvious that Chinese in all parts of Europe have immigrated from many different parts of China and other places (like Southeast Asia, the South Pacific and South America), and that there are great linguistic differences between them. Why do they overwhelmingly refer to themselves as Chinese and contend for status with Chinese of different provenance and speech? Chinese live in many different parts of Europe, and some are organised in associations that link them to local authorities. Why is it that community leaders in local settings, from Barcelona and Birmingham to Bologna and Bonn, know community leaders across the continent? Chinese in all parts of Europe are naturalised, have permanent or temporary residence, or are illegal immigrants. Why do they interact across these divisions?

The themes of diversity and division must be juxtaposed against the huge homogenising forces that work on the Chinese in Europe. The nature of the European states' and the European Union's relation with their ethnic groups has changed in the 1980s and 1990s, contributing to pan-European community structures. At the same time, the overseas Chinese policies of the People's Republic of China (PRC) and of the Taibei government help forge a general Chinese identity. Europe's Chinese react politically and socially on these influences and they interact with each other across Europe. Their shared conditions and the avenues through which they can assert their identity become increasingly homogenous. The idea of a European Chinese identity reflects one of many dimensions of the Chinese communities in Europe. The fact that Chinese traversed Europe without much regard for national borders, and that they interacted privately and in business in Europe as a whole, made them stand out from other, more parochially based, European populations; Benton and Vermeulen (1987) jestingly referred to them as the 'first and best Europeans'. This proposition can since the mid-1990s be expanded in terms of the overseas Chinese's political interaction in pan-European organisations. As the analysis in this book will make clear, the Chinese communities in Europe also react to and reflect the emergence of global Chinese identity-formation and their active wooing by local governments in China. These multiple and countervailing forces are observed from the perspective of Europe.

The title 'Chinatown, Europe' seeks to capture the many dimensions of Chinese ethnic identity in Europe. 'Chinatown' in the abstract is an emblem of Chineseness constructed and manipulated by the overseas Chinese, an emblem that mobilises cultural stereotypes. 'Chinatown' in the concrete is an urban space for people from different Chinese backgrounds at the same time as it is a miniature replica of an imagined 'China'. The address 'Chinatown, Europe' does not refer to a geographic place, but to an imaginary realm of assets shared and utilised by the Chinese in Europe.

Is there a shared Chinese identity across Europe? The following chapters reflect on conditions for such a shared identity. The Chinese nationalist project is a strong unifying factor; yet the overseas Chinese are, at the same time, divided by seemingly immutable bonds with their native places in China and by differences in speech that impede communication among them. They live under hugely different conditions in a large number of European states. Can there be a shared identity under these circumstances?

The first chapter will set out some of the main issues and approaches of this book. The analysis aims to identify both the interaction with 'host' societies and between the various diverse groups of Chinese in Europe. Identity-formation is, accordingly, regarded as a *social process between ethnic groups and within them* and forms the core of a theoretical debate in the first chapter.

The second chapter, on Chinese migration to Europe, considers some myths on how Chinese arrived in Europe before the Second World War, gives an overview of the main streams of migration, and finally examines some cases of how the migrants' identity was framed by a variety of factors related to their passage. Chapter 3, on Chinatowns in Europe, analyses how symbolic representation, political expedience and collective status interact to form a 'cultural space' for Chinese identity. Chapter 4 uses two case studies of immigrant communities from China to explore the interplay between general and sub-ethnic Chinese identities. Chapter 5 examines how overseas Chinese associations and their leaders develop Chinese ethnic identity in Europe. Chapter 6 discusses how Chinese authorities influence Chinese identity. Chapter 7 looks at how the economic activities of the overseas Chinese form an important determinant for the formation of ethnic identity. The final chapter draws conclusions from the book.

1 European Chinese identity in the 1990s

Blood descent, nationality and nationalism

Almost any Chinese discussion of overseas Chinese claims that genetic heritage defines who is Chinese. Blood descent (xuetong), the idea that people born of Chinese parents are ethnic Chinese, seems powerful because it is intuitively right and because it is simple. It is also part of what has been termed Chinese 'racial nationalism'.[1]

When we look at the Chinese in Europe, however, blood descent is not a useful way of defining the overseas Chinese, for it is hard to use for anything. The interviews made for this research revealed that while they cited blood descent as a criterion for defining who is Chinese, our interviewees found the idea inadequate, and they also used other criteria. The more one looks at 'blood descent' as a criterion for Chinese ethnicity, the more it seems meaningless in its own right: it is a criterion the Chinese themselves use, and it is their interpretation of it that counts. That interpretation is different from person to person and from situation to situation.

Blood descent is used as the basis for China's nationality law and for China's policy-making on overseas Chinese. The concepts of huaqiao (i.e. Chinese citizens residing abroad) and huaren (i.e. Chinese who have assumed foreign nationality), both based on genetic descent, accordingly define specific administrative and legal statuses of overseas Chinese vis-à-vis China.

Chinese nationalism and blood descent are closely linked. Overseas Chinese, who emphasise their genetic heritage, accordingly, imply that they are members of the Chinese nation. The imagined community of the Chinese has a strong affective appeal and is politically important.[2] 'Overseas Chinese' are linked to Chinese nationhood, so that is where our analysis begins.

The Chinese nation and the overseas Chinese

The origin of the Chinese revolution in 1911, and of earlier uprisings and attempts, lay in popular opposition to Qing rule and resentment towards the presence of foreign powers in China. The 'fan Qing fu Ming' ethos (to overthrow the Manchu Dynasty and restore the Ming Dynasty) was alive and strong in the popular movements and organisations that the revolutionaries around Sun Yat-sen and

Huang Xing mobilised for their revolutionary cause during the last decade of Qing rule. The anti-foreign sentiments, and the attacks on foreign churches and missionaries, as well as on their Chinese proselytes, had formed a core in the Yihetuan uprising in 1900–1. Nationalism arose from the assertion of a popular common cause against the Qing dynastic rule and foreign presence.

Sun Yat-sen mobilised the overseas Chinese in Southeast Asia and the Americas in support of the revolutionary enterprise; his networks of allies abroad, apart from a handful of intellectuals, were the leaders of the Hongmen secret societies, which existed as Zhigongtang (Che Kung Tong) all over Asia and in America. Their aim was to overturn the Qing dynastic rule and to restore the Ming dynastic rule, and they provided Sun with money and organisation for the revolutionary endeavours.

Intellectual circles in China and in exile in the late 1890s began to formulate the idea of a Han nation, a unity of the descendants of the Yellow Emperor. This idea incorporated the opposition to the Qing and the foreigners, but went much further in proclaiming a new unity of all Chinese, who had until then been divided and linked by particularistic bonds. The history of the Han was reinterpreted and reformulated. Frank Dikötter (1996; 1992, 97–125) has in detail described the evolution of radical reformist ideas, which emerged as 'racial nationalism' around the turn of the century. These ideas were explicit reflections of Western racism, inspired by Darwin's theory of natural selection, and by Spencer and Huxley. The Chinese idea of 'bloodline ethnicity', which still exists today, sprang from these racial nationalist ideas as formulated by people like Liang Qichao and Zhang Binglin, and later rephrased by Sun Yat-sen. Racial nationalism, rather than restoration of the Ming dynasty formed the basis for early Chinese revolutionary ideology.

State-building after the 1911 Revolution, however, forced a third perspective onto nationalism. The 1911 Revolution was weak; the Provisional Government in Nanjing, headed by Sun Yat-sen, could not hold out against the force of Yuan Shikai. Yuan not only represented the Imperial Court and the infant emperor Pu Yi, but was also a strong bureaucrat with immense patronage networks, commanding respect among the Han bureaucracy that was freeing itself from the imperial yoke. In addition, he commanded huge, modern armies that easily matched the armies that had joined the revolution. The revolutionaries had no option but to yield power to Yuan Shikai in early 1912. The nationalist foundation of the new republic was not the Han racial nationalism of the intellectuals and the revolutionaries, but the unity of the five great nations, the Han, the Manchus, the Mongols, the Moslems, and the Tibetans. The Republican authorities issued two declarations, assuring equal treatment of the five nations within the new state.

The Han bureaucracy under Yuan Shikai understood that Han nationalism as a state-founding principle, from the point of view of Realpolitik, was divisive. It was likely to lead to independence efforts by Moslems in the whole of the North West (religious and ethnic insurrections during the nineteenth century were still fresh in their memory), and at the very least Russian attempts to sow the seeds of discord. Although the Mongols mainly had been docile and accommodating, they had attempted several insurrections. But more importantly, Mongol nobles were so in debt to Chinese merchants and to the Qing state, that they hoped to forfeit those debts by a declaration of independence. The Mongol nobility was also open to inducements from Russian agents. The North East was old Manchu land, which until the 1870s had been excluded from Han immigration by the segregation policies of the Qing empire. These vast under-populated regions had attracted the attention of Russia and Japan. Even with a rising Han population (migrants from Shandong and Zhili), it was essential to formulate a claim on the region, which went beyond actual Han settlement. State-building in 1911 based on Han nationalism would have been foolhardy, giving the expansionist Russian empire and Japan a carte blanche to divide the fringe territories of the Qing Empire between them. The state-building coalition of the revolutionaries and the powerhouse around Yuan Shikai chose to declare that China included the combined territory of the five great nations.

The fact that the revolutionaries around Sun Yat-sen, the core of the Tong-menghui and later the Guomindang, had to a large extent been exiles, living in Japan and other foreign countries, and that Sun Yat-sen's revolutionary cause had received huge amounts of money, logistic support and organisational aid from innumerable overseas Chinese, meant that the overseas Chinese from the very beginning were included as a part of the post-revolutionary state-building ideology. This, of course, was easily accommodated within the notion of racial nationalism or bloodline nationalism. This 'modern' nationalism could not accommodate the ideology of restoring the Ming Dynasty and the obscurantist ways of secret societies, so Sun Yat-sen sought to force overseas Chinese into a new, politically oriented relationship with the new state, urging them to establish a revolutionary party on the foundations of their old-style tangs. An overseas Chinese leader in San Francisco, Huang Sande (1936), in his *Revolutionary History of the Hongmen*, gives a vivid account of how he was pushed around by Sun Yat-sen and the republican bureaucracy when he sought post-revolutionary recognition of the American Zhigongtang.[3] But the state-founding nationalist ideology of China included overseas Chinese.

Constitutionally, overseas Chinese have been regarded as a part of China ever since. This follows the logic of 'bloodline nationalism'. However, this must be examined from several perspectives. The claim to integrate overseas Chinese is important to gauge the nature of their relationship with China, and the policies to cement this relationship are important for the examination of the community they imagine.

Citizenship through the blood-line

The Chinese state, unlike many other states, includes its compatriots who live abroad as part of the nation. This extends much further than the *jus sanguinis* underpinning some countries' nationality laws. The overseas Chinese have since the founding of the Chinese Republic in 1911 habitually been seen as a factor in Chinese political life and as an element to be included in the constitutional context and in decisions relating to the fate of the nation.

Overseas Chinese had or could claim citizenship of the Chinese Republic, and could have the right to vote and be elected to the two-chamber parliament of the Early Republic, according to the Organic Law of Parliament of 10 August 1912 (Tung 1968, 33). This situation basically continued through the tumultuous constitutional history of the Chinese Republic. Overseas Chinese, for example, elected some of the members of the People's Political Conference in 1938–48, which was under Nationalist domination, but included Communist members until 1945 (Tung 1968, 188–91). Overseas Chinese political participation also exists in Taiwan today, even after the revision of the Constitution of the Chinese Republic in the early 1990s.

The founding of the People's Republic of China (PRC) in 1949 was based on the inclusion of overseas Chinese in the process. The state-founding coalition of parties, organisations and individuals under the leadership of the Chinese Communist Party included a number of overseas Chinese. They formed part of the Chinese People's Political Consultative Conference (CPPCC). They gave credence and legitimacy to the new state by taking part in setting it up: they were constitutionally involved in its formation. The CPPCC is the prime layer in China's political constitution, being the body which founded the state, gave it its first constitutional framework (in the form of the Constitution which was passed in 1953), and passed the most fundamental special laws of New China, namely the Marriage Law and the Land Reform Law.

However, the integration of overseas Chinese in the political system of the People's Republic of China is ambiguous. First, Chinese nationality law was not strongly and explicitly regulated for a long time, even though it always rested on the principle of *jus sanguinis*. After concern expressed by the Indonesian government around the time of the Bandung Conference in the mid-1950s that the large overseas Chinese population in Indonesia, due to the dual nationality, might have split loyalties, the Chinese and Indonesian governments in April 1955 issued a joint declaration terminating dual nationality of the overseas Chinese. This established the policy of not allowing dual nationality, which now forms Article 3 of the Nationality Law of the People's Republic of China of 1980. As a consequence, the People's Republic recognises two types of overseas Chinese; namely, citizens of the People's Republic of China who reside abroad, so-called huaqiao, and Chinese by bloodline who have acquired citizenship in a foreign state, huaren.

Representation of overseas Chinese within the Chinese political system is indirect, through the so-called 'returned overseas Chinese compatriots', guiguo qiaobao. The CPPCC includes representatives of this group among its members; in addition overseas Chinese, living anywhere, may be 'specially invited persons' (tebie yaoqing renshi). The political system of the People's Republic has to a radical extent based itself on a division of the population in ideal-type segments, to whom different rights accrue. This is particularly evident in the 56 officially recognised minority nationalities, in the division of holders of agricultural household registration, and urban household registration, and so on. Legally and practically, returned overseas Chinese compatriots, are such a group apart: they are subject to special rules and treatment, and there are even differences between the treatment of those who are Chinese citizens residing abroad and those who are bloodline Chinese. The status of citizens in China is, thus, mediated by individual attributes other than citizenship which determine the scope of people's rights: are they Han, or Tibetan, or Zhuang? Do have agricultural or urban resident household registration? Are they returned overseas Chinese compatriots? Viewed from within the Chinese political system this division into ideal-type segments is rational. For overseas Chinese, however, this fine-meshed categorisation indicates the constraints they are under. If they return to China to settle, their political participation will be guided and determined, or at least influenced, by their status as returned overseas Chinese compatriots. Their social status is defined largely by their ideal-type role.

What is the political concern of the CPPCC with the overseas Chinese? The CPPCC has as one of its declared functions to

> utilise its members' historical links and social relations to, on a broad scale, deploy the links with Taiwanese compatriots, Hong Kong compatriots and overseas Chinese compatriots [so that they] make contributions to support the modern construction of the motherland and to realise the great cause of the unification of the motherland.
>
> (Huang Daqiang *et al.* 1993, 26)

This is the closest one comes in terms of political inclusion.

The notion of imagined communities indicates the construction of common cultural and political interests in an environment where these are not yet realised, a transient situation where visionary activists create generalising nationalist norms based on shared rudimentary social institutions. Benedict Anderson (1983) in his book *Imagined Communities* describes the unifying forces that created nationalist bonds where none had been before the beginning of nationalism. He emphasises the career patterns, the 'apex of the pilgrimage' of the young and educated. To put it crudely, if the highest attainable social position and official post is within a narrow region, then that narrow region will emerge as a 'nation'. Anderson (1983, 119–23) discusses why Sumatrans 'have come to understand Ambonese as fellow-Indonesians, the Malays as foreigners'. The career patterns of young educated people in the Dutch Indies were universal in all parts of the colony, and they came to feel Indonesia as the wider area for their ambition, thus shaping their nationalist bonds across language barriers and cultural difference. The opposite was true, says Anderson (1983, 125–31), in French Indochina, which limited the 'apex of the career pilgrimage' of young Cambodians to Cambodia, even though many were educated in Vietnam or even in France. As a consequence, French Indochina developed divided nationalisms and later formed different nation states.

The overseas Chinese do not have educational and career patterns that integrate them at a national level in China, but the continuous promotion of first a revolutionary nationalism at the beginning of the twentieth century and later the official integration of overseas Chinese as part of the Chinese political system (albeit more symbolic than real in some periods) has contributed to the emergence of an imagined community based on the idea of a Chinese nation that integrates people of different origin in one national teleology.

Inclusion at the symbolic level gives overseas Chinese official recognition. This recognition gives them status and power in the overseas Chinese communities. Their membership of the national and provincial CPPCC, and their appointment as consultants, board members, or honorary citizens, or in Taiwan as Overseas Chinese Affairs Commissioners or any of the many official and semi-official posts specifically directed towards them, sets them apart and outside real influence on the 'home' polity, but allows their political cooptation, and provides a channel for influencing the nature of overseas Chinese identity.

The rise in Chinese nationalism at the turn of the century that changed overseas Chinese around the world into carriers of a synthetic and general Chinese national identity still sets the norm. Duara (1997, 1998) examines how late Qing reformers, revolutionaries and imperial representatives competed to create national allegiance among overseas Chinese. Lynn Pan (1990, 168–9) in *Sons of the Yellow Emperor* describes how, in the 1910s, the majority of locally assimilated Chinese in Southeast Asia, the babas and peranakans, suddenly regained their Chineseness under influence of Chinese nationalism, learning Mandarin (while some few acquired education, skills, lifestyles and tastes inseparable from the British and Dutch colonial masters). An event of great influence in overseas Chinese communities (including those in Europe) was the sustained campaign for supporting China in the period up to and during the Anti-Japanese War 1937–45. The cause of national salvation joined all segments of the Chinese communities and ran parallel with the anti-fascist movements in Europe at the time. The emergence of China as a member of the world community (with a seat in the Security Council of the United Nations since 1945) and the rise of strong totalitarian state systems in the Mainland and in Taiwan in 1949, both of which promoted visions of a linguistically, culturally and politically unified China, further cemented the mirage of a general Chinese community. Conversely, the nationalist policies in Southeast Asian states which contributed to exclusion of and prejudice towards ethnic Chinese, forced them into precarious management of 'identity politics', balancing a 'host' state identity with sub-ethnic Chinese identities and, importantly, a *general* Chinese identity. The assertion of Vietnamese, Indonesian and Malay nationalisms thus contributed to the consolidation of a Chinese national identity among Southeast Asia's overseas Chinese.

Ethnic Chinese confronted with exclusion and racism in the nationalising ex-colonies in Southeast Asia were forced to embrace the notion of a general Chinese identity.

Chinese national identity among overseas Chinese is thus strongly supported by the history and political practices of shifting government authorities in China since the nineteenth century.

Concepts of ethnic and sub-ethnic identity

Dealing with Chinese ethnic identity in this book means accounting for the *heterogeneity* of Chinese communities, as well as their divisiveness and emphasis on the local. The concepts of ethnicity that we use to understand the differences between Chinese and other groups must, accordingly, also explain sub-ethnic diversity *among* the Chinese.

Sub-ethnic identity, i.e. identity at a level below that of the general Chinese group, has long been recognised as important among overseas Chinese. One could consider such sub-ethnic forces so strong as to throw doubt on the very usefulness of the concept of a general Chinese identity. Crissmann (1967) has suggested that segmentation based on speech, local origin, and lineage, is a universal characteristic of overseas Chinese everywhere. This implies that sub-ethnicity would be a defining and immutable feature of Chinese identity.

The existence in China of strong local cultures and identities gives some credence to Crissmann's understanding. Myron Cohen (1994) has explored the relationship between the unifying, general Chinese identity and culture and the existence of local cultures, and he sees the two as complementary. Local culture was a necessary aspect of the wider Chinese culture, an expectation that worked both ways:

> At all levels of society, and among those serving or representing the state, it was considered that one dimension of being Chinese was to have a place of origin somewhere in China. It was therefore as important for a region to have its own personality as it was for it to manifest its Chinese character.
>
> (Cohen 1994, 96)

Tao Tao Liu and David Faure (1996) make a similar argument. They note that certain aspects of local culture are universally identical in all Han Chinese communities (like burial rituals), and that other aspects of local culture (like food) diverge radically. They understand the link between the general Chinese culture and the local cultures as a two-way process. Universal state-unifying orthodoxy is absorbed by local elites and emulated by the common people, while the very same elites create and assert local uniqueness vis-à-vis their neighbours. Far from being an immutable and original condition in conflict with a unifying Chinese identity, local identity is created by elites. These elites play both the local and the central cards in their quest for power and dominance. Local and national cultures, therefore, are creations of history and resources available to elites. In the context of Chinese communities in China, local identities should not be perceived as primeval conditions, and the inclination to create or emphasise local identities should not be seen as an archetypal reflection of Chinese culture.

Discussing Chinese communities overseas, Gary Hamilton (1977) has criticized studies that suggest that 'intracommunity differentiation' is a primordial condition of the Chinese, and has argued that it was a continuation of practices that had a background in earlier history and were used with great ingenuity by the Southeast Asian Diaspora.

The interviews revealed that sub-ethnic identities play an important role among European Chinese and also that sub-ethnic identities are often considered complementary to a general Chinese identity. Chapter 4 of this book, therefore, analyses the genesis of sub-ethnic divisions in two highly distinctive cases. The Siyinese are a closely-knit group of people whose social structures and status are, in part, the outcome of century-long struggles with other groups; Siyi identity weakened after 1949, but is now reviving. The Qingtianese case illustrates how two initially close and mutually dependent groups (originating from Qingtian and from Wenzhou) suddenly began to diverge after almost a century in Europe.

Sub-ethnic identity, like ethnic identity, is a resource available for mobilising members of the ethnic group. In that sense, the approach here stands in the tradition pioneered by Fredrik Barth (1969). It seeks to understand Chinese ethnic identity as an outcome, in part, of interaction with other ethnic groups (cf. Barth's 'boundary maintenance'). However, Barth fails to discuss the deeper sources of ethnic identity, which for him are constants that 'may be called upon when the need arises' (Hylland Eriksen 1993, 54). For Barth, ethnic identity has no history.

Abner Cohen (1974, xii–xvi) criticises Barth's failing in this respect. For Barth, says Cohen, ethnicity is a given, an 'organisatorial vessel' that acquires 'varying amounts and forms of content in different socio-cultural systems', an ascription of the 'basic most general identity' of an ethnic group. In other words, ethnicity, pliable and negotiable across ethnic boundaries, is for Barth a pre-existing fact.

Paul R. Brass (1991, 19), in critical dialogue with Barth's approach, considers ethnic groups not as givens but as conscious communities, whose identity consists of the 'subjective, symbolic or emblematic use' by 'a group of any people … of any aspect of culture, in order to [create internal cohesion and] differentiate themselves from other groups' (Brass 1991, 19). Brass emphasises the active management of group membership by the group, as opposed to Barth's inert ascription of people to their roles (Barth 1969, 13; Hylland Eriksen 1993, 54–5).

These theoretical concerns are critically relevant to understanding sub-ethnic identities among the Chinese. Are Chinese sub-ethnic identities primordial, immutable, and prone to 'manifest' themselves in response to certain circumstances? Or do they develop over time, as a reflection of past divisions and struggles, in a never-ceasing process of flux and change? Do ethnic divisions precede other social relations or do they emerge from nothing when the context so requires? Can ethnic division cease? The direction of one's enquiry will be strongly influenced by the answers to such questions.

Sub-ethnic divisions emerge as reflections of struggles about resources. The interaction between groups is a historical process in which each group collectively manipulates and manages its ascription. Groups not only create but continually revise the rules that define membership. The 'cultural substance' of an ethnic group is the volatile product of a shared history of inter-ethnic struggles rather than something primordial or immutable.

On the one hand, ethnicity is rooted in history, the product of past struggles; on the other hand, it is constantly reshaped. How to reconcile this idea of historical heritage with that of the constant reshaping of the group's value system by its individual members? Different sub-groups and individuals in an ethnic group may perceive such shared cultural values differently, use their ethnic identity in pursuit of interests different from those of the majority, or entertain deviant opinions about who is or is not of the group. This ambiguity makes it hard to understand the group's coherence. Finally, some may argue that to define ethnic identity as the outcome of struggles over resources is to reduce the issue to the level of economic determinism.

Pierre Bourdieu's *Outline of a Theory of Practice* (1977) provides perspectives that help to resolve these theoretical issues. According to Bourdieu, social behaviour follows shared sets of rules that constrain people's choice of action, but that can also be manipulated and interpreted. Those who have most power have most influence on that process. Within ethnic groups, too, contradictory interests are mediated through the groups' shared rules and norms. Some can interpret the cultural heritage and influence the membership better than others. Sub-ethnic difference and contradictory interests are the norm.

Different groups and individuals use the cultural value system in their pursuit of particular interests. Ethnicity can be understood as a set of rules by which material or political conflicts can be mediated and people's positions on the group ladder can be negotiated. The relationship between the ethnic rule set and economic interest is not deterministic but dialectic; the rules raise such conflicts into a different realm of discourse. According to Bourdieu, structures are created through continuous use. To map the structures that guide behaviour is, therefore, pointless. To focus instead on how people manipulate and use the rules of behaviour makes ethnic identity transparent not as an 'objective' reality but as practice constructed collectively by real people in actual contexts.

Sub-ethnic identities arise when conflicts over resources divide a group into opposing sub-groups. The new distinctions are collectively constructed from each side of the emergent boundary. Each group stereotypes the other, creates a new mythology for itself (and for the other), and sets up new political organisations where appropriate.

Gary Hamilton (1977, 347) observes that

> as subethnic distinctions became the most meaningful form of intracommunity differentiation, ethnic identity as Chinese became a part of one's taken-for-granted existence. In other words, Chinese identity was nonproblematic.

Chinese identity gained meaning, so Hamilton, for historical reasons in specific economic settings in Southeast Asia. Chinese merchants took advantage of the regionally-inclined forms of social organisation among new migrants to divide the markets among themselves. Even if regional divisions among Chinese in Southeast Asia radically expanded after 1850, Hamilton (1977, 347) does not see that as an obstacle to a generalised Chinese national identity:

> Chinese nationalism was not built on the cohesiveness of overseas Chinese communities. Instead it was built on their extreme segmentation which occurred along subethnic regional lines.

The theme of sub-ethnic diversity among Chinese is persistent in Europe for at least three reasons. First, because it is established in social discourse as a resource that can be mobilised when needed. Most Chinese are likely to recognise the force of sub-ethnic divisions. Where regional, sub-ethnic distinctions among Europeans have almost died out as distinguishing factors,[4] the Chinese take them seriously. Second, strong extant sub-ethnic bonds were imported to the French Chinese communities with the Chinese immigrants from French Indochina (and to a lesser extent to the Netherlands with the Chinese immigrants from the Dutch Indies). Third, sub-ethnic divisions to a certain degree coincided with the time and path of migration (e.g. accounting for differences between for example natives from southern Zhejiang and Guangdong) and with class difference among overseas Chinese arriving in Europe (accounting for differences between peasants from Zhejiang and the New Territories on the one hand and merchants, professionals and industrialists whose ancestral origin was in Chaozhou, Guangdong and other places, on the other). Various waves of immigration have reinforced sub-ethnic identity as an important resource that both overseas Chinese organisations and authorities in China can manipulate.

Sub-ethnic difference among overseas Chinese adds to the register of identities they can play on: they can both be Chinese in a general sense and belong to sub-groups of Chinese.

Sub-ethnic divisions: sub-ethnic identity?

Overseas Chinese in Europe are diverse. Their differences have many different dimensions: speech, place of origin in China, path of migration, generation, occupation, religion and political allegiance. The following outline will provide a background for understanding the dynamics of the differences, and strategies for conceptualising them.[5]

Speech

We do not know how many Chinese dialects are spoken in Europe, and how these dialects are used for different social purposes. Language and dialect combine into a fluid and complex world of social group distinctions. Mandarin and Cantonese are the most important vehicles for public communication among overseas Chinese in Europe. For most overseas Chinese, Mandarin (Putonghua) and Cantonese (Guangdonghua) are not the languages of their parents, but were acquired independently. Two other large speech groups exist in Europe, Hakka (Kejiahua) and Teochiu (Chaozhouhua). Hakka is normally not learnt by non-Hakka speakers, although several of our interviewees who are Cantonese speakers of origin claim to be fluent in Hakka because they were brought up in bilingual villages in the New Territories. The large number of Hakka-speakers among the immigrants to Great Britain in the 1950s–70s has kept Hakka alive as a language of common social use (i.e. a language used outside the family and a circle of close friends). Teochiu has a similar function in France, due to the large immigration from former French Indochina in the 1960s–80s of Teochiu speakers. Mandarin, Cantonese, Hakka and Teochiu are all used in large regions in China for communication across local dialects. Mandarin was developed as China's national language during the first decades of the twentieth Century. Cantonese was a spoken language of administration in the former prefectures Guangzhoufu and Zhaoqingfu in Guangdong, and gained supra-regional usage as the main spoken language of the south Chinese merchant class during the nineteenth century, and as the *de facto* official language of Hong Kong and as the most dominant language among overseas Chinese. Hakka is a dialect of an ethnic group with a long history of migration and aversion to assimilation, and therefore wide geographical dispersal; in the twentieth century, the speech of Mei County in northern Guangdong emerged as a sort of ideal standard for Hakka. Teochiu gained early dominance as an administrative and trading language in the Shantou region. Several centuries of Teochiu communities in what is now Thailand, Vietnam, Cambodia, Myanmar, and Laos consolidated Teochiu as a speech group. Other supra-regional dialects like Hokkien (Minnanhua) are not represented in Europe in common social communication, and neither is Toysanese (Taishanhua), which had such a function in North America's Chinatowns before the Second World War.

There is a ranking between these languages. Most overseas Chinese agree that Mandarin has the highest status (as the national language), even in Great Britain and some other places in Europe where Cantonese dominates (for example in Antwerp in Belgium). Most Hakka speakers tend to use Cantonese in mixed company, where Teochiu speakers, according to several interviewees, use Mandarin. This reflects, of course, how people choose their business partners and social companions.

The largest new waves of migrants to Europe are mainly from southern parts of Zhejiang, from Qingtian, Wencheng and Wenzhou, all speaking various sub-dialects of the Shanghainese dialect group (Wuyu). These immigrants, especially in Southern Europe, tend to use their local dialect in situations of social communication. People from Qingtian and Wencheng claim to understand the dialect spoken in Wenzhou, while native speakers of Wenzhouese cannot understand them. A hierarchy has therefore emerged among Zhejiang immigrants where Wenzhouese is gaining a position as a language for limited social communication in large concentrations of new Chinese immigrants in Southern Europe. These, however, come directly from the mainland, and are generally literate and able to use Mandarin in social conversation. Recent chain-migrants from Fuzhou, speaking dialects from northern Fujian, can also use their home dialect for social intercourse; most speak Mandarin as well.

In Europe, the Chinese live among a dozen major national languages, and most learn the main language of the country of residence. This diversity has great implications. Communication among overseas Chinese across borders in Europe cannot easily lapse into English (as in the USA), and Mandarin and Cantonese therefore have a stronger position. At the same time, many parents are careful to encourage their children to learn Chinese (Mandarin and/or Cantonese), the local national language (like French, Dutch or Spanish) and English.

Some European Chinese become speakers of many languages and Chinese speech-forms because there are so many Chinese dialects and host society languages in their environment. For many overseas Chinese knowledge of several languages and dialects is an important avenue to influence and status. Doing the interviews, we met one overseas Chinese who claimed to be fluent in 13 languages and dialects, and others who had five or six languages.

Speech difference works in two ways. In one sense it divides the Chinese into segments, creating 'speech communities' because Cantonese speakers, for example, feel more at home with each other and because they trust each other more than they trust non-Cantonese speakers. Yet in another sense it generates strategies to overcome language difference; it creates a need to know more dialects and languages in order to survive, to achieve status and influence or to make money. The fact that many overseas Chinese in Europe are multi-lingual may indicate that the pressure to overcome the limitation of one's own speech is great.

Speech segmentation in Europe undergoes changes over time. Until the 1980s, for example, there was a great unwillingness among Cantonese speakers in Europe to use Mandarin, a situation that rapidly changed in the late 1980s and 1990s due to the growing global importance of China and because of Hong Kong's return to China in 1997. Social Cantonese speakers whose first speech is Hakka have mused that they have an advantage above Cantonese speakers whose first speech is Cantonese or Toysanese; Mandarin, they say, is closer to Hakka, and so easier for them to learn. Specific language environments can have diverse effects on different people. In Belgium, the two major communities are divided into Cantonese/Flemish in Antwerp and Mandarin/Walloon in Brussels; settlement of people from different speech groups has been directly influenced by speech segmentation. Yet this 'typical' speech division covers a complex pattern of linguistic abilities and cooperation between people from the different language segments. Instead of focusing on the segmentation, it is germane to consider that Belgian overseas Chinese in reality have a linguistic scope of operation which spans the Netherlands, Belgium and France as well as Cantonese and Mandarin as social speech forms; this does not imply that all have these linguistic skills, just that these skills are available in many combinations among large numbers of Belgian overseas Chinese.[6]

Place of origin in China

Ideas of nationalism normally consider village and sub-national identities as primitive bonds engulfed by and eventually dissolved in nationalism. Chinese nationalism tended to subsume regional and village identities rather than dissolve them, regarding them as extensions of the central state.[7] This means that the Chinese still have a local ancestral home with two dimensions, administrative and affective. The place of family origin (jiguan or zuji) is officially registered and accounted for as the place where one's father or his forefathers were born. Family origin is entered in official documents and is part of the official identity of a person. The affective dimension of the native place of the forefathers is often referred to as 'down in the country' (laoxiang or xiangxia). For most people family origin is not of practical importance. The urbanisation and the huge movements of the population during the last 50 years, the suppression of ancestor worship for long periods, and the melting together of people in the work units, in military service, in the movements to send young intellectuals to the countryside (1962–78), and in higher education during the 1950s–70s in China somewhat reduced the significance of the native place. Reinforced migration and urbanisation in the 1980s and 1990s have further weakened it.

Migration may, however, invigorate the affective value of ancestral origin.[8] For some people whose native place as an official classification is obsolete because their fathers and grandfathers and perhaps even earlier generations of ancestors were born somewhere in Southeast Asia, it can still have a strong affective value. Overseas Chinese in Paris, whose ancestors several hundred years ago migrated to what is now Cambodia or Thailand from Chaozhou, still maintain ancestral halls in their 'native place'. Affinity among co-natives is common, even when the shared native place is never visited and no relatives remain in the native area.

Such culturally imagined belonging to a distant village where no relatives live any more also extends to the wider jurisdiction of the native village, so that fellow-'natives' may stem from not only the same village, but also from the same county, group of counties, city or province. The people involved often see native-place bonds as primeval. They provide a socially established channel for contact between people who otherwise have little in common. In the case of chain migration they provide some form of social network for new migrants. In other situations they give local officials in the 'native place' of overseas Chinese a peg on which to hang their overseas contacts. They also provide overseas Chinese with an avenue to status-enhancing activities.

One British-born Chinese business manager told me how his father had gone back to the native village somewhere in Fujian's remote mountainous regions to worship his ancestors, and that he himself wanted to go there, at least to have a look; but also because there was a pressure from the lineage spread around the globe to invest in an ancestral hall. No relatives were known to live in the place.[9] Yet this successful businessman was attracted by the idea of an ancestral hall because it was a status marker among overseas Chinese. The lineage was one realm in which to compare status within a framework of set rules for seniority and prominence given to affluence and business prowess. The ability to point at an ancestral hall in a specific village (with the implied antiquity and social status of one's provenance) would also give a social edge among peers in Britain.

Native place bonds span the whole register from sentimentalism and vanity to political and economic utility. Building ancestral halls and restoring the graves of the forefathers have become status markers. Erecting a grave for oneself or one's deceased parents in the native village has similar significance. A veteran overseas Chinese leader tersely assessed how tombs can furnish fulcrumage to the power of overseas Chinese:

> All these overseas Chinese who can't find enough to spend their money on go back to their native place and establish graves. These graves are really big. The mountain between X and Y – it's not really beautiful – is full of graves.

Each grave costs a fortune. From the aeroplane you can see them scattered like small dots all over the place, they spoil the forests on the mountain. So recently they said they'd create this 'serene mountain environment' of Y and not allow good land to be used for graves any more; they wanted to weed out in them. So if something comes up, an overseas Chinese can seek the help of the leader of an association, and as his relative [in China] you can get some leverage through the foreign affairs office. For example, if you are a chairman of an association, and there is an amnesty [for illegal immigrants], you have more clout vis-à-vis the consulate, so they issue or extend passports faster.[10]

(057//061)

As a result, local officials in China are more flexible towards overseas Chinese and their relatives when it comes to protecting the graves from destruction. Using this flexibility to intervene on behalf of overseas Chinese to protect existing graves or to establish new ones, overseas Chinese leaders could reinforce their status even more (057//061 ... 065). The link with the native place is one aspect of a multi-faceted system of power and status.

The reality and the imagination of community overlap in a peculiar sense. The bond with China for many overseas Chinese is through the native place, even if it does not exist as a living reality; the bond, however, is often not with China but with other people sharing the native place, as lineage members or as total strangers.

The place of ancestral origin is an aspect of a multi-layered and multi-faceted identity system that divides people into a large number of different categories. While it is defined as a specific village or city in the household registration documents, it is reduced to a county or prefecture-level city in other documents, like degree certificates, and to the provincial-level administration in passports.

The speech and native place divisions among overseas Chinese are fluid and overlapping, giving rise to creative shaping of multiple personal identities. An interviewee in Denmark was born in Shanghai and had ancestral origin there, but was raised in Fuzhou, and married to a Fuzhouese, and so could play on two identities, interchanging them according to the situation (009//002):

Yes, I am a member of (the Fuzhou association). They said, please come, be a member. I have a good relationship with them, so I felt uneasy about refusing. In reality, I am not Fuzhouese, but that doesn't matter. My husband is. I can't speak proper Fuzhou dialect, but I can understand it, so I said, 'OK, no problem, I'll join you'. I am both a member of the Chinese Association,[11] and the Fuzhou association[12] but not the Teochiou association.[13]

(009//058)

Even though speech and origin do not form essential categories of a primordial nature, they do constitute important borders between the members of the Chinese communities in Europe. Some Chinese have the capacity to transcend them and use them to their advantage, while others' social sphere is to some extent limited by them.

Primordialism and instrumentalism: assimilation, integration, exclusion

Are the overseas Chinese a separate ethnic group in Europe? What are the mechanisms by which immigrant groups are made out to be different?

The primordialist school tends to regard culture as fundamental patterns that distinguish ethnic groups. It holds that cultural systems are defined in their own right, and descend from an original cultural core closely related to an ethnic group. Ethnicity is defined as pertaining to and partaking in this cultural stock. The most important claim of the primordialist school is that ethnic identity is affective, is an inexplicable and intense feeling of belonging to an ethnic group and its culture.

The instrumentalist school understands ethnicity as a construct of circumstance. Ethnic identity and ethnic characteristics are defined by contact and interaction between ethnic groups. Ethnicity is created as a result of the contrasting interests of such different groups, and it is used and manipulated by strong persons in the groups. The forms which ethnic identity takes, the cohesion within the ethnic group and its links to other ethnic communities, define community power. Ethnicity and cultural identity, therefore, are volatile and malleable, but also very powerful, 'instruments' for social interaction.

What do these two perspectives mean for the Chinese communities in Europe? With the risk of over-simplifying the policy agendas, European host societies send out signals and stipulate policies that are intended either to

1 integrate the overseas Chinese, that means giving them a place in European societies as a distinct ethnic group, whose characteristics are recognised as distinct, and who are given specific policies, administrative bodies, state support, group representation and so on; or to
2 assimilate the overseas Chinese, that means ignoring any ethnic characteristics they have, not treating them as a special group, and demanding that they adopt the norms and languages of the host societies, ensuring that their opportunities are equal to those of other citizens.

These two trends are not mutually exclusive. They tend to coexist; integration tends to require active decisions by politicians, the allocation of resources, organisation and monitoring, while assimilation normally is characterised by non-action, and the attitude that perceived problems will go away if they remain unresolved. Active efforts towards cultural assimilation of ethnic groups (through compulsory language programmes and suppression of cultural expression) are generally regarded as oppressive, and it was until recently difficult to imagine such policies being openly promoted within the European Union (although they were on the agenda of right-wing parties and organisations). Initiatives during the last few years, when immigration and political asylum became prominent in public debate, moved assimilative ideas towards the centre of politics. The British Home Secretary David Blunkett (Labour), for example, in early 2002 proposed legislation that implied greater pressure to assimilate. Broadly speaking, the measures, rules and laws, administrative attitudes and policy statements as they exist in Europe today represent a mixture of integrationism and assimilationism, and cross-border comparisons indicate huge differences between countries.

For example, naturalisation in Denmark requires permanent residence in Denmark for at least seven years, a documentation of special links with Denmark, a probable intention of permanent stay in Denmark, and fluency in Danish; foreigners are made Danish citizens by law. Denmark does not allow dual citizenship.[14] In Britain, a foreigner must have been a permanent resident for at least four years before applying for British nationality; naturalisation is an administrative decision. Britain allows dual citizenship.[15] There is a formal, but in practice not strictly enforced, requirement that a person knows sufficient English, Welsh or Scottish Gaelic before he or she acquires British nationality.[16] These rules do not reflect policies towards ethnic groups; they take the individual as their target. But indirectly they exert different pressures on ethnic groups. Danish rules encourage assimilation, while British rules do so less.

Often the integrationist policies emerge not as the outcome of moral and political choices, but as a result of the situation governments find themselves in. In France, the emergence of large Chinese communities in certain parts of Paris and Lyons, and the nature of immigration (from French Indochina, over a short time-span, due to de-colonisation) created a *de facto* integrationist policy. The sudden concentration of large numbers of Chinese in the 13th arrondissement and in Beaux-Arts in Paris made assimilation attempts difficult as a choice, and issues had to be dealt with by recognising the internal structure of the Chinese community. The French policy had been to disperse the large numbers of immigrants to the provinces by accommodating them in reception centres; most had means of their own and moved to Paris almost immediately. When the ethnic Chinese boat refugees from Vietnam arrived in Denmark in large numbers, the Danish government likewise decided to disperse them to all parts of Denmark, and sought to prevent them from clustering within any part of any town. One rationale was to distribute the economic burden on all local governments in Denmark, but a deeper rationale was to promote assimilation, an effort supported by the active provision of Danish-for-foreigners courses. After a decade, few remained in small towns, while many lived in the two largest cities or had migrated onwards to the USA or France.

European countries have widely diverging traditions for dealing with strangers. For example, France is by many considered state-centred and 'assimilist', while Germany cherishes an 'ethno-cultural' and 'differentialist' attitude to immigrants, so that it is easier for an immigrant to be awarded citizenship in France than in Germany (Brubaker 1992). The Dutch political tradition of 'pillarisation' (verzuiling), a sort of political cohabitation between Protestant, Catholic and liberal segments of society, has been used to explain the emergence of an integrationist ethnic minority policy (Guiraudon 1998, 279). British multicultural society is said to allow political concessions to the communal forms of distinct, racially classified ethnic groups in a system distinctly different from other countries in Europe (Favell 1998, 322–3).

Global ideas of primordialism: clash of civilisations

Primordialism asserts that ethnic identity has sprung from an original cultural root that defines the characteristics and behaviour of the members of the ethnic group. Primordialism is common and is reinforced from three sides, which all give it credence. These are (a) the post-Cold War debates on the 'new world order', (b) Chinese nationalism, as promoted by think tanks and functionaries of the governments, as well as independent intellectual circles, in the Chinese Mainland, Taiwan and Singapore, and (c) overseas Chinese communities in Europe themselves. These are all more or less formalised and articulated political ideas that reflect intellectual choices and deliberations, and are seriously debated among people who are normally considered to be leading figures and those who formulate policy.

Primordialism is a strong trend among influential circles. The struggle for supremacy of major civilisations, the Christian, the Islamic and the Sinitic, with an alignment of other, lesser, civilisations became a theme in global debate in the 1990s (Huntington 1996). The 'Sinitic' sphere, in this way of thinking, is built around a core of Confucianism, a history of authoritarianism, ancestor worship, religious pluralism and other general features and is a threat to Western, Christian civilisation because the growing populations in the East are poised to engulf the declining populations in the West. The overseas Chinese, according to this view, form a fifth column in the Western world that can be mobilised by the power-holders in the Sinitic sphere. The fundamental assumption is thus that there exists a primordial cultural identity that all 'Sinitics' share. All Chinese share this culture, and they are defined by it.

Strong circles in the Chinese Mainland, in Taiwan and in Singapore mobilise the Chinese in a pan-Chinese nationalism, whose roots are complex. This nationalist idea also assumes that Chineseness is a primordial quality. Its main structuring element is the common racial origin of the Han people, as the descendants of the Yellow Emperor. The Confucian tradition stands at the centre of this nationalism, generating social order and harmony through moral norms, and by ranking the individuals in firm familial and social roles. Confucianism asserts an order beyond political divisions, is native to China, and represents a political and rational alternative to the Western liberal-democratic statehood.

As a response to segmentation and diversity, overseas Chinese often define ethnic unity, using generalising cultural assumptions and stereotypes. Chinese community organisations represent different interests in the communities, yet many interviewees indicated that they cooperate across them. 'We are all Chinese' is a phrase used not only to paste over the diversity but to incorporate all Chinese into one ethnic group sharing a community. Persons belonging to very different segments of the Chinese community express similar stereotypes about the nature of Chineseness – 'hard working, frugal, loyal, family-oriented' and so on.

The European nation states are receptive to primordialist claims of ethnic identity. Europeans tend spontaneously to regard ethnic homogeneity as the natural foundation of the nation and the social community (Gellner 1983). Claims that Chinese ethnicity also reflects such a pattern are easily accepted and promoted among Europeans, so many people are willing to regard each individual Chinese as a manifestation of an ethnic core, as a stereotype.

What are the consequences of adopting a primordialist concept of ethnic identity as a norm for ethnic policy? Integrationist policies are considered benign by many because they supposedly protect the ethnic groups from cultural dominance by the majority ethnic group (or host society) and respect and protect their ethnic 'core'.

Primordialists seeking to integrate ethnic minorities as groups are likely to emphasise stereotypical difference and create social barriers between ethnic minority groups and the 'host' society. Primordialism may also create stereotypes by inferring social roles from the culture or 'innate character' of the group. Organised crime, social destitution, unemployment, unreliability, ghetto mentality, violent behaviour, dominance in specific trades and other socially undesirable aspects are ascribed to the group itself, rather than to the political, social and economic environment from which these phenomena spring. The ethnic character is considered violent, crime-prone, lazy and so on, and so the relative isolation from the 'host' society becomes a self-fulfilling prophecy.

Equally primordialist is the wish to construct Chinese as Confucians with conservative moral norms and averse to democratic principles and equality, a construction that bears in it the message that the Chinese are incompatible with modern Western states.

Instrumentalism as a norm-setting understanding of the ethnic group recognises the interaction between the ethnic group and the 'host' society as an important factor framing the nature of the ethnic group. Such an approach is difficult to handle for the 'host' state because it involves a continuous criticism of the institutions dealing with ethnic minorities and a questioning of the national and ethnic self-perceptions of the 'host' society.

The structuring influence of the European states on the Chinese communities

European overseas Chinese communities are creatures of the interaction of Chinese migrants with European states. They make claims on society in step with dominant attitudes, and they reflect immigration, race relations and minority policies. Such attitudes and policies differ across Europe and have particularly evolved since World War Two. I will discuss two main strands of the issue here, (a) the welfare state's institutionalised concern for minorities, and (b) the 'sovereignty deficit' of the 'host' societies.

The institutionalised concern for minorities in the European welfare states is a development of public policy between the 1960s and the 1980s.[17] Large waves of migration to European countries from the 1950s to the 1980s, due to decolonisation, labour recruitment and political asylum led increasingly to institutionalised approaches to deal with large groups of people perceived as strangers living within the nation-states. The individualised, ad hoc and short-term approaches that had been prevalent during the prelude to World War Two, during the huge displacements of people after World War Two, and during the early part of the Cold War between the allied victory in 1945 and the Berlin Wall in 1961, were in the 1960s gradually replaced with more elaborate systems and rules for dealing with long-term resident populations of non-natives. The systems that emerged were different in the major receiving countries like Britain, France, Germany, Belgium and the Netherlands, while countries like Spain, Portugal and Italy were countries of large emigration and insignificant immigration until the 1980s, and so did not develop special systems for dealing with immigrant groups.[18]

'Host' societies, generally speaking, began to see non-natives as culturally distinct groups sharing a range of problems; the development of institutions matched the specific issues of immigration and the composition of the non-native population in the different countries. In no European country were the Chinese an important immigrant group. British race relation policy, accordingly, was mainly directed towards 'Afro-Caribbeans' and 'Asians' (i.e. Indians and Pakistanis), German policy towards Turkish guest workers, and French policy towards North Africans from Algeria, Morocco and Tunisia. Policy changes were accompanied by 'racialisation' of the ethnic minorities, meaning that cultural and racial essence became a dominant criterion for constructing the groups at the receiving end of the policies. Policy concern was preoccupied with the largest ethnic groups, but included lesser groups like the Chinese.

At the time when the large Chinese immigration in Britain, France and the Netherlands began, ethnic policy in these countries was emerging. Culturalist attitudes and the provision of services to ethnic minorities went hand in hand to align the Chinese with other ethnic groups. This has to a large extent defined how their social needs were perceived, and how their associational life became structured. The situation was different in each country due to the major sources of immigration, the status of the immigrants and the perceived social problems caused by their arrival, and so the situation also differed for the Chinese.

The French had a history of easy naturalisation and aversion to treating immigrants as groups representing non-native cultures and political interests (perhaps most significantly symbolised in the interdiction against political associations of immigrants that was not lifted until 1981),[19] whereas the British and Dutch embarked on a cooperation with immigrant associations, which were considered to represent a wider set of cultural and political interests particular to the groups they represented. In Germany, conversely, policy towards immigrant groups did not rely on their own organisation or on assumptions about their cultural cohesion. In Italy, immigration laws created the conditions for the emergence of hierarchical structures of dependency within the Chinese community. The systems emerging in European countries varied and created vastly different types of interaction between the Chinese and their 'hosts'.

Britain

The British system was highly ambiguous. On the one hand it was dedicated to the idea that the ethnic groups embodied non-native cultures and to providing them with opportunities to give internal coherence to their collective difference from the surrounding society – the dominant doctrine ordained that Britain was a multicultural society (Favell 1998). On the other hand, the high number of British citizens among the ethnic groups, combined with their large concentration in some parliamentary constituencies and local government polling districts meant that the 'black' vote became worth vying for, so leading to a certain level of political integration (Adolino 1998). The Chinese were relatively insignificant in the British political and social policy landscape and by the 1990s only mustered a handful of Chinese elected to local councils.

In 1984–5, a Home Affairs Committee hearing in the British Parliament led to a formulation of policy concerns (House of Commons 1985). The five main obstacles to 'full participation in British life' faced by the Chinese were identified as lack of English language skills, ignorance of social and other rights, cultural differences, scattered settlement and the long, unsocial working hours in the catering niche. The 'cultural differences' were mainly ascribed to the Chinese's unwillingness to have contact with official authorities, and their feeling of 'shame' when seeking help beyond the Chinese community. This statement was supported by anecdotal evidence and some adages current among Chinese (House of Commons 1985, xii–xiv).

The policy was bifurcated. Public authorities, mainly local councils, were to funnel more services directly to the Chinese, through information campaigns, use of bilingual staff where appropriate, publication of Chinese-language information materials and advertising in and manuscripts provided for Chinese newspapers. Local government should make provisions in accordance with Chinese tastes, like serving Chinese food to Chinese inpatients in hospitals. They should also establish and fund Chinese community centres and similar institutions, and they should establish frameworks for liaison with the Chinese communities. The 1985 enquiry into the state of the Chinese in Britain did effectively release more funds for which Chinese community organisations could apply. This in spite of a comment in the proceedings from the hearing on grants to the Chinese community that said that a 'substantial component of people' had prospered in Britain, and some had land holdings in the New Territories that had 'vastly increased in value'. These

> wealthier Chinese could well afford to do more to assist community ventures than they do at present.
>
> (House of Commons 1985, xxvii)

The 1985 inquiry was instrumental in shaping the approach to the overseas Chinese in the years to come.

This liberal thinking dictated that the community was considered a separate segment of society, and (in spite of an awareness of its heterogeneity) as rather undifferentiated. Transient problems of language and lack of information – which disappear gradually as migrants gain more language competency – were understood more in cultural than in practical terms (the proposed policy was to let local authorities culturalise the issues and direct specific ethnic resources towards them). Instead of providing large resources for English language training for all age groups and expecting that fluency in English would be achieved for all but the frailest elderly, the policy *de facto* perpetuated the problem by providing official services in Cantonese.

Chinese community centres, Chinese health clinics and other ethnically directed provisions by the local authorities aimed at acculturation, at building bridges between the Chinese and the host community. The emphasis on addressing the Chinese community with special institutions, even with the intention to do away with ethnic disadvantage, helped reinforce it, adding to its institutional logic and dynamics. The involvement of Chinese community leaders as advisers and board members in such projects further enhanced their community standing.

Some wealthy Chinese (both those who had profited from increasing real estate prices in the New Territories and those who had been successful businessmen in Britain) took their responsibilities towards the community seriously, and so there emerged a political structure among the overseas Chinese communities in Britain, where the wealthy could afford the expense of taking leading posts in community associations, where their prowess was measured in their ability to secure government grants for community projects, and where these community leaders entertained ceremonial links with mayors and local councillors.

British public policy towards ethnic minorities had a homogenising effect on the community (because people of different status and background were rolled into one by the authorities), generated resources and statuses for which leaders in the Chinese community could compete, provided career opportunities for second-generation Chinese as officially-employed 'cultural brokers', and manifested itself in a generalised Chinese symbolism (like adorning Chinatowns with Chinese arches).

Germany

The German system differed from the British. Few Chinese were naturalised, so they were regarded as politically insignificant. The policy towards foreign citizens resident in Germany was mainly directed towards the large numbers of Turkish guest workers, and only gradually developed during the mid- and late-1970s when family reunion and unemployment began to generate social problems. Foreigners tended to congregate in certain areas where they constituted a large segment of the resident population, in some areas in Baden-Württemberg even more than 15 per cent (Blotevogel, Müller-ter Jung and Wood 1993, 91). The issues of ethnic groups were to a large extent devolved to the federal states (Länder) and the local councils (Gemeinden), but overall administration was in the hands of the Ministry for Labour and Social Organisation and broader policy formulation was vested in the post of the Federal Government Commissioner for the Interests of Foreigners. Policy concern at federal level was concentrated on monitoring the situation and describing developments. Local councils did not rely on the 'internal' organisation of the ethnic groups for their contact with them.

For political liaison many councils established elected 'foreigners' committees' (Ausländerbeiräte), in which resident foreign citizens had the right to vote. Councils produced information materials in some minority languages (mainly Turkish), depending on the local need, and employed some staff to deal with specific problems. In addition to direct service provision by local authorities, some charitable organisations carried out social welfare tasks among migrants on behalf of local councils. The official attitude towards migrants' organisations was that they were single-issue interest groups like so many other, and that they in some cases had a cultural and social function, giving the groups some coherence. Unlike in Britain, there was great reluctance to afford them any role in public policy. They were bypassed in terms of liaison and representation of interest through direct elections to the local foreigners' committees, and they were given little if any government support for social projects. For the overseas Chinese, a small and scattered group in Germany, this has meant that their associations are scarce and have less crucial functions than in Britain. There is a broader tendency to treat different groups of foreigners as one than in Britain and so to distinguish less between different ethnic groups in public administration.

The reluctance of German authorities to issue residence permits to Chinese nationals meant that the migration of ethnic Chinese to Germany in the 1960s and especially the 1970s was dominated by people holding Dutch or British passports (who had the right of labour mobility under European Community rules). As European Union citizens, they are eligible for elections to the foreigners' councils, but they are not considered in the same categories as non-European Union citizens for the purpose of social policy. With the right of European Union citizens to vote in local elections in Germany, introduced in the 1990s, the foreigners' committees are being reconsidered. It is generally opined that extending voting rights to European Union citizens for both foreigners' committees and local elections violates natural justice. In some areas local politicians therefore propose to limit voting rights for foreigners' committees to non-Community citizens or to abolish them. In either case, the few ethnic Chinese members on the foreigners' committees are likely to lose their official representation.[20]

Italy

Italian concern with ethnic groups largely emerged in the 1980s when a census revealed a growing presence of people from outside the European Union; this led to a examination of Italy's 'new position in the international labour market' (Pugliese 1991, 5). Previously a country of emigration, Italy was suddenly becoming a major country of immigration. The policy reorientation and the whole debate surrounding it were dominated by ideas of labour market adjustments. Pugliese (1991, 43–8) criticises the immigration legislation of 1986 for basing itself on the false premise that immigration was a response to a need for labour in Italy. The law aimed at setting foreign and native workers on an equal footing, and at curbing clandestine immigration. To that end it included an amnesty for all non-European Union citizens working in Italy on 31 December 1986. The legislation was followed up by more restrictive rules under the 'Martelli Law' in 1990,[21] and by detailed provincial legislation (Venturini and Bonini 1993). Further provisions at national level were made in 1996.[22] Each new immigration law included an amnesty for illegal immigrants, a fact that caused great political controversy. Italy thus experienced three major amnesties for illegal immigrants between 1986 and 1996, all of which had an important impact on overseas Chinese in Italy.[23] The labour market philosophy behind the immigration policy has had a great impact on the structure of Chinese immigration and the composition of the Chinese community in Italy.[24] Residence permits to non-European Community citizens were given almost exclusively to dependent workers.[25] Non-European Union citizens were not allowed to register new enterprises. In the case of the Chinese this contravened an agreement between the Chinese and Italian governments about mutual recognition and protection of foreign investment by their respective citizens. Although the law was a couple of years later altered to allow investment migration, it barred new overseas Chinese immigrants from registering their own enterprises during a period in which Italy experienced large immigration from China. Naturalised Chinese entrepreneurs or early immigrants whose residence permit had not barred them from registering enterprises were thus able to employ Chinese with the aim registering for an amnesty; they were under great social and moral pressure to do so for the sake of their fellow countrymen. At the same time it put them in an advantageous position to enjoy a large supply of cheap labour.

The Italian immigration laws thus created dependency among recent Chinese immigrants on their employers, a dependency that translated into acceptance of hard working conditions.[26] Large numbers of Chinese immigrants, however, chose not to opt for an amnesty for fear of rejection and expulsion, or because they feared losing their income from irregular labour relations. A third tier of the Chinese community in Italy is therefore irregular workers in sweatshop factories or street vendors held on a short leash by their 'protectors' and suppliers of goods. The fact that new Chinese immigrants are unable to register their own enterprises means that the common pattern for the ethnic economy in other parts of Europe cannot be realised in Italy; shopkeeping, catering and small-scale services are not viable options for the new immigrants (Ceccagno and Omodeo 1997). By 1996, only 377 out of 2,919 Chinese (or one-eighth) with residence permits in Prato (Tuscany) had permission to register enterprises (Ceccagno and Omodeo 1997, 68). An estimate by a local overseas Chinese leader indicated that for each overseas Chinese with a residence permit there were at least two 'illegal' immigrants from China, so that the real Chinese population in Prato approached 10,000. On average more than 20 Chinese were dependent on each Chinese employer. High dependency rates and illegality have led to a siege mentality in the Chinese community and the Italian press has linked the Chinese with organised crime, leading to mutual suspicion and further closure.

Local government in Italy has, since the beginning of the 1990s, sought to deal with social problems, issues of schooling and medical provisions. The central state does not provide strong guidelines and policies, and most approaches have been to set up ad hoc offices to deal with specific problems encountered by migrants, providing advice and administrative assistance (Ceccagno 1997). Although the Chinese community in Italy tends to be relatively closed and relatively homogenous in origin (most immigrants stem from Wenzhou, Wencheng and Qingtian in Zhejiang province, and arrived over a short span of years), there is no structured contact between the Italian state and the community; existing contacts are sporadic, local, individualised and of a practical nature. There is no institutionalised participation or liaison between the authorities and the Chinese community. Chinese associations are not afforded a specific official function or status.

Playing the minority rights card

Soysal (1996) has observed that immigrants use their rights to make collective claims on society as minority groups. The European states include interdictions against discrimination on the basis of race, origin, nationality, creed, gender, sexual orientation and so on. Constructing ethnic rights as cultural group rights affirms and helps institutionalise ethnic difference, allowing groups to formally interact with authorities or to fight for recognition through political activism.[27] Group rights are Janus-faced, for they strengthen the group, thereby *both* inadvertently facilitating discrimination and stigmatisation, *and* creating the only credible framework for overcoming stigmatisation and discrimination, namely collective action. The benign, liberal-egalitarian ethos of culturally-defined ethnic group rights in this sense sets the scene for essentialising the group in terms of both outside prejudice and inside claims to nature-given difference. Individual citizenship on the one hand and group rights of ethnic minorities on the other, however, create a particular space for playing the ethnic card vis-à-vis the European Union and its member states.

Citizenship of a European state (Soysal 1996, 4) does not any more determine the status of the individual, for non-citizen immigrants normally enjoy a range of rights traditionally considered exclusive to citizens, such as civil rights, social rights and some political rights like local voting rights in many countries. Individually, they enjoy the 'rights of the person', and collectively they have group rights.

The European Union authorities have, in their effort to accommodate non-community citizens, adopted institutional frameworks and policies aimed at some form of integration. Riva Kastoryano (1999) has examined the Migrants' Forum, an institution established under the auspices of the European Parliament. This Forum aims to be a place 'where immigrants from non-European countries can express their claims, but also a place through which European institutions can diffuse information concerning them'. These non-European citizens should have 'the same rights and opportunities as the autochthon citizens of the Union', and the Forum should compensate for 'a democratic deficit'. The immigrants should be represented through voluntary organisations fulfilling four sets of criteria: each association (a) must be supported and recognised by a member state; (b) must prove its capacity of organisation; (c) must define its objectives in universal terms and abide by universal values such as equality and the respect for human rights; and (d) must represent populations originating in non-European countries.

Kastoryano points at the ambiguity and inconsistency of this structure. Each nation state in the European Union has its ways of defining citizenship and ethnicity.

Legal status is different in each European Union member state, yet the Forum aims to be autonomous in relation to the member states and induces the immigrants to situate themselves beyond them. Kastoryano rightly questions the nature of the membership of and representation through the Forum, both of which are highly ambiguous. It is not clear whether membership is based on nationality or culture. Immigrant communities in Germany consist of a majority who have not obtained German nationality, whereas in France and Britain, members of ethnic groups with full citizenship in these countries dominate similar communities in Britain and France; the different member states also differ in their recognition of ethnic and cultural difference. The criteria are vague, and so seems the practice of the Forum to be. Its subtext and self-understanding are permeated by the notion of group rights, as amply documented by Kastoryano (1999); but when the Forum in May 1995 issued some 'Proposals for the Revision of the Treaty on European Union at the Intergovernmental Conference of 1996', it proposed a separate citizenship of the Union for Third Country Nationals who had been residing in a member state for at least five years. This proposal was unsuccessful. It did, however, define rights in terms of individual citizenship of the Union, and not as cultural or group rights.[28]

The structure of the Forum until its suspension in 2000 was, in practice, based on delegation from 'support groups' constituted in each member state and integrating a certain number of voluntary associations of 'third country' nationals.[29] Membership and discourse were therefore shaped to aggregate at member-state level general concerns of dominant populations of 'third country' nationals. The formulation of agendas, accordingly, was directed towards general themes like European coordination of immigration policy initiatives against racism, and labour market exclusion. The concerns were with policy towards ethnic groups that were important due to their size and their activism, e.g. the Turks in Germany, the North Africans in France or the Caribbean and South Asian communities in Britain. On the basis of group rights ideology, and thereby a recognition of cultural distinctness of ethnic groups, Europe institutes structures of semi-official representation that homogenise group articulation across difference.

The European Union, through its Directorate General for Labour and Social Inclusion, has, in the mid-1990s, begun to communicate with the European Federation of Chinese Organisations (Ouzhou Huaqiao Huaren Shetuan Lianhehui). It allows, in that sense, the overseas Chinese in Europe to aggregate the political issues across European borders, and perceives them as one ethnic group with shared characteristics. This structure is not concerned with the nationality issue, but with the culturally distinct representation of ethnic interest. It therefore allows and forces the Chinese community to present itself in such terms.

Europe is one of several agencies setting the terms for the overseas Chinese when they negotiate their identity. The construction of a common 'other' in the form of 'people originating in non-European countries', of course, reflects the concerns raised by the demands for a restrictive European immigration policy (popularly referred to as 'Fortress Europe') and racist movements in European Union member states.[30] This is based on the premise of ethnic and cultural distinction vis-à-vis the European 'us'. The 'other', consisting of many different groups, is constructed to be homogenous, to be a mass of blacks, Muslims, and Asians who constitute one policy field. However, when it comes to actual policy measures and remedies, the European Union and member states can only act on nationality status and individual rights. Simultaneously, the European Commission does recognise the existence of culturally distinct groups like the Chinese and seeks to interact with them.

To the European Union, the Chinese are three things: people 'originating in non-EU countries' (irrespective of their nationality), 'third country' nationals, and a culturally distinct group. The first notion is conceptually vague, the second not or only minimally true (large groups of Chinese in Europe are nationals of European Union member states) and the third a self-fulfilling prophecy (if the European Commission accepts a dialogue with the European Chinese community, such a community will emerge).

The ethnic triangle: 'community', 'home', and 'host'

The overseas Chinese in Europe extend metaphorically into three distinct realms. The three realms are: the 'community', that is the dimension of interaction between the overseas Chinese; the 'home' country, that is the dimension of their interaction with China; and the 'host' society, that is the dimension of their official interaction with their country of residence.[31] These three realms expand and shrink as required by the circumstances. The community can have the shape of a group of Chinese in one locality; it can include all Chinese in a nation state or in Europe. The 'home' can be a place or region in China, China as a political unit (like the Mainland or Taiwan) or it can be a greater, culturally-defined China that extends beyond political borders. The 'home' has an imagined character; many overseas Chinese have not lived in China, but feel strong bonds there. The 'host' can be a local government, a nation state or Europe; it may also for example be a charitable organisation or private institution directed towards the overseas Chinese.

The three dimensions can give us a good impression of the development of the overseas Chinese communities in Europe. The extremes of the community formation in this triangle are:

- Overseas Chinese communities, representing people of common local origin in China, living in one small area in Europe, recognised by the local authorities of one European city.
- Overseas Chinese communities, representing people from all over China, including both the Mainland and Taiwan, living scattered in all parts of Europe, and relating to Europe or the European Union as a whole.

European overseas Chinese formulate their identification in many dimensions and scales between these extremes. The extremes do not exist. Historically, the former probably did exist as an approximation, when in the early 1900s the large majority of the overseas Chinese in Liverpool came from a cluster of villages in

Taishan, few people from that area lived in other parts of Europe, and the main relationship with 'host' authorities was with Liverpool. Yet, these people were drawn, one way or another, into China's national movement and so had to deal with issues of Chineseness beyond their 'home' village identification. Their status in Britain was deeply affected by nationwide issues (especially the labour issues of the time), and so Liverpool was not the only area of official interaction with the 'host'. Liverpool's overseas Chinese from Taishan, of course, did have links with their few fellow villagers in London and in other European ports. Their community did stretch beyond Liverpool. The dominance of the Taishan Chinese in Liverpool did not last long, and even in the period where they were dominant, people hailing from other parts of China did live in Liverpool.

The ethnic triangle can indicate some developments of importance. One common pattern is that co-natives from a Chinese locality tend to be scattered around Europe, so that a narrow 'home' dimension is linked to a broad 'community' dimension. Conversely, a local overseas Chinese community tends to comprise people from many different parts of China, so that a narrow 'community' dimension is linked to a broad 'home' dimension. The greater assertiveness of overseas Chinese affairs offices in Chinese counties and cities in the 1980s and 1990s enabled a whole range of new 'home' identifications different from the old village (mainly related to villages in the New Territories like Lin Village and Ji'ao Village) and speech group (for example Cantonese, Teochiu, Hakka, Foochow, Hainan, and Toysanese) affiliations. People gained the ability to point to their roots in Nanhai-Shunde, Shenzhen, Qingtian, Shanghai, and so on. Speech group identities were also reinvigorated by the same policies.

The 'host' dimension also reveals change over time and difference between national systems. For example, Europe has only emerged as a structure dealing with Europe's overseas Chinese in the 1990s, long after parts of the Chinese communities began to regard themselves in a Europe-wide context. In some settings, like in the Netherlands and Britain, the 'host' dimension is very intensive, and situated at all levels of government, while it is scant in Denmark, highly localised in Italy, and so on.

The three dimensions do not predetermine overseas Chinese identification, but they define how overseas Chinese can position themselves in ethnic terms.

China's national minorities and the overseas Chinese in Europe

The homogenising nationalist project of the Chinese state in its relations to overseas Chinese faces a specific problem in the case of national minorities. As the most substantial part of the overseas Chinese of national minority stock live in cross-border communities and originate in relatively few communities in the north west (relating to Khazaks, Tadjiks, Kirgiz, Mongols etc.), the issues tend to be handled as separate from overseas Chinese affairs in general. The Tibetan Diaspora is centred on India (and a cross-border community) and under a strongly politicised, anti-Chinese leadership.

Except with regard to the cross-border communities, the minority diasporas are numerically insignificant and very diverse. Some national minorities are highly assimilated with the Han (like the Manchus or the Zhuang) and are fully integrated in the general overseas Chinese communities. On the individual level, many individuals of national minority background mix with other overseas Chinese, so for example a Tibetan qigong master in Manchester who is fluent in Cantonese serves important functions in the local Chinese community, and identifies with other Chinese. Mongols whom we have come across in Europe during the research seem to display the same features. They are by their passport and other attributes categorised as Chinese. Their Mandarin skills, learnt in school, are often their only or best access to social interaction; their access to society in that sense is dominated by their belonging to China. The research for this book did not include these groups, but impressions from individual cases indicate that such migrants normally are too scarce to form communities in Europe beyond the frailest private networks, that they look to Chinese consulates and embassies for official documents and assistance, and that those who have arrived from Mainland China since the early 1980s due to their Mandarin language skills, training and experience have much in common with overseas Chinese of Han stock.

There exist few, if any, genuinely separate Chinese national minority diasporas in Europe. One small community of this sort is the Nung (Nong) community in France. This community comprises the descendants of a tribe of Nung speakers in northern Indochina who according to one interpretation formed the backbone of French colonial troops in the region. The Nung, although not speakers of a Han Chinese dialect, pay allegiance to the Han Dynasty general Fu Bo, and see themselves as the heirs to Chinese militaristic and moral virtues. Fu Bo was the hero in the pacification of South China and Annam, known for his loyalty, fierce bravery and patriotism. With the decline of the French colonies in Indochina, the Nungs were likely to face allegations from the new power holders of treachery and collaboration with the colonial power. The French therefore decided to settle them in France, where they are seen as a part of the Chinese community and use Chinese speech in social interaction (Yuan Guoen 1991, 386–7). The term Nung, according to another account,[32] seems to have been used to circumscribe not only the speakers of a language of that name which belongs to the Thai language family, but also certain groups of early twentieth century labour migrants from Guangdong to Annam, which the French authorities for diplomatic reasons referred to as Nung tribal people. Whether or not the Nung community in France forms a separate ethnic group or consists of descendants of Chinese immigrants is not very important. Obviously, they are not a minority in the formal terms set by the Chinese authorities. Their lore indicates that they are included as a part of the overseas Chinese community more by subscription than ascription.

Another group of European overseas Chinese of national minority stock is the Uighurs. A study by Frédérique-Jeanne Besson indicates that a small Uighur Diaspora emerged in Istanbul in the 1950s and 1960s, who organised themselves in the Association of Immigrants from East Turkestan. This community led to the emergence of a small Uighur community in Germany:

In the 1960s, a tertiary migration steered some Uighur families from Turkey to Germany in the wake of the emigration of Turks. This migration at the outset followed economic and professional objectives. It gained a political dimension when Radio Liberty began to employ Uighur staff ... They formed the kernel of a community that provided sufficient structure to concentrate later migrations on Munich. The community was not large, 50-odd people, but after 1992, individual migration originating in East Turkestan[33] quadrupled the numbers.

(Besson 1998, 168)

The Uighur Diaspora's Cold War origins are an important feature. Exiled Uighurs found in Turkey a co-ethnic sympathy based on the popular belief that 'East Turkestan' was the original homeland of the Turks, and that the Uighurs were part of a greater Turkish nation. There is some linguistic affinity between Turkish and Uighur, making the two languages mutually comprehensible (albeit with some difficulty). The wish to restore 'East Turkestan' as a separate state was one of the aims of the Diaspora leaders.

Their migration to Germany after the end of the Cold War is significant, and the post-Cold War situation has changed the parameters radically. The Uighurs of Xinjiang have in the 1980s and 1990s gained greater self-confidence due to the increased religious freedom in China and due to the greater direct cross-border contacts. An opposition movement pits itself against the Chinese authorities. Uighurs arriving in Europe from China during the 1990s may therefore be receptive to secessionist ideas and visions of 'East Turkestan'. If that is so, they are provided with a focus of identity that allows them more easily to assert themselves as non-Chinese. Their discourse of opposition to communism and of secessionism provide them with 'host' state recognition as a separate (political) group, distinct from the Chinese.

Their diaspora is torn between several forces. Their anti-Chinese tendency links them with general dissident movements and the cause of the Dalai Lama,[34] and gains them recognition by European human rights movements and by the media. Their 'East Turkestan' secessionism gains them recognition by conservative ethno-nationalist movements in Turkey that hope for the ultimate emergence of a greater Turkey. Their religious inclination means that various Islamic movements seek to win them over. When Islamic leaders publicly make claims like 'Uighurs are in their Islamic belief an example for and an elite of the Umma',[35] they court them for a religious cause. Their beliefs and political objectives (and those of other religious leaders) are anathema to the fundamentals of the human rights discourse, and also to the ideal of a secular 'East Turkestan'.

The Uighurs in Munich established in 1990 the Union of East Turkestanis in Europe, an organisation which has outposts in Britain and Sweden, and is linked with the East Turkestan Information Centre in Munich, which has established a web site. According to Besson (1998, 183), the leaders of the Uighur movement in Europe, especially in Munich, were trained in the 'American school' of Radio Liberty. Even though Radio Liberty did not broadcast propaganda to China, the leaders of the Uighur community 'show how the Uighurs used this American political instrument to enlarge their audience and gain an international stature' (Besson 1998, 183).

As a movement they sought, in the 1990s, to regroup as an international lobby with a global strategy. They are in that respect hemmed in by governments (in Europe, Turkey and in Central Asia) that give their official links with China higher priority than the support of East Turkestan secessionism.

The European overseas Chinese communities are in the main subjected to the homogenising logic of the Chinese nation. Only the small Uighur community in Europe has a cultural, religious and political frame of reference that draws it away from a Chinese identity.

Forging overseas Chinese identity in Europe

The forces that work on overseas Chinese identity are enormous and many issues and conflicting interests are involved. The following chapters will examine some of the ways in which the Chinese have shaped their identity in Europe. The themes chosen are broad, and the examples originate in many countries. This gives the advantage of broad comparisons and makes it possible to structure the discussion around the process of creating identity; the drawbacks, of course, are that historical perspective to a certain degree is sacrificed, and that many issues relating to specific communities cannot be dealt with.

Chinese nationalism and the political, social and economic environments in Europe are at the centre of the discussion, which will take us through migration, community-building, sub-ethnic divisions, organisations, patriotic politics and ethnic business.

2   Chinese migration to Europe

There is no common myth of Chinese migration to Europe. No 'Angel Island' legend serves as a shared experience of entrance to Europe.[1] Spurious anecdotes, scant traces in European archives, and some stereotyped reports in newspapers are the main sources on overseas Chinese in Europe before the Second World War: not reliable, and not very interesting.

Chinese migration to Europe is divided into many histories. Different waves of Chinese arriving in Europe followed diverse tracks. Each stage in the migration process shows difference rather than uniformity. The migrants came from a variety of coastal places between Guangdong and Shanghai, former French, Dutch and British colonies, and smaller numbers from all other parts of China. They arrived in European cities that embodied cultures and political systems that bore little resemblance to one another. Some remained in one place, others moved between places in Europe, some went back to China or onwards to North America in search of the best place to make a living.

Early migration to Europe in small numbers dates back to the eighteenth Century. The numbers were so small and the circumstances now seem so obscure that they mainly have antiquarian interest. The scattered individuals and tiny groups in question left few, if any, traces.

Myths

Walking the Silk Road and trekking along the Siberian Railway

Some myths about migration in the late nineteenth and early twentieth centuries still live among overseas Chinese in Europe, but their permanence has more to do with frequent repetition of uncertain tales that appeal to the imagination than with historical substance. The oldest myth, whose origin is hidden in a distant and nebulous past, is the account of the Chinese who arrived in Europe walking along the Silk Road. Some old members of Chinese communities still remember in their youth having met or heard about somebody who had come by that route. Details of the route and the hardships are vague and can only be imagined. The early migrants walking across the continent are normally thought to be from Qingtian in Zhejiang or from Tianmen in Hubei.

Such narratives are part of the way many Chinese talk about their identity, even among those whose own migration is later and much better documented. An interviewee who had arrived in the Netherlands from Hong Kong's New Territories at the end of the 1950s:

> It was easy get to Holland, you just needed someone to invite you. However, at that time there were many outsiders[2] in Holland. The outsiders were people from Zhejiang in the Chinese Mainland who had arrived, begging for food. Most of them had come from China begging all the way to Holland, they made some clay figurines for a living. I've heard that it took them three years to get to Holland, I talked to them then, and they told me some of their stories ... When I arrived in Holland several decades ago, these first-generation people were all in their seventies and eighties ... They did not go by ship, they walked through the Soviet Union [*sic*] to Holland. It took them three years, begging all the way.
>
> (006//004)

The lack of sympathy in the statement is not only rooted in contempt for the 'outsiders', but also in the interviewee's own experience of hardship and poverty. Their feat of traversing the continent as beggars is stated laconically; the interviewee thinks that their misery does not deserve pathos, and that begging is indicative of these people's low character. The statement asserts both continuity and difference: those people came before us, but they belong to a different category. Implicit in the statement is also similarity and discontinuity: their poverty and hardship and ways of overcoming them were nothing special, it is an experience shared with other generations of Chinese immigrants to Europe, but that generation has gone now and all we know about them is hearsay.

Pamela So (1997) has a different perception of those who walked across. A third-generation Chinese now living in Glasgow, she has traced her ancestry back to itinerant artists who walked from Hubei to Germany and France in the first years of the twentieth century. With very few clues, based mainly on the story of the only member of the troupe still alive, she describes their itinerary in heroic terms, especially the bravery of the women who not only bore children en route, but also began to release their lotus feet. So's family eventually began a laundry in Liverpool. Her grandfather, an opium addict, suddenly fled to Holland and never returned, leaving her grandmother alone with four children, of whom the eldest son was only 14. One of the original troupe members returned to Hubei with her husband in the 1930s and experienced such abject conditions that they eventually returned to Liverpool to run the laundry with So's grandmother. The troupe members eventually settled in London, Birmingham, Leeds and Newcastle, so the families rapidly lost their Hubei speech and began to speak English. Her focus is on the strong women, who stand for continuity and family cohesion, even across the loss of language:

The four children of the family loved to speak English, so Grandma had to communicate with her children in her stiff and awkward English.

(So 1997)

So's story may be private, but it is published in Chinese in the Liverpudlian periodical *Brushstrokes*. *Brushstrokes*, a 'collection of British Chinese writing and drawing', records daily experiences of second-generation Chineseness, local Liverpudlian Chinatown reminiscences and personal histories of ordinary Chinese with some link to Merseyside or, more broadly, Britain. It is part of an effort to give substance to the identity of young second- and third-generation Chinese in Britain.

The veracity of these myths, therefore, is not so important as the fact that they are used; those involved are all dead, most details are lost, and the imagination has free play. Some interviewees (like −/064/017) refer to books like the *Local History of Qingtian County* (Chen Murong 1990) as the main source of their knowledge of early migration by foot. Some stories are conveyed between generations in families. An example of this tells us that a Chinese silk trader by the name of Liu walked from Shandong along the Silk Road through Turkey to Germany in the 1930s, married a German woman and opened the Taidong Restaurant in Munich (020/ /009). Many such vignettes of family histories exist among European overseas Chinese and they are important elements of personal identification. It is, however, almost impossible to see them as reliable historical accounts; often they contain few concrete details, and if they do, the details may be distorted.

Mette Thunø (1999, 159–67) provides an overview of the early migration from Qingtian to Europe, critically examining the few reliable written sources available, including some reminiscences recorded in local publications of historical miscellanies (wenshi shiliao). The beginning of what developed into chain migration from Qingtian to Europe was based in local handicraft, carving ornamental figurines in soapstone. Foreigners in treaty ports and vacation resorts in China developed an interest in the figurines, an interest which brought some artisans and traders to Europe after 1893. A stream of migrants slowly gained impetus in the early 1900s, making use of improved travel connections by rail and by sea. The fact that a Qingtianese before the turn of the century ran a boarding house in Marseilles (Thunø 1999, 164) and acted as a shipping master for a European shipping company may indicate which way the first large contingents of Qingtianese came in. When European lines hired Chinese crews they normally went though a shipping master who almost invariably employed people from his native village. The fact that 2,000 Qingtianese worked in France during the First World War, and that perhaps 1,000 stayed after 1918, added to the migration. Migration became institutionalised and commercialised in the 1920s and 1930s, allowing the Qingtianese to arrive in Europe in ever-increasing numbers. Thunø's (1999) investigation of the sources allows us to understand in rough terms how the migration took place. It was chain migration, facilitated by means of transport, and a gradually improved infrastructure, evolving from a boarding house just before the turn of the century, to an elaborate system of credit-ticket packages provided either above board by high street financial institutions or secretly by illegal organisations by the 1930s.

Waves

Migration from China to Europe is a process that follows many patterns. Rather than regarding migration as numbers in statistics, therefore, I examine the diverse main waves of migration and their concrete contexts. The process of migration is fluid, some Chinese migrants stay in Europe, some migrate onwards, some go back to China, some who arrived with the view to work or study for a short time settle down, some retain an economic base in China or Southeast Asia and travel back and forth, some are sent back to China to go to school and return to Europe as adults. Some Chinese immigrants firmly settled in Europe imagine themselves as sojourners, as 'guests passing by' (guoke), and hope to be buried in their native soil.

The flows of immigrants reflect many different concrete circumstances and individual opportunities, reflected in the common Chinese formulation 'if there's a hole, they'll slip through it' (wu dong bu ru). Even the main waves of migrants consist of many individual cases, responding to individual conditions. Even so, I will consider the main migration waves under large summarising headings: (a) labour recruitment, (b) resettlement of refugees and political asylum, (c) trade and investment, (d) study, (e) chain migration, and (f) 'snakeheads'. In real life, the decision to migrate and the paths chosen are likely to span several categories.

Labour recruitment

One of the important concessions the British negotiators wrested from the Manchu Government after the Opium Wars was that Chinese subjects should be allowed to go abroad to work. Before, emigration had in principle been interdicted. The abolition of slavery in most of the world had just been achieved, and the British looked for new sources of cheap labour to replace black slaves. The effect of this was that Hong Kong, and later other treaty ports on the China coast, became entrepôts for the coolie trade. There was no significant effect on migration to Europe, but later some of the coolies thus exported to the colonies would percolate into the European metropolitan areas.

The recruitment of Chinese labourers with the greatest impact on Europe in the nineteenth century was the use of Chinese to carry out menial tasks on board ships. The numbers of Chinese seamen in Europe remained low, until steamship transport between Europe and the Far East became feasible in the 1870s and 1890s. European lines then began to hire in crews of cheap workers to stoke the boilers. The infrastructure surrounding the use of Chinese seamen sustained small immigrant communities and transient populations of sailors waiting for a new hire in ports like Marseilles, London, Liverpool, Amsterdam, Rotterdam, Antwerp, Hamburg and so on.

French, British and American military operations in France and Flanders during the First World War relied on approximately 140,000 Chinese ancillary workers (Summerskill 1982). Although most were repatriated immediately after the war, a few thousands are believed to have stayed in France.

Chinese were recruited on some scale for hard physical labour in Russia at the beginning of the twentieth century, but many were repatriated during the Russian Revolution. It is likely that some found their way to Western Europe in spite of strict border controls.

The need for civilian labour on merchant fleet convoys in the North Atlantic during the Second World War was partly solved by accommodating a large pool of Chinese seamen in Liverpool. Most left after the war, but some remained in Britain.

Between the 1950s and the end of the twentieth century, Chinese specialised cooks were recruited from Hong Kong, Southeast Asia and Mainland China to work in the expanding Chinese catering sector. It is difficult to establish the numbers of cooks thus migrating. Restrictive rules helped limit this avenue of immigration to Europe.

The migration of cooks and other workers to the expanding Chinese catering sector in Great Britain was in the 1960s based on labour vouchers under British immigration rules and on organised migration structures. The decline of agriculture in the New Territories and the rise of opportunities in Britain were important factors, as was the fact that the migrants held British passports. The migration was mainly to Britain, but there was some onwards migration to Germany and the Netherlands.

From the beginning of the 1990s, large numbers of Chinese workers have been attracted to work in sweatshop factories in Italy, Spain and France. Much of this migration is irregular.

Resettlement of refugees and political asylum

A substantial part of the Chinese communities in Europe consists of refugees from the former colonies. Ethnic Chinese in many former British, French and Dutch colonies were to various degrees exposed by post-colonial nationalism, and either expelled or forced to assimilate. At the time of de-colonisation, few Chinese migrated or were relocated to the metropolis, but warfare and ethnic policies later created large-scale migration. The main migration streams were from Vietnam, Laos and Cambodia to France, from Indonesia and Surinam to the Netherlands and from East Timor to Portugal, while minor and scattered migration of Chinese took place from various overseas possessions, territories and protectorates to France, the Netherlands, Portugal and Britain.

Some ethnic Chinese refugees from former French Indochina were not resettled directly in the metropolis. Many of those who escaped by boat were picked up at sea; when vessels registered in European states rescued boat refugees, these were normally offered refugee status in that state. International refugee organisations facilitated family reunion for refugees who were stranded in Hong Kong or other Asian countries, and who had family in European countries.

Between the 1950s and the 1980s a constant trickle of political refugees arrived in Europe from Mainland China. The numbers were small. Countries in Europe offered political asylum or 'leave to stay'.

The clamp-down on the protest movement in Beijing and other major cities in China on 4 June 1989 caused European states to provide various forms of political asylum or 'compassionate leave to stay' to students staying in Europe during the events. Some countries, in particular France, also gave political asylum to activists escaping from China after the events.

In the 1980s and 1990s when travelling outside China became easier, Europe has experienced more applications for political asylum, many of which reflect persecution due to the rigid implementation of family planning policy, corrupt leadership and infringements of the freedom of belief. I will not discuss the related problems in detail here, as the problems are commonly known; it is difficult to differentiate between those who are in genuine personal danger due to their politics, religion and so on, those who make an application for political asylum because they have been told by 'snakeheads' that it is a way of obtaining residence, and those whose application *de facto* incriminates them vis-à-vis the Chinese authorities so that their extradition becomes impossible. In spite of the fact that less than two per cent of all asylum applications by Chinese are granted, they continue to be made. According to *Ouzhou Shibao – Nouvelles d'Europe* (04.11.1999), the number of applications by Chinese for political asylum in France suddenly rose in 1999, especially in the third quarter, to the effect that the number of applications in 1999 was likely to treble, compared to 1998:

Periods	Asylum seekers
January–December 1998	1,560
January–March 1999	849
April–June 1999	1,057
July–September 1999	1,729

The trend predates the clampdown on the popular semi-religious Falun Gong organisation in China in July 1999 (Vermander 1999), and most likely reflects other dynamics that could have to do with the operation of human trafficking or with issues particular to the French amnesty for illegal immigrants. No doubt, however, the clampdown on the Falun Gong organisation, and the subsequent declaration by international human rights organisations that this represents an infringement on the religious freedom and the human rights of the adepts, creates a new framework for political asylum-based migration.

Trade and investment

Chinese civilians serving United States military personnel in China and the Pacific during the Second World War as purveyors, tailors, hairdressers and so on, were partly able to relocate to Europe with military units between 1944 and 1950. Once they were in Europe, they invested in trading, catering and other services.

The opening of China towards the rest of the world in 1978–9 was the backdrop for new waves of business migration. It is possible to detect three main forms of this migration.

One type of investment was the opening of offices and trading branches of Chinese state-owned enterprises and government agencies in major cities. That means that in addition to some few handfuls of offices in Europe that had existed during the Cultural Revolution, like those of the Bank of China and New China News Agency, a range of new offices and branches emerged, representing everything from transport and trading companies to pharmaceutical retailers. Managers and other personnel were stationed in the European locations. The employees in many cases worked on conditions specified for civil servants stationed abroad, and although enterprises and offices were locally registered, their affiliation to bodies in China was evident. Their operation was in most cases under central planning and budgetary control by the Chinese parent.

The second type consisted of various forms of direct and indirect investments outside official planning procedures by Chinese state-owned and other companies under various regimes of ownership, control and regulation by Chinese authorities. Investments were of varying size, and in many cases were a stake in companies co-owned with overseas Chinese. In particular the ability of enterprises to invest in activities outside the state plan and to use foreign currency quotas made such investments possible. Their impact on migration is hard to ascertain. One may assume that the companies often had multiple purposes, such as to earn a profit in hard currency, to cut costs of foreign travel for Chinese delegations, to have people on the ground in Europe to represent interests, and to perform specific services directed at overseas Chinese. Although there was some migration linked to such companies (for example overseas posting of staff), their overall impact on migration was limited.

The third, and most important, type of investment was the establishment of many small Chinese import-and-export companies in Eastern Europe after the fall of the Berlin Wall in 1989. The liberal conditions for immigration in Hungary at the beginning of the decade helped a large market for such small enterprises to grow, but Chinese traders were active in Russia, Poland, Yugoslavia, Czechoslovakia, Romania, Bulgaria, and Albania (and the states they split into) during the 1990s, occasionally interrupted by warfare. When the market contracted in the late 1990s, some of the investors sought to gain a foothold in southern Europe, especially Italy. The traders represented investors or enterprises in China as agents, acting on their own risk, or they were independent. They profited from a main historical coincidence, namely that the markets in Eastern Europe immediately after the fall of the communist regimes were craving all sorts of commodities, ranging from brand-name fashion wear to electronic gadgetry, and that such goods were available from Chinese enterprises specialising in sub-contracting manufacturing for department store chains in the West. The Chinese moved in fast, taking greater economic risks and responding more flexibly to the market than companies from western Europe and North America, and so could carve out a niche for themselves. The migration related to this investment type was large, but highly fluctuating. Migrants often moved on to new destinations, conducted their trade while commuting back and forth between, for example, Hungary and China, or returned to China after some time. The fate of many companies was short-lived, and some operated in an environment of high risk and illegality that prevented their growth and stability.

Taiwanese businesses were another source of new migration in the 1990s. Taiwan's economy changed rapidly in the 1980s away from export-oriented assembly and manufacturing towards becoming a high-tech metropolis. Assembly and simple manufacturing were increasingly located in the Chinese Mainland and in export-production zones in the Asia-Pacific region, and export gradually switched towards advanced high-tech products. Taiwan's enterprises began to see investments in Europe as important for maintaining both the technological edge and market competitiveness. The process began slowly, in the beginning of the 1980s, when a few Taiwanese companies had branches in Europe, mainly relating to air transport. In the Netherlands, for example, there were around 40 Taiwanese companies in 1991, increasing to almost 100 by 1996 (027//006), and the scale of the individual companies grew. The other main destinations of Taiwanese investment were Germany and Britain. The main growth was in the computer trade, including transport, storage, marketing, wholesale, retail and service (027//008–009). In Britain, several large investment projects were aimed at the manufacture and assembly of computers and computer accessories. This investment brought thousands of Taiwanese managers and top-level business employees to Europe. The business settlement was both concentrated in large cities and more scattered, reflecting how local governments in underdeveloped corners of Europe sought to attract foreign investment with preferential treatment and development funds. This was also reflected in the residential pattern. The Taiwanese in the Netherlands would concentrate in a few middle-class suburbs like Amstelveen (near Amsterdam) and Capelle aan den IJssel (near Rotterdam). One interviewee found it 'only natural' that they would live close to each other, as they formed a 'social group' (027//017, 020). This transient population – mainly employees sent out for a few years – already to some extent shows the signs of long-term settlement, when Taiwanese employees establish their own European firms or decide to stay for the sake of their children's education or due to local family relations.

Study

From the 1920s and 1930s onwards, small numbers of Chinese students arrived in Europe on various schemes. The student-worker programme in France gained particular fame because it was closely linked to early Chinese communism. Inititated by the Chinese anarchist Li Zhizeng and the Chinese intellectual and educationist Cai Yuanpei (who had both lived in Europe before 1911, in France and Germany respectively), it consisted of a number of diverse programmes, one of which was to educate wartime workers in France and Flanders 1917–19, bringing Chinese students over to France to work in factories while studying, and operating the Institut Franco-Chinois in Lyons which was largely financed by Boxer indemnity funds. Due both to the political climate of the time and the poor management of the programmes, many of the over 2,000 young Chinese staying in France in this way were radicalised, and many participated in communist organisations; several, like Zhou Enlai and Deng Xiaoping later rose to the highest ranks of the Chinese Communist Party (Live 1994; Costa-Lascoux and Live 1995; Chen Sanjin 1986).

However, Chinese students of many different subjects were enrolled at universities in all major European countries, in particular Germany, France, Britain and the Netherlands.[3] The origin of these students was very mixed; they came from colonial dependencies (like French Indochina, the Dutch Indies or Hong Kong), from foreign concessions (like those in Shanghai and Shandong), and from other places in China; they were financed by government schemes, paid from their own means, or received grants from missions and churches. The Anti-Japanese War in the 1930s rapidly depleted the numbers of Chinese students in Europe. Many saw it as their patriotic duty to return to China and fight. In that way they reflected the anti-fascist mood of the time in Europe. The war years 1939–45 and the first post-war years saw a disruption of university education for Chinese in Europe. The Civil War (1945–9) in China and the ascendance to power of the Chinese Communist Party in 1949 made studies abroad increasingly difficult to pursue for people from the Mainland.

In the 1950s, the Nationalist authorities in Taiwan awarded scholarships to some Chinese students to study in Spain. A number of these students settled in Spain after completing their studies.

Since the 1950s, many students from Hong Kong have gone to study in Europe, mainly in Britain, and some have settled in Britain. Especially after the decision on Hong Kong's retrocession in 1997 had been taken in principle in 1983–4, many students from Hong Kong used their study in Britain to obtain permanent residence rights in Britain, but once these were obtained most returned to Hong Kong to profit from much better career prospects there.

This process can be explained by the growth of Hong Kong's population and the sudden rise in economic welfare and stability that gradually emerged after the unrest in Hong Kong in 1968. The new and large middle class sought to secure a good education for the young generation, and Hong Kong's higher education system did not develop fast enough to absorb the large cohorts. In Britain, the higher education system in the 1980s became increasingly aggressive in marketing higher degrees in overseas markets. Chinese from Hong Kong, Singapore, Malaysia and Taiwan were systematically targeted by British universities, polytechnics and colleges. The new Chinese middle class in these places had the spending power, was (except in Taiwan) used to a British-style education system, and had few problems with the English language.

Among the perks of senior Hong Kong civil servants was the provision of boarding school places for their children. During the colonial era, thousands of Hong Kong boys and girls went to school in Britain on that account and thus gained a cultural and affectionate foothold and in some cases the basis for an academic or professional career in Britain.

The 1970s saw a slowly increasing number of Chinese students leaving the Mainland to study in Europe. In the early and mid-1970s, the number of students was very limited, and strong efforts were made to ensure that they returned to China after completion of their stay abroad. In 1979, several batches of very young students were sent to European countries. They were picked from among the best candidates who had passed the university entrance examination. These 17-, 18- or 19-year-olds were to spend at least five or six years in the foreign country, reading for their undergraduate and postgraduate degrees. Many of these students later found employment in Europe and North America. From 1980, the general pattern was to sponsor students who had already passed their undergraduate degrees in China.

China depended on a wide range of bilateral agreements with European states for sending advanced Chinese students abroad on short stays. Arrangements with different countries diverged in content, but resulted in many grants being made available through the Ministry of Education (during long periods called the State Education Commission). At the same time, the Chinese authorities instituted a unilateral grant system for visiting scholars, by which Chinese academics were given the opportunity of stays at foreign universities.

This official system began to function in the 1980s and rapidly developed into a springboard for students who wanted to study for foreign degrees. They used the year abroad to obtain placements and grants at European institutions. Different regimes in European countries relating to work permits for foreign students and their spouses influenced their living conditions. Those staying in European countries in June 1989 were in most cases given some form of 'compassionate leave to stay' including a work permit. Those who arrived later in many cases also sought to gain permanent residence permits or foreign passports in order to improve their status and chances of occupation. They formed a stratum of highly educated people with good access to information and the ability to communicate globally. Chinese scholars formed a community across Europe and beyond, and migration became an important aspect of study abroad.

China sought to limit the brain drain. However, their measures had little impact. Some Chinese institutions, for example, sought to bind their employees by demanding that they sign bonds of seemingly astronomical sums that would be forfeited if the employee did not return before a specific date. Once the employee had gone abroad, the money lost on the bonds appeared an affordable price for the 'freedom' to stay away. Institutions saw their employees' stays abroad as an investment in their own future, but many who did return to China went into more attractive jobs in other enterprises or institutions; the new employer would pay the former employer an amount to cover the loss. Why did many choose to stay abroad? Many, after all, never gained positions and responsibilities in Europe commensurate with their qualifications and often felt pushed aside. But the alternative of going back to China rarely appeared attractive. Rumours spread fast about negative experiences of those who did return to China. Tensions relating to promotion, work organisation, housing, salaries, perks and colleagues' jealousy caused unease.

Many returning with foreign degrees, a good publication list, and work experience in foreign work teams were dissatisfied with subordinate positions where their further academic achievement was stymied by superiors with poorer qualifications. Recruitment campaigns aimed at solving these problems foundered because good intentions could not change the fact that the institutional dynamics of universities, research institutes and other work units were unable to smoothly accommodate scholars returning with foreign degrees.

An increasing number of people from the Mainland went abroad to study on their own accord. In the late 1980s, the category of 'self-financed students' grew rapidly. From the mid-1980s, private passports and exit permits could be issued for the purpose of studying abroad at one's own cost. The main condition was that Chinese higher education graduates must have fulfilled five years' employment by the state (or pay an 'education fee' of up to 10,000 RMB to be released from this obligation).[4] The sudden rise in affluence among certain groups in China made study abroad a viable option. The cost of studying abroad for one year seemed very expensive; in Britain at the beginning of the 1990s, a fee of GBP 5,000 and estimated living expenses of another GBP 5,000 would total around 140,000 RMB according to the official exchange rates. Add to this the 'education fee' of 10,000 RMB and travel costs of around 10,000 RMB. Depending on the black market exchange rates for RMB (it was impossible to change RMB to foreign currencies at official rates for study abroad), the first year at a British institution could cost in the range of 180,000 to 250,000 RMB, equivalent to ten years of earnings in a good job in China. However, people wanting to go abroad to study could often be sponsored by kin or borrow money from friends. Some worked hard in the new sectors of the economy to save enough funds to go abroad to study. There is some anecdotal evidence that 'money clubs' came into existence among Chinese graduates, by which a number of people pooled their money to allow one to go abroad first, and when he had paid back the pool, the next would leave, and so on.

'Study abroad' also became part of the business interaction between foreign and Chinese firms. Many joint venture and other investment and trade activities included arrangements for training or grants to study abroad for staff members. Sponsorships to family members of officials to study abroad were in some cases used to facilitate the smooth running of business deals.

The United States of America was the preferred destination, but Europe also received its share of these self-financed students. In this group, the incentives to migrate were very high, as the cost of studying abroad could more easily be recouped through working in foreign countries, and because the self-financed students tended to be younger and have less commitments at home. They often chose the path of foreign study in response to poorer educational and occupational opportunities in China. In spite of this, many of the self-financing students did return to China. The burgeoning labour market in private and foreign-invested companies provided ample job opportunities. Their expectations and ambitions often accorded with the new sectors, as many had read for professional degrees (in business, finance, design, and management).

Chain migration

Waves of chain migration had as their starting point some early immigrants from Zhejiang and from the Pearl River Delta. The main waves were from Qingtian, Wenzhou, Wencheng and Ruian in Zhejiang, from Baoan and Taishan in Guangdong and from the New Territories in Hong Kong. Of these, those from Qingtian, Wenzhou and the New Territories were the largest and most persistent. Chain migration has also taken place on a small scale from many other places in China.

Chain migration from Dapeng in Baoan originated in a shipping master in the Netherlands, who hired in crews of sailors from his home district. A steady flow of migration from Dapeng to the Netherlands and Germany took place in the 1950s and 1960s, but seemed to have died out by the end of the twentieth century. Migration from Haiyan in Taishan was centred on shipping masters in Britain (mainly London, Cardiff and Liverpool), who hired in fellow-villager crews. Migration took place in the 1950s, 1960s and 1970s, and gained a boost through secondary migration of Haiyan people who had originally migrated to Nauru in the Pacific. By the end of the twentieth century, there was no substantial chain migration from Taishan to Europe, although in the 1980s and 1990s some Chinese men settled in Britain would still be introduced to potential spouses in Taishan villages. Early migrants (from Taishan in the nineteenth century and from Dapeng in the early twentieth century) created cores for chain migration that picked up in the 1950s. Most of this chain migration took place through Hong Kong. As living standards in Hong Kong improved, migration stopped.

Early Qingtian and Wenzhou migration to Europe formed a core for chain migration that began in the early years of the twentieth century and gained momentum in the 1920s and 1930s. Chain migration to Europe never stopped, but fell into a trough between 1949 and 1986. After 1986, it grew quickly again. Qingtian and Wenzhou have contributed large quantities of migrants to Europe. Chain migration from Wencheng and Ruian followed similar patterns, but was of a lesser scale.

Chain migration from the New Territories began in the 1950s and stopped sometime in the 1980s. This migration originated in social upheaval in the New Territories that was caused by agricultural policy, shift in land use patterns and urban development in new satellite towns. Strong lineage structures were able to facilitate the social transformation of the peasants by helping them to migrate to Britain to work (as Hong Kong from the 1950s to the 1970s did not provide many prospects). Migration was intensified and institutionalised by determination to beat immigration restrictions imposed by the British government in 1962.

The essence of chain migration is kinsfolk and friends, and by extension fellow villagers, who help each other to migrate in a highly organised way. The whole process of providing information, papers, permits, tickets, and jobs is tried out and systematised, involving people both at the place of origin and the place of destination.

Snakeheads

Illegal immigration of Chinese to Europe has taken place since the nineteenth century, and still continues. Illegal migration is organised, but unlike ordinary chain migration it is not run by relatives and friends, but by strangers who seek a profit by providing passage. In the 1980s, gangs in various parts of China began to provide migration services on a large scale, most notably in Fujian and Zhejiang provinces. The gangs in Fujian involved in the smuggling of migrants are called 'snakeheads' (shetou), and this term is often used as a general name for human traffickers in China. Many methods are employed in a continuous struggle to evade detection by border police. Illegal passage in the 1920s or 1930s as a stowaway in a steamship arranged by gangs was in principle not different from illegal immigration at the end of the twentieth century, but the techniques employed and the barriers to be overcome have become much more sophisticated.

Karsten Giese has observed that the distinction between legal and illegal immigration is blurred:

> Migration and employment take place in the context of a multiplex network of social relations that includes contractual arrangements with hardened criminals and corrupt officials as much as social ties with family, kin and friends. The boundaries between benevolence and profiteering, mutual assistance and exploitation, and chain migration and human trafficking are fluid and often indistinct; it is only rarely possible to tease them apart.
>
> (Giese 1999, 211)

Cases

The rest of this chapter will examine migration issues through concrete cases as they were captured in the interviews. Other chapters also treat migration from various angles, so I will restrict myself to three of the migration waves, and also present a case of illegal Chinese immigration to Italy.

New Territories to Britain

One of the largest and most important flows of Chinese immigrants waves to Europe was from the New Territories in Hong Kong to Britain. When this migration was at its height, British anthropologists analysed it (a major work is Watson 1975). It attracted intense attention from both Hong Kong and British home authorities, and is perhaps the best-documented case of Chinese migration. The background, mechanisms, social organisation, and course of the migration have been traced in much detail. Here, not the details but the wider significance of this migration flow is explored. The material at hand lends itself to a comprehensive understanding of migratory processes. Migration from the New Territories to Britain was chain migration. Families, large parts of clans and whole villages were gradually summoned to Britain by the pioneers and those who followed. Most settled in different parts of Britain, while some moved to the Netherlands and Germany. Reverse migration played an important role. Some children of the migrants went to school in Hong Kong. The second generation, raised in Britain, went to Hong Kong to seek their roots, or responded to better job opportunities there. Land entitlements in the New Territories kept material bonds with the 'home' area alive.

Five large clans, the Deng, Hou, Wen, Peng, and Liao,[5] provided many migrants, but there were other surnames among them. The five clans had, in pre-colonial times, been the elite, whose power lay in their ownership of the 'sub-soil' land rights and their roles as village leaders (Chiu and Hung 1997, 12–14). Colonial rule, according to Chiu and Hung (1997), broke their original, all-pervasive power bastions, but at the same time allotted them functions as co-opted village leaders in the political structures of the colony. Their role as political intermediaries gave them new power and status. Many of the overseas Chinese in Britain from the New Territories are still today organised in five 'clansmen's associations' corresponding to the five clans; in addition, a sixth 'clansmen's association' of the Zhangs (Cheung) also organises many immigrants from the New Territories.

James Watson sees the migration process as a conjunction of political economy in Hong Kong and the way in which the clans used their organisation and resources to initiate migration. Watson (1975, 30) dates the major shift to the period between 1957 and 1962. In that period, the village San Tin suddenly changed from an agricultural village to an emigrant community. Agriculture, in that period, collapsed as a major source of income, and the peasants were forced into other activities. The rice culture on which the clans had built their economy gradually became inoperable, and vegetable farming gained strength. In parts of the New Territories, like San Tin described by Watson, rice farmers were unwilling to change to vegetables because they were used to the cycles and intensity of labour in rice cultivation, finding it difficult to adapt to the all-year toil in the vegetable fields, and because they were reluctant to invest labour and money in the land to make it suitable for vegetables (Watson 1975, 46–7). The political and economic status of Hong Kong changed in the early 1950s. The communist takeover in 1949 in the Mainland caused refugees to swarm into Hong Kong on an unprecedented scale, and the colonial authorities were concerned that the supply of vegetables and meat from the Mainland might be cut off at a time when the population was growing quickly. They therefore established an infrastructure for vegetable farming, including technological extension, transport and market facilities. International market prices of rice fell and consumer tastes moved away from the types produced in the New Territories, while production costs rose. This scenario pressed peasants to switch, and those who did not lost out. The newcomers from the Mainland took over land and developed it for vegetable farming. Therefore, in San Tin and many other places in the New Territories, conflict started between old clans and newcomers, where the latter were more able to adapt to the new patterns (Watson 1975, 48–50). Watson describes how one clan, the Wen,[6] in one small area of the New Territories was pushed out of farming in just a few years. Specific conditions differed from one community to another in the New Territories, but the general picture was that economic change forced certain groups out of agriculture and did not provide acceptable employment opportunities in nearby areas. For many, emigration to Britain appeared to be an alternative.

Chain migration at the end of the 1950s was based on a core of perhaps 60 fellow villagers from San Tin already in Britain. They were seamen who had jumped ship in the 1940s and 1950s. When demand for Chinese sailors declined after World War Two, some went into the early Chinese restaurant business (Watson 1975, 56–62).

The jumped-ship sailors were in the early 1950s followed by a small contingent of enterprising, middle-aged fellow-villagers who regarded restaurants in Britain as an investment opportunity. They invested money earned through smuggling activities along the border between Hong Kong and China. During the Korean War, when the Mainland was hit by an embargo, smuggling petrol and other things yielded great profits for traffickers. By investing in London, they responded to better investment opportunities than in Hong Kong with its weakly developed economy and uncertain political future. The new entrepreneurs soon outclassed the earlier sailors-turned-restaurateurs. They employed relatives in a number of successful restaurants.

When the economy changed in the New Territories in 1957, the restaurateurs began to summon jobless young relatives from the New Territories, providing them with low-paid and hard jobs in their London restaurants. They were allowed entry without problems, for they had British passports, albeit a type issued to subjects in colonies and dependent territories. The Hong Kong authorities encouraged migration and readily issued passports in order to take pressure off the local economy and alleviate unemployment and poverty. Between 1959 and 1961, the annual migration from the New Territories grew from 900 to 2,270 persons. The passage of the 1962 Commonwealth Immigrants Act aimed at restricting the immigration of colonials into Britain (Watson 1975, 59–60 and 72–8). It gave rise to a race to 'beat the ban', so that 1961 and the early months of 1962 saw a surge in immigration. Watson dryly remarks, 'It is ironic that, in the long run, the first Commonwealth Immigrants Act did more to encourage emigration from San Tin than to discourage or curtail it' (Watson 1975, 78). Several of our interviewees claimed they were on the 'last plane out' of Hong Kong. The Act did slow down the rate of migration, but did not stop it, for people from the New Territories were able to fulfil the requirements for migration.

Migration to Britain before 1960 was normally a long and tiresome journey by boat, but after 1960 most migrants went on charter flights from Hong Kong to London. This much easier form of travel lowered the barriers to migration. It was not tainted with the image of 'coolie trade' (mai zhuzai) that still stuck to transport by ship, and the migrants had the feeling that it was possible to return to Hong Kong every so often.

Most of the early migrants were young, unmarried men, including perhaps some young husbands who left their wives at home. Before 1965 few women left the New Territories for Britain. These young people worked hard, both saving money for themselves, and remitting some back to their families. After some years, to judge by the pattern described by some of our interviewees, they would invest in a restaurant together with a brother or cousin and use this as a base to summon more relatives over. When they had saved enough, they would go back to Hong Kong to find a suitable spouse and establish their own business. Many restaurants were run as man-and-wife businesses. Once in Britain most wives were strongly involved in the running of the restaurant. Children were often raised in Hong Kong by relatives and joined their parents later.

Many of the early investors returned to Hong Kong to live, and every so often went to Britain to look after their property (Watson 1975).

Most of those whose forefathers or who themselves lived in the New Territories before it was leased to the British crown in 1898[7] had an original lease title to land, and had prerogatives to build a small 'village-style' house (dingwu). It was important to assert these rights even while staying in Britain. With the expansion of new towns in the New Territories in the 1970s, the lease rights became the object of speculation, and the small houses became useful sources of rent income.

The immigrants from the New Territories were, to judge by Watson's analysis, part of a system of authority that stretched from the villages in the New Territories to Britain. The forms and expressions of authority underwent fundamental changes and gained new dynamics during the prolonged process of migration. But it remained an authority spanning the two places.

When a large number of New Territory villagers in a short span of years migrated to Britain, their villages were already in a process of change. Migrants from the Mainland were supplanting the original inhabitants, agricultural production and fishery were changing, and core frameworks of the social structure were changing; for example, when families allowed all sons, even the only son, to migrate. Loans, remittances, marriages and visits kept the formal structures intact, albeit over a distance, while rural production and fishery declined. In Britain, many people from the same villages settled near each other and formed small communities of fellow-villagers and some established voluntary organisations representing tiny hamlets. The meaning of community changed as people at a far distance remained bound to each other through resources, social obligations, and common concerns arising from the protracted migration process.

The New Territories provided exceptional opportunities for building a separate identity. The Chinese inhabitants in the area leased to the British in 1898 and their descendants were, by treaty, protected from eviction from their land and their traditions and lifestyles were guaranteed for the duration of the lease. They were, in that way, given special collective rights. The British takeover of the New Territories began with a peasant uprising that marked collective protest. The uprising was firmly quelled, but tensions continued to exist between the peasants and the colonial authorities. Although there were splits and suspicions among different New Territories clans, they understood themselves to be opposed to the British, and they were forced to cooperate with them as a group, for example, from the 1920s onwards, through the representative organ, the Heung Yee Kuk (Xiangyiju). From the beginning the peasants in the New Territories had a formal political status, centred on the protection of their group rights. In the 1950s and 1960s, the Hong Kong authorities played various fractions within this polity en miniature against each other. The climax was reached in 1957, when the Hong Kong government, following social unrest caused by the building of a dam, forced a coup in the Heung Yee Kuk, which became a more cooperative organisation. These events reinforced the political ramifications for a shared identity among people in the New Territories (Chiu and Hung 1997).

Not only the political organisation and the group rights but also social stigmatisation and exclusion gave a sense of common identity. The Hong Kong Island elite considered the New Territories rustic backwaters. The Chinese who had gained a foothold in Hong Kong from the 1840s regarded themselves as more sophisticated than the inhabitants north of Kowloon; the differential treatment of the groups by the colonial administration added to this social distance. In the 1920s, the Hakka bourgeoisie in Hong Kong became aware of its peasant cousins, the Hakka families in the New Territories. It established schools and charities for them, and sought to help them in many other ways. The general attitude towards the people in the New Territories thus ranged from charitable paternalism to disgust and arrogance.

In the 1950s, the fact that the descendants of the indigenous villagers in the New Territories held British passports made them different from the new inhabitants who had fled the Mainland. In particular, the descendants had the option of migrating to Britain. The newcomers, renting their land or buying their land leases, were in conflict with them.

The policy on 'village-style' houses and the practice of issuing land vouchers (documents promising future land leases to replace land that had been resumed by the government in order to construct new satellite towns in the 1970s) were directed towards the descendants of the indigenous villagers, irrespective of their present place of residence or job. They did not include New Territory residents who had arrived later than 1898 or their descendants. Common descent, therefore, became a distinguishing factor of the group. The claim to be descendants derived its vitality from their economic and juridical claim to assets, and was expressed in the assertion of group rights.

The migrants not only retained the claim to an asset in the New Territories, but were under pressure from the family to assert it. One of the major tasks of the Hong Kong Government Office in London (established in 1957) was to identify owners of New Territory land leases living in Britain in order to ensure that the land resumption policy of the 1960s, 1970s and 1980s could proceed. Leaseholders had to be found and given compensation before new town expansion could go ahead (064//002...003). The firm control with land leases and the official restrictions on 'village-style' houses also gave work to the Hong Kong Government Office, as even simple transactions had to be verified by a public servant and acknowledged by the land authority. This incremental process of identity construction relied on political organisation, descent, legal status, social divisions, land rights, migration, and the leadership of the 'five great clans'.

Political activism among New Territory migrants was important. Some migrants of the 1960s, whose background in Hong Kong had been characterised by the poor conditions and political crises there, had an ambivalent attitude to Britain and were politically active. Several of the interviewees told us that they had been active in leftist political work in Hong Kong before they went to Britain, and some had even been educated in the Mainland before the Cultural Revolution. One interviewee had fought among the East Lake Guerrillas during the Anti-Japanese War. The Chinese Embassy in London provided a secret focal point for political propaganda during the Cultural Revolution, and many of the restless young inclined towards Chinese communism.

The migrants from the New Territories were not drawn into the schism between Beijing and Taibei. The Nationalists on Taiwan did not have any influence in Britain, and although the diplomatic relations between Beijing and London were strained, the Mainland gained importance among the overseas Chinese in the 1960s, just before the Cultural Revolution. One immigrant from the New Territories said:

> At that time there wasn't even a chargé d'affaires, nothing, not to speak of an ambassador. When in nineteen-sixty-something a Chinese chargé d'affaires, Song Zhigang, arrived, we were so happy.
>
> (006//032)

However, the Representative Office of the Hong Kong Government in London served as an active force, providing a focus point for overseas Chinese organisations, aid to Chinese mother tongue schools and a political antidote to communism.

Political activism grew after 1983, when it became clear that Hong Kong would revert to China in 1997. The identity of the descendants of the 'indigenous villagers' stood at the centre of the activism. Several issues overlapped during more than a decade of lobbying, demonstrations, media struggles and petitions. The major issues were male inheritance in the New Territories, rural elections in Hong Kong, and their status as Hong Kong residents in Chinese nationality law after July 1997. The descendants of the 'indigenous villagers' in both Hong Kong and Britain were active in these activities.

In Hong Kong, political change, especially during Chris Patten's incumbency as governor, inflicted serious blows on the descendants. Democratic reform decimated Heung Yee Kuk's political status, among other things through changing procedures for elections and political representation. Streamlining the administration, the Hong Kong government aimed to remove what seemed anomalies in the laws; the fact that inheritance laws in the New Territories excluded women from inheriting land, while there was gender equality under general Hong Kong law, turned into an important rallying point for the descendants all over the world.[8] A delegation from Heung Yee Kuk travelled to Britain, the Netherlands and Belgium to seek support for the cause.[9] The problem was that the land laws, the land resumption policy and the rules on 'village-style' small houses as the material core of the descendants' identification would disappear with female inheritance. According to the logic of the large lineages, such assets would then be forfeited to people who were not members of the lineages. Through very elaborate action, including large demonstrations, the descendants sought to prove that female inheritance would deprive them of their birthright; the media depicted Heung Yee Kuk and the people in the New Territories as retrograde and sexist.

The greatest problem that faced the descendants was the issue of Chinese nationality law. Chinese nationality law does not allow dual citizenship. The Joint Declaration of 1984[10] and the Basic Law of 1990[11] solved most issues of nationality, permanent residence and use of travel documents for people in Hong Kong. Those who were of Chinese stock (in the official Chinese formulation, 'Hong Kong Chinese compatriots') were Chinese nationals.

Those who had been 'British Dependent Territories citizens' (BDTCs) were allowed to use British-issued passports after 1997, but these passports gave no British consular protection in Hong Kong or other parts of China. Article 24 in the Basic Law spelt out the eligibility for permanent residence in Hong Kong. The formulation excluded Chinese holding foreign passports (other than the British Dependent Territories citizens' passports) from automatic permanent residence in Hong Kong because they were not technically Chinese citizens under the provisions of Chinese nationality law. Many of the Hong Kong migrants to Europe did not hold BDTC passports, but full British passports, so neither they nor their children were Chinese citizens. Their only way to obtain permanent residence in Hong Kong would be through seven years of continuous residence in Hong Kong.

In the mid-1990s, this problem provoked a spate of political lobbying. The Heung Yee Kuk and overseas Chinese organisations sent delegations to Beijing to secure a solution, and were received positively. They carried forward a range of arguments, of which the most important was that they thought of themselves as Chinese and had never actively sought to change their nationality. Ultimately, in May 1996, the Standing Committee of the National People's Congress reiterated and explained the rules, allowing people of Hong Kong origin living abroad and holding foreign passports to be considered Chinese citizens. The solution was that Chinese citizens with permanent residence in Hong Kong could use foreign passports for foreign travel, but that such a document could not be used as proof of nationality in Hong Kong or the rest of China.[12]

This political rallying around perceived collective rights at a time when they were threatened by political circumstance invigorated the sense of a separate identity. These sentiments were reflected in the interviews with overseas Chinese in Britain:

> Because we people from the New Territories incessantly have struggled against the British colonial rule, we have been able to sustain the basic rights of the indigenous villagers up till today. But these last two years, Christine Loh proposed to amend the Land Exemption Bill, that's to say to further mess up the lineage traditions of the indigenous villagers. They use the human rights issue to talk about gender equality, and think that women should have the same (land inheritance) rights as men ... The traditional lineage system will be destroyed.
>
> (002//062)

At the moment, the Heung Yee Kuk struggles with all means and, of course, we as people from the New Territories say: 'These are our rights, we must protect them'. However, some compatriots in Hong Kong say: 'We are all Chinese, why should we accept [that they receive] such special treatment?'

(002//069)

Under the protection of the colony, we citizens could freely leave and enter Hong Kong, why should we overseas Chinese go through a visa formality after 1997? That would not be fair. So when I went back (to Hong Kong) this time, I fought for these rights, I suppose (the papers have) already published it.

(005//005)

Over two years ago (when Christine Loh proposed to amend the Land Exemption Bill), I personally and Mr. XXX received many letters from (overseas Chinese originating in) the New Territories who did not understand what was going on. We answered them all.

(006//048)

One interviewee explained that until the 1990s, there were only a few links between the Heung Yee Kuk and the overseas Chinese (064//038). The perceived infringement on the rights of the descendants of the indigenous villagers was the major catalyst for the new activism spanning Europe and Hong Kong. Familial, social, economic and political bonds have played an important role during three decades, and in the 1990s, the Heung Yee Kuk made a deliberate effort to canalise and interpret some major issues of the community. The migration from the New Territories was a long and complex process of building a community that spanned people in Europe and Hong Kong.

Southeast Asia to France

The migration from Southeast Asia to France was an outcome of de-colonisation and the rising nationalism and wars in former French Indochina. The migrants were ethnic Chinese, but they normally did not hold French (or other European) passports, but the passports of their state of origin, Cambodia, Laos or Vietnam. Unlike the migrants from the New Territories they were refugees, and although they came from large Chinese communities, they and up to several generations of their forefathers had never been in China. Another important dissimilarity with the people from the New Territories was their social status and relationship with the colonial power: they were not peasants and fishermen, but merchants and professionals, who had held core functions in society, and workers.

The Southeast Asian Chinese saw themselves as separate from the indigenous societies of Indochina, and emphasised their internationalist merchant status. One interviewee enumerated the eight languages he knew, Teochiu, Cantonese, Mandarin, French, Cambodian, Vietnamese, Laotian and Thai. As he said, 'overseas Chinese all do it to earn a living, so we are relatively fast at everything', including learning languages (038//006). Eight languages may seem many, but the interviewee claimed that most of his fellow migrants know between five and eight languages. Their realm was not one segment of one Chinese community in one country, it was French Indochina with its various peoples and Chinese communities, it was neighbouring Thailand with its abundant trading opportunities, and it was France as the metropolis. The interests of Chinese businessmen in French Indochina spanned borders and languages.

The migration from former French Indochina therefore created a different community. The community of origin was torn apart, and the vestigial groups of co-ethnics left behind in former French Indochina went out of contact. The migrants in France, holding refugee papers, could not return to the region (including Thailand) without forfeiting their refugee status. The migrants did not see their country or area of origin in Southeast Asia as a major focus of identification. On the contrary, they gathered together in communities reflecting their ancestral place or dialect group.

Migration was, from what can be inferred, not as straightforward and uniform as the migration from the New Territories to Britain. For some it was a gradual retreat, cutting losses, moving from, for example, Cambodia to Thailand, and from Thailand to other places in Asia, before ending up in France, maintaining as much business as possible. For others it was a hasty flight, during which they lost everything. Some escaped by boat and were rescued by European ships, or they fled to Hong Kong. One interviewee arrived in Europe at the age of 16 and only during subsequent years gradually located his parents and siblings (all still in Asia, some in refugee camps) and summoned them. Some were rich on arrival in France, while others were poor.

Migration from French Indochina began in the 1950s during the first wave of de-colonisation, but it intensified between 1975 and well into the 1980s. The early migration to France determined the direction of identity formation. The ancestral-place identification that had been a strong factor in all Chinatowns of French Indochina was replicated in France. Later Chinese refugees from the new nation states Vietnam, Cambodia and Laos joined these patterns of group formation. The first immigrant organisation of refugees in France, the Association des résidents en France d'origine indochinoise (Huzuhui), incorporated Chinese refugees from all parts of French Indochina, irrespective of their ancestral places, but gradually divided itself into associations reflecting ancestral origin. While the main stream of migrants went to France, many found their way to other European countries, including Germany, Britain, the Netherlands, Belgium and the Scandinavian countries. In Britain, immigrants from Vietnam have formed a separate organisation, based on the country of origin rather than ancestral place. Their experience of being pushed out by the communist government of Vietnam created a point of shared identification (058//155–63).

The migrant community of Chinese from French Indochina in France is centred in the 13th arrondissement of Paris. Their large numbers and relative importance as merchants mean that they form a natural centre for fellow refugees in the rest of France and other parts of Europe. Unlike the migrants from the New Territories they do not have a common set of economic interests, political organisation and strong political causes around which they can build a functional identity. Their strength is derived from two main sources, namely religion and lobbying to improve the conditions of their refugee status. The major associations of refugees from French Indochina have established Buddhist shrines or temples. In 1999, for example, two associations, the Association des résidents en France d'origine indo-chinoise and the Amicale des Teochew en France, were instrumental in securing permission for Indochinese refugees in France to travel and do business in Thailand (*Ouzhou Shibao – Nouvelles d'Europe*, 03.06.1999).

The fact that the refugees had been driven out of Vietnam, Cambodia and Laos by communist regimes in the 1980s inspired the Nationalists in Taiwan to seek to organise them. They established a Taiwan-inclined pan-European association, which in the 1990s became defunct, as Taiwan's policy towards overseas Chinese changed. In Britain, Belgium and elsewhere, the Taiwanese also created local Vietnamese associations that aimed at rallying the refugees in 'anti-communist' organisations (035//125). In response, pro-communist organisations sprang up in order to counter the Taiwanese efforts. Voluntary organisations in Taiwan providing a 'home' for such organisations declined in the 1990s, as Taiwan's political reforms lessened the need for such channels of informal contact.

The refugees from French Indochina were 'discovered' by the government of Cambodia after the political normalisation that took place in the years 1991–3. Towards the end of the 1990s, politicians and senior officials from Cambodia visiting Paris routinely met with leaders of associations of Chinese from French Indochina.[13] Cambodian officials were invited to Chinese New Year Celebrations in Paris, and overseas Chinese were consultants to the Cambodian government (*Ouzhou Shibao – Nouvelles d'Europe* 20.02.1999, p. 5). The sixtieth anniversary of a school in Cambodia was used as an opportunity to establish an alumni association in Paris, consisting of refugees from French Indochina who had originally attended the school. This created an informal framework for semi-official contacts between Cambodia and its Chinese refugees in Paris. The alumni organisation encompasses people across the ancestral-place boundaries. The chairman of the preparatory committee of the alumni association is a leader in the Cantonese camp, while business leaders in the Teochiu camp are also involved, in particular with financial support (*Ouzhou Shibao – Nouvelles d'Europe* 27.11.1997, p. 5). There is no doubt that the overseas Chinese merchants, with their deep knowledge of Cambodia, their language skills and vantage position in Europe, are an important potential bridgehead for Cambodia, whose economy is one of the poorest in the world. For Cambodia and the merchants, courting each other is a rational calculation. The interest is expressed in ceremonial terms that construct native-place bonds. The emerging relationship with Cambodia thus provides material for a reinterpretation of community among the refugees.

The internationalist, cross-border bonds are, of course, also cemented by the many dialect-group or ancestral-place organisations. The remainder of the Chinese community in Cambodia, for example, is linked to the refugees in France through such organisations. The Teochius in Phnom Penh maintain contact with their fellows in Paris through the Teochiu Association (Chaozhou Huiguan) and the Amicale des Teochew en France. (Teochiu organisations also exist in other European countries, e.g. Denmark.) In the 1990s, these associations, which originally regarded themselves as neutral in the Taiwan–Mainland schism, became increasingly involved with the Mainland authorities (*Ouzhou Shibao – Nouvelles d'Europe* 20.11.1997).

The ethnic Chinese refugees from Southeast Asia living in France are not only different from their New Territories counterparts in terms of migration history and original social status. The circumstances of their migration have also created fewer points of identification, save for a commercial cosmopolitanism. The formation of their identity in the process of migration has happened under different pressures and as a result of this taken more diverse directions. In the case of the New Territories migrants, economic assets, political rights and the principle of descent were tangible unifying factors, while such elements hardly played a role among the refugees in France. One interviewee, outside the interview, indicated that he retained his Southeast Asian passport and avoided naturalisation in France, because as a French national living in France he would have to report his overseas capital holdings and incomes to the French tax authorities, but as a resident refugee he was exempt from this obligation. But such an individual business decision, even if many take it, does not constitute a focal point for identity based on group rights.

Illegal immigration and the Zhou Yiping case

You apparently haven't discovered – there is a question you haven't asked me – China now does not any more put restrictions on those compatriots who are leaving. But if the foreign countries do not give you a visa, do not allow you to apply for migration, how do you get out? I need to give you an answer to this question: of the people who come here, very few have formally applied for work permits.[14] Perhaps one in five hundred has. That is, firstly, because it is difficult, and secondly, because the difficulty is huge. Most of the people who have come during the last seven or eight years have had to pass immense barriers. They could not go by plane, for if you have no visa, you are not allowed to. From the moment the Berlin Wall fell, the East European political systems collapsed, and the door of the Soviet Union was opened, the door to Chinese migration to Europe stood wide open … This is how they came. They had to pay 20,000 or 10,000 or 30,000 US dollars for the passage. It takes somebody to do this work. So that is how Zhou Yiping emerged as the boss.

(051:87)

This interviewee claims that large numbers of overseas Chinese were able to go to the Soviet Union (later Russia) on false papers, from where East European organisations transferred them to the Czech Republic, Hungary and Yugoslavia (before the Balkan wars of the 1990s), and later through Austria or directly to Italy.

This is one of the many ways used to migrate illegally into Europe. Using real passports, it is possible to travel to a number of countries outside China without visas, from where it is easier to get access to European countries. The Czech Republic, Hungary, the Baltic states and the Balkans have been access points for human trafficking across borders (Giese 1998). Some migrants even pass through African countries (*Le Monde* 20.08.1998, p. 8). Other methods include obtaining fake visas and residence permits, using false passports from other Asian countries, obtaining genuine tourist visas and overstaying, and obtaining visas on false pretexts (e.g. false certificates for qualified cooks) or false identities (e.g. using the papers of deceased persons).

Moscow is a major port of transit for illegal migrants to Western Europe. An account in *Ouzhou Shibao – Journal d'Europe* (13.01.1994 and 14.01.1994) written by Ma Zhuomin describes the Moscow connection in great detail. When Hungary and Romania withdrew visa-free access for Chinese citizens in 1991 and 1992, human trafficking relocated to Moscow. The advantage for traffickers was that they had a more concentrated market with a greater supply of customers. They could (in the early 1990s) demand between 7,000 and 8,000 USD per transit from Moscow to Italy or Spain, where the in the past, the income from smuggling between Budapest or Bucharest and southern Europe had ranged between 4,500 and 5,000 USD. Also, lax security in Moscow made it a safe place for traffickers, who could better control their customers.

In the early 1990s it was estimated that the illegal transient population of Chinese in Moscow exceeded 30,000 at any given time. Several dozen snakeheads based in Moscow had specialised in smuggling Chinese to western parts of Europe, and some snakeheads had specialised in transporting people from China to Moscow. Middlemen operated to link customers with traffickers for a fee. Some people specialised in providing all sorts of false passports, others in making false visas and entry and exit stamps from various countries, and some in doctoring documents, like replacing photographs in passports and residence papers. The snakeheads charged their customers for living expenses. They spent 120 to 150 USD renting a flat, and charged each migrant 500 USD as a one-off charge for meals and accommodation; between 10 and 30 persons lived in the flat at a time. They charged several hundred USD commission for Russian exit visas (for which they only paid about 1,000 roubles); those who had arrived legally in Moscow paid 320 to 400 USD, those who had arrived illegally paid 500 to 600 USD. The expense of transit was 5,000 to 6,000 USD to reach Moscow from China; living expenses in Moscow amounted to 500 USD; various paperwork, 320 to 600 USD; transit to Western Europe cost 7,000 to 8,000 USD. An additional tax on the migrants was that Russian thieves and policemen often targeted them and stole or confiscated their money and belongings. Some lacked money for onward travel and were stranded in Moscow for several years, living in squalor. Giese (1998), using mainly German federal police agency reports, largely confirms Ma Zhuomin's description, and also discusses other types and examples of illegal entry.

European governments' procedures and measures aimed at preventing illegal immigration may make it more difficult for a while, but it often returns in other areas. Frequent changes in policy and detection methods also contribute to confusion about the definition of legal and illegal immigration.

Illegal status is subject to change. Many respected pillars of society in overseas Chinese communities in Europe came as illegal immigrants, but now have permanent residence permits or the nationality of their country of residence.

The main rules concerning migration were different in the past, so the forms and channels of human trafficking differed from now. One of our interviewees told about the route to the Netherlands from China in the 1950s and 1960s. The first step was to go to Macau in order to obtain a Macanese identity card. One had to contact specialist contractors to get such a paper. Using the identity card, one could apply for a Republic of China passport, so the next step was to go to the Taiwan government's consulate in Hong Kong to obtain a passport. With a Republic of China passport one could easily get a tourist visa for Germany or Switzerland. One then went there by plane and slipped illegally across the border to the Netherlands. The interviewee arrived in the Netherlands in 1965, and stayed there without a residence permit for three years. In 1968, he registered for a residence permit under an amnesty scheme. Other illegal immigrants had their status legalised during a large amnesty in 1975 or later in 1980–3 (021//046–47; see also 041// 030). Such migration normally depended on middlemen, and people who provided information and helped with procedures for a price.

Illegal immigrants can be legalised in many ways. Illegal entry may be *de facto* legalised by administrative procedure. A false identity may be officially declared the real identity or may become the officially recognised identity. An illegal status may become legal because the person in question becomes entitled to residence (e.g. through marriage or amnesty). One interviewee told us that while his parents had a permanent residence permit in Germany, he was unable to get one, so he went to Belgium, because at that time it was possible to settle down without applying for a residence permit (034//055). In that way, his illegal immigration status in one country could be changed for a legal status in a neighbouring country. Lack of papers proving one's identity and nationality may in some cases protect one from repatriation or expulsion, and so provide a *de facto* 'legal' basis for residence. Some illegal immigrants, therefore, destroy their papers, lest they be repatriated to China (037//046), and Chinese diplomats insist on clear identification before they accept responsibility for illegal immigrants (037//050).[15]

I shall in the following examine how the activities of one person, Zhou Yiping, helped increase illegal migration, and how they affected the Chinese community in Italy.

Zhou Yiping was an immigrant from Qingtian, who during the late 1980s and early 1990s gained prominence in the Chinese community in Rome. He owned several prestigious restaurants and became the chairman of an influential association. His wealth, status and influence stemmed from the fact that he provided false residence papers for illegal Chinese immigrants in Italy (–/086/079). His services were only one part of the system of illegal immigration.

Various interviewees in Italy, some of whom knew Zhou Yiping personally, provide some glimpses of this affair. The main impression is that his actions were both resented and admired. Some of his fiercest critics among the overseas Chinese are ready to level charges against the whole community for accepting him:

> He gathered so much money for himself, but in the eyes of the local overseas Chinese he did many good deeds, they did not think of it as criminal, they thought he did good deeds by helping so many people out (of China).
>
> (051:89)

However, one may ask what the odds were for those who opposed him.

> This man, how can I say it, there were many guys – he had charm and the gift of the gab. He could put things very pleasantly. He would say, OK, these poor buggers are all friends, we share what we eat with them, and we share our money with them. So he had this entourage, they stayed at his place, ate together, and they did whatever he told them to. Many people said he was good.
>
> (057//077)

> As for his insiders, he had ten to twenty youngsters, they were very united, and they said he was good. They said that he was just and upright, like (the heroes of the classical novel) the *Three Kingdoms*, and (the hero) Wu Song in (the novel) *Water Margin*. In reality they did not think a step further, how such actions would affect the reputation of our China.
>
> (057//082)

He was a charismatic person who used his associates to terrorise the community; he was a man it was not wise to oppose. He took his share of the booty when he intervened to solve disputes; he would, for example, be the benign force helping to negotiate the release of people held for a ransom, and part of the ransom would end up in his pocket (057//083–86). He endorsed, behind the scenes, the fact that gangs demanded 'loans' from people in the community, threatening them. He did not organise these gangs himself, they were spontaneous mobs of youngsters, but he taxed them (057//089–94). His main crime was that he printed residence permits indistinguishable from the official ones on a computer (051:89), and that he handled false passports (057//081–82).

Zhou Yiping struck a clever balance between criminal activity that he construed to be to the benefit of all Chinese, and the public appearance of community spirit and leadership, combined with secret profiteering. One may imagine the ambiguity and the undercurrent of terror that he produced among Chinese in Rome in the early 1990s. What brought him down? One interviewee suggests that his hubris was to build a Chinese restaurant so ostentatiously decorated that

> the foreigners[16] became jealous: this Chinese from the Mainland, so shabbily poor, how come he has got so much money, millions of USD? Investing hundreds of thousand dollars? Where did the money come from? Of course

they were to target him. When they searched his home and his restaurant they found piles of passports, fake and real mixed together.

(051:89)

However, it is more likely that the conflict between people from Wenzhou and Qingtian sealed his fate (051:139; 052//040). In 1992, the elections to the major Chinese community association in Rome were the cause of his downfall. The leadership team elected consisted of Qiangtian people, and the Wenzhouese were kept out. Interviewees imply that the vote had been rigged to that effect. The disagreement between the two groups flared up because a compromise on the leadership of the association had fallen through, and the Wenzhouese felt cheated. The row escalated, Zhou Yiping lost control of the situation, and incriminating evidence became so hard that the Italian authorities arrested him. He was sent to jail for about four years, and after completing his sentence, he was deported to China in 1996.

The case created distrust among overseas Chinese in Italy and also became a topic for negative media reportage on the Chinese community. The case was presented as a part of worldwide triad activity, and headlines implied that all Chinese represented a 'yellow invasion' (on related issues, see *Le Monde* 02.07.1997, p. 14 and Marsden 1997).

Several interviewees politely refused to comment on the case. One answered the question about what impact the case had had on the Chinese restaurant business by saying, 'I've heard that he's already been sent back' (056:236).[17] However, all interviewees who spoke about the case indicated how negatively it had affected the overseas Chinese in Italy.

Zhou Yiping's ability to facilitate illegal immigration relied on the facts that (1) the Florentine leather and garment sweatshop industries need cheap labour to provide fashion houses across Europe with their wares, (2) the Italian state, despite its rhetoric, condoned and encouraged illegal immigration, and (3) as Giese (1998, 203) points out, local authorities in China see emigration as a source of extra-budgetary income.

Some interviewees blame the Italian authorities for lacking initiative:

Italy hasn't achieved anything, there are so many (illegal immigrants) coming, and they haven't caught any, so we must conclude they haven't got the abil … er, haven't got the means to understand how our community works.

(053//048)

Interviewees believe that the inaction of the Italian government towards illegal immigration is harmful. They argue that on one hand there is rhetoric and public debate against illegal immigration, and that on the other nobody is deported. This means, so the interviewees claim, that the whole Chinese community is made to suffer intolerance and suspicion:

If, for example, you have a residence permit, you run a leather workshop or whatever, and hire in a lot of black (i.e. illegal) workers. If the police target you, they take the black workers away. Italy has got the problem; if they catch people in France or other countries, they send them home to China, but here they haven't got the money to send them home. They give you 15 days to leave the country. When the Chinese receive the order to leave, they throw it in the waste bin. In the past, they'd put you in jail for four days and then release you.

(057//074)

In Britain, the late 1990s witnessed a sudden rise in illegal immigration from the Fujian Province in China. Within a decade, Fujian migrants rose from 10 to 10,000, mainly arriving from Fuqing and Changle counties under the jurisdiction of Fuzhou (the capital of Fujian). The migration, as *Ouzhou Shibao – Nouvelles d'Europe* (04.12.1999, p. 5) comments, mainly consists of men in their twenties and thirties, but also some teenage boys and a young woman. They 'arrive in a strange country to a harsh life, but for the Chinese restaurant managers they are the core troops that provide fresh labour'.

A newly established Fujian native-place organisation provides legal aid and gives publicity to the misery of the Fujian migrants, for 'since 1993 there has been little chance of obtaining long-term residence for political asylum seekers', and 'only few new migrants are likely to find jobs, as the Chinese restaurant labour market cannot absorb them, so that some people go without work now' (*Ouzhou Shibao – Nouvelles d'Europe* 04.12.1999, p. 5).

Amnesties

Illegal migration to Europe has created a wave of amnesties, especially in Southern Europe, mainly in France, Italy, Spain and Portugal during the 1980s and 1990s (earlier on, countries in Northern Europe carried out amnesties, like the Netherlands in 1975 and in 1980). The amnesties (in Chinese, dase) aim at legalising the status of illegal immigrants. Amnesties reflect the realisation that the illegal immigrant population has grown to a large size due to an improper or too lax immigration regime. More effective and stringent laws on or measures towards immigration are accompanied with the decision to allow those already present to stay. Illegal immigrants are allowed to apply for an amnesty before a specific date; they must fulfil some criteria (e.g. being able to prove that they have lived in the country for a certain period, have work or capital and a place to live) and be able to prove their identity. An amnesty for illegal immigrants is, therefore, wiping the slate clean and bringing an unstable situation under control.

Although the number of illegal migrants from China since the 1980s has steadily increased, the Chinese only constitute an insignificant part of third world immigration to European countries. The Chinese are not considered to be among the largest groups of immigrants (in statistics they are surpassed or equalled by people from various North African and sub-Saharan African countries, Turkey, ex-Yugoslavia, Albania, the Philippines, and Sri Lanka), and they have, generally speaking, not caused major crises in race relations or social policy. (Two book titles, one on French and one on Italian Chinese, convey the impression of quiet and peaceful entry: *L'intégration silencieuse*[18] and *L'immigrazione silenziosa*.[19]) Initiatives in Europe during the 1980s to introduce stricter immigration rules were not primarily aimed at solving illegal Chinese immigration, but in the event, the Chinese profited from the amnesties.

For example, during the French amnesty in 1998–9 many Chinese immigrants obtained residence status. The French authorities initiated a new immigration law in 1997, combined with a circular on an amnesty. The estimated 300,000 'sans papiers' (the French term for immigrants without proper residence papers) were allowed half a year to apply for an amnesty. Restrictive and inconsistent implement-ation of the amnesty caused popular resentment, voiced in demonstrations, hunger strikes, the occupation of churches by sans papiers and their supporters, protests by concerned intellectuals and sharp media reactions. Public pressure on the government forced the authorities to adopt a more liberal implementation of the amnesty, for which about 143,000 people had applied. According to press reports, the Chinese stood out as a 'surprise' when in the first round 10 per cent (or 2,350) of all permits were given to Chinese and they turned out to have the lowest refusal rates (*Le Monde* 23.02.1998). When the final results were published about a year later (*Le Monde*, 20.01.1999; *Ouzhou Shibao – Nouvelles d'Europe* 24–26.01.1999), 9,000 of the total of 80,000 residence permits were given to Chinese, and 87 per cent of the Chinese who applied were granted an amnesty.

This success can partly be attributed to the high degree of organisation among the overseas Chinese, which may have been an important contributing factor. One association was given the task by the Chinese embassy of attesting the identity and other details of all applicants, and the Embassy used these as the basis for issuing relevant papers to the applicants.[20] This procedure was carried out rigorously, so that those who applied were more likely to submit proper material to the French authorities. Those who were not likely to meet the criteria were told so at an early stage, and refrained from applying. Another factor contributing to the success was that many illegal Chinese migrants had relatives in France. This probably made it easier for French officials to fit the Chinese into the categories used for the amnesty. The informal organisation among the overseas Chinese in France also made it easier for the Chinese illegal immigrants to meet the criteria, for co-natives were in many cases able to help with work, accommodation, and even marriage arrange-ments. Many of the Chinese sans papiers participated actively in hunger strikes, civil disobedience actions, demonstrations, and other protest forms together with sans papiers of other nationalities. Through this they gathered a profound knowledge of the issues involved and they were part of sophisticated information networks on how to beat the system.

One purpose of the amnesty was to create better and more just conditions for those affected. The sweatshop industries where the sans papiers earn their living play an ambiguous role. On the one hand, they provide work and subsistence for the sans papiers; work and a place to live were among the the conditions for an amnesty. On the other hand, the amnesties aim to liberate the sans papiers from the low wages, long working hours, poor work conditions, and exploitative conditions in sweatshop industries.

The Chinese sans papiers in France who were given amnesty established the Association sino-française d'entraide et d'amitié,[21] that aims at providing people with social security and better working conditions (*Le Monde*, 20.01.1999; *Ouzhou Shibao – Nouvelles d'Europe* 20.02.1999, p. 5). For the former sans papiers, their legal immigration status places them at risk of losing their job to those illegal immigrants who did not apply or who arrived later.

The amnesties in France, Italy, Spain and Portugal have given rise to 'amnesty nomadism', to groups of Chinese travelling in Southern Europe, seeking entitlement to apply for amnesty somewhere. Those who are rejected in one place may try in the next country. Decreasing border controls between European states make such movements increasingly viable.

3 Chinatown, Europe

Centres of community-building

Chinatowns are symbolic centres of overseas Chinese communities. Even small places with few Chinese restaurants and shops are referred to as 'Chinatowns'. In Europe there are not many large Chinatowns, and most of them do not have the ghetto functions the American and Southeast Asian Chinatowns once had. This chapter will explore some of the aspects that keep the Chinatowns together and make them a focal point of ethnic identity.

One interviewee, talking of the situation in Hungary, where the Chinese only began to arrive in large numbers in the early 1990s, said:

> Our aim is to have a Chinatown after some years, a Chinatown that belongs to the Chinese and is managed by ourselves. In this Chinatown, on foreign soil, it must be like walking down our own street, and we'll create it as a comprehensive thing with eating, drinking, leisure and culture. I believe it can be ready in two or three decades' time.
>
> (047//178)

The interviewee emphasised the ethnic significance of the Chinatown and the pride that would be associated with it. Ownership and management by the Chinese community would be the source of pride, 'like walking down our own street'. The aspiration links ethnicity, Chinese culture, leisure and catering. Does he mean culture, leisure, eating and drinking mainly for the Chinese community? Or does he refer to business activities directed towards Europeans? Is it a cultural space and emblem for the Chinese, a cultural refuge from the outlandish Western society? Or is it an ethnic ambience for Chinese business? He does not say and he does not make the distinction. Either way, the emblematic significance is obvious, made up of symbols aimed at evoking feelings of cultural home and Eastern mystique, respectively.

The ethnic pride and symbolism of Chinatown are important rationales for overseas Chinese leaders. The belief that the Chinese, wherever they live on foreign soil, tend to settle in Chinatowns and lead culturally distinct lives provides powerful ideals for overseas Chinese in Europe. Some have lived in the large Chinatowns of Phnom Penh or Vientiane, and others regard the Chinatowns of San Francisco and New York as an ideal. The old Limehouse Street Chinatown of London's East End that served as the backdrop of Sax Rohmer's Fu Manchu novels (Pan 1990, 84–90; Clegg 1994) may have added a spicy tinge to the notion of Chinatown. Creating Chinatown, projecting its roots back into history and asserting that it is an essential characteristic of Chinese culture, are ways of claiming authenticity and the right of leadership among overseas Chinese.

The Cantonese term 'Tong yan gai' (in Mandarin pronounciation ('Tangrenjie')[1] has gained almost universal usage as the affective, colloquial term for 'Chinatown', while 'Zhongguocheng'[2] is by many considered a poor translation of the English word. However, Zhongguocheng appeared in several interviews, and even occurs on signposts throughout Europe.[3] The Mandarin word 'Huabu'[4] is only used in written style, for example in official names of organisations. An alternative to 'Tangrenjie' is to use the English word 'Chinatown' in the flow of Chinese words. In France, the terms 'quartier chinois' and 'la petite Asie' are common. Costa-Lascoux and Live (1995, 16) regard the use of the English term 'Chinatown' in the context of a Parisian Chinese quarter as aimed at making it more 'exotic in the eyes of visitors', as it connotes places like the New York Chinatown. The names reflect the variety of meanings and feelings attached to Chinatowns, as needed by the concrete circumstances.

How do the Chinatown idea and the managerial issues of Chinatown interact? Chinatowns have physical extension, are made of bricks, mortar and tarmac, are subject to town planning initiatives, and embody investment and business interests. The men and women who involve themselves in the management of Chinatowns and their activities face practical issues beyond caring for their cultural heritage. Local politicians and overseas Chinese leaders regard the European Chinatowns as political and economic assets; they form an intersection of 'host' and 'diasporic' activity. For local politicians, Chinatowns are not ghettos or derelict problem areas, but are a source of pride and a monument of achievement. For the overseas Chinese leaders, they provide incomes and structure to the community.

Amsterdam

Even in Amsterdam, where Chinatown is interspersed with the red light district (run by non-Chinese) and other ethnic enclaves in the Wallen area of the city centre, the Chinese restaurants, shops and associations create a special atmosphere, acknowledged by city council planners. The area is a major tourist attraction because of its unique mixture of picturesque sixteenth-century buildings, shop-window prostitution, oriental mystique, drug pushers, and ethnic diversity. The visitor is captured by curiosity for the exotic and a subliminal feeling of danger that comes close to the classical image of Chinatown as immoral and unsafe. Yet Amsterdam Chinatown's existence does not only rely on being a tourist attraction; it is also a shopping area:

> Earlier on, the [local] government changed the traffic conditions, because the city councillors wanted there to be fewer parking spaces in the city centre. All

of a sudden, several hundred parking spaces were taken away. When that had happened, many people stopped coming to Chinatown to do their shopping. After many contacts with the government, where we threatened to move away if the traffic conditions weren't improved, the government gave us many parking spaces back, and promised to build a subterranean parking lot within the next two years.

(028//016)

Chinatowns are assets for local government, they are objects for development by Chinese entrepreneurs, normally in conjunction with city planners and local politicians, and they are investment objects that have to go with the market. Their affective value is a real and significant economic issue, for the ethnic emblem is what makes the Chinatowns special. How can a Chinatown develop when it is squeezed into a narrow space?

Overseas Chinese leaders voiced the need to place a residence for elderly Chinese in the Chinatown area, and in an attempt to find a solution city planners suggested that further development could be placed in a derelict harbour area. One interviewee told us that the idea had apparently not been to move Chinatown, but to situate an old people's residence and a significant number of shop and catering premises in a disused harbour area at some distance from the existing Chinatown (028//104). The new area was being developed for mixed residence and services anyway. The interviewee had been involved directly in the negotiations with the city council. He felt that the idea was absurd, but he went along with it. He had said to the city planners that it was not a good idea to move Chinatown in order to serve the interests of the elderly, but he encouraged them to get on with the planning, saying:

> When you've finished with the plan, you tell me where, at what rent or at what buying price, and then you tell me which facilities there are. Then my members and I make a decision. I have no reason to move, for I've invested so much in this area, the foundation of my members is in Chinatown; it's big, there are more than sixty businesses in Chinatown. After we've invested so much, suddenly to say we have to move to a new area for the sake of the elderly – first, there's no public transport, second, there's no metro station, just some empty buildings – that we have to make a new big investment and compete with our old area.

(028//104)

He added that if the businesses in the 'old' Chinatown were not inclined to make the move, nothing would come of the 'new' Chinatown (028//105). However, the interviewee was not the major negotiator. The person in charge was a more successful and influential businessman and a community leader with greater political clout, and he carried the talks with the city council further, reaching the point where senior politicians got involved. The main opposition to the plan was based on the prospect of lacking facilities and public transport and parking space problems, so we all think, OK, if it turns out to be attractive, we will certainly not allow this opportunity to slip away, So I say, our attitude must not be to participate directly, but to keep track of developments, to maintain contact, that's our attitude.

(028//109)

This interviewee considered Chinatown decisions on the merit of economic viability. In fact, it did not seem to him to be much of a political decision, as investors would be attracted if the conditions were right.

We also interviewed the person who was the major negotiator on behalf of the Chinese, a man whose personal economic interest was closely linked with the opportunities a new Chinatown might bring. He thought that a new Chinatown would solve the image problem of the old Chinatown, namely that it was meshed in with the red light district, so that people confused going to Chinatown with going to the sex market, and he complained about 'all the Negroes (heigui) and drugs dealers loitering all day', the lack of public order, the petty crime, addicts taking their drugs in the streets and so on (023//088). However, the main point was that there was nowhere to rent or buy property in the area; it was impossible for new Chinese businesses to establish themselves or old ones to expand. Looking for a new Chinatown would not be a matter of competition; it was rather a responsibility to ensure the opportunities for the next generation. The opportunity posed by the current redevelopment of harbour areas was precious, as land for development was so scarce in Amsterdam that other opportunities might not arise again soon. Also, people from China wished to invest directly in Amsterdam and did have money, but there were too few areas available. Investors from the Mainland with the money to invest were keen, for it was a way of getting a residence permit:

For example, it would help them to apply for residence permits, if you start an enterprise, you certainly need a temporary residence permit. Even if it's temporary to begin with, a year at a time, after some years it'll be permanent, you see.[5]

(023//089)

Commenting on the problem that the majority of the leaseholds in London's Soho Chinatown are held by a property company owned by 'foreigners' (guilaoren) who allegedly keep increasing the rent year after year, the interviewee said:

So, with this experience in mind, we definitely must control our own business rights. Yes, you Chinese have buoyant [business], but your profit doesn't go to the Chinese, but to others, the landlords take it. That's a lesson to be learnt. Apparently, this is also an issue in France these days. We have talked extensively with the [Chinese] community leaders in France and Britain about this, so now we have become wiser; we don't want to be bought up by those foreigners (guilao). Everybody's feeling is, we hope those westerners will not buy us out, that the Chinese can buy back a part of the trade. Perhaps we can't buy it all, for we lack the money, but at least a part of it ... so we will fight for this. Once we Chinese have created this [new] Chinatown, it will be buoyant, that's the case with all Chinatowns in the world. They prosper.

(023//098)

He thought of the Chinatown autonomy in terms of the difference between Chinese and 'foreigners' (Chinese landlords were to be preferred above non-Chinese), but in other respects had a totally commercial attitude. Creating a Chinatown was a question of whether or not the business people involved could earn money. Negotiations were based on whether or not a sufficient critical mass of new investments could be targeted in an area experiencing urban redevelopment in a highly competitive setting where other buyers were lining up. Both local politicians and Chinese community leaders had an interest in the spatial focusing of ethnic business.

In the event, the building of the new Chinatown did not get off the ground. The interviews cited above were taken in 1996, and two years later, we were told that the ideas had taken a new direction. Amsterdam's central post office on the Oosterdokseiland immediately to the east of the Central Station closed and the site was to be redeveloped. Due to the failure to find a way to create a feasible new Chinatown in the harbour district, overseas Chinese entrepreneurs were drawn into informal discussions about the future of Oosterdokseiland. The Chinese restaurant Sea Palace is anchored on the south side of the Oosterdokseiland, and the site is not that far away from Chinatown. Between 1998 and 2000, some Chinese community leaders and business men were involved in negotiations on this project, which came up for public planning procedure in June 2000. Chinese entrepreneurs had got their act together and formed an association called Stichting New Chinatown (New Chinatown Foundation) to engage in the negotiations:

The New Chinatown Foundation, a business initiative with Asian members, has indicated that it will develop the Network Facility Centre, offices, a hotel and residences in collaboration with MAB Development b.v. The Foundation will, based on the existing Chinatown around Zeedijk and Nieuwmarkt, create more space and opportunities for business activities and to this end cooperates with entrepreneurs and authorities in China and Europe.[6]

The 800 million guilder project of 180,000 square metres plus 1,000 parking spaces, in addition to the parts the New Chinatown Foundation participate in, may also include new office space for the PTT, the Amsterdam Conservatoire, a National Archive for Images and Experiences and a new building for Amsterdam's Public Library.

The idea of a new Chinatown in Amsterdam, in other words, has grown from an idea of coordinating individual investments in a development scheme in disused harbour areas to be the 'ethnic' aspect of a high-powered, big-builder, big-finance inner city development scheme on the most coveted development location in Amsterdam. The participation in such a project does not imply ethnic autonomy, and it does not allow much focus on the ethnic origin of investments. There is no doubt that MAB Development b.v.'s collaboration with the New Chinatown Foundation contributed to the success of MAB's bid as opposed to the two other invited bids. This co-operation symbolised a development concept or a focusing theme that fitted within city planners' broader vision of the regeneration of the southern IJ bank, of which the Oosterdokseiland is a part. The project incorporates various big players in complex constellations, including the real estate branch of the Dutch post office PTT Vastgoed and the Amsterdam City Council, MAB Development as the main contractor, the New Chinatown Foundation as an associate contractor, and probably a range of financial investors and contractors. It is likely that the New Chinatown Foundation is a preparatory structure for the formation of an investment company or of an operating company that contracts or purchases part of the estate. While it is impossible to have a clear understanding of the contractual arrangements at the present stage, and even more impossible to presage the eight years that will elapse before the project is completed, or the management structures likely to be implemented after completion, there is no reason to believe that the term 'ethnic capital' will be able to describe the reality of this Chinatown project.

The Amsterdam Chinatown development began, so to speak, with the perceived need for a residence for elderly Chinese, and dissatisfaction with the existing ambience and lack of development potential on the existing site. It later involved largely unfeasible ideas of creating a new Chinatown in areas with access problems that were being developed mainly for residences. It finally took shape inside the framework of a major real estate project that was part of the huge city planning scheme to restructure the southern bank of the IJ.

Concerns for the elderly, the investment and trade patterns of Chinese shops and catering outlets, the ethnic ambience, the function of the tourist trade, the transport and parking space issue involve people and organisations with many different interests and agendas. The point made by one of the interviewees, that 'Chinatowns always prosper', indicates the strength of the ethnic emblem. The critical mass of enterprises that in combination create wealth is at the core of this. The concentration of ethnic shops, restaurants and other services on a small area is the result of individual business decisions; the individual business decision thus depends on a collective trend; for Chinatowns to do well, agreement and coordination are needed in some measure, and this is something that can ultimately only be delivered by a city council.

On a question relating to a Chinatown in Britain, which in reality only consists of a handful of businesses and situated in ungainly surroundings, we received an answer that illustrates the issue. We asked whether the local Chinese association had not sought to get the city council involved in the development of the Chinatown; the answer was:

> The city council has approached us in the past. In my opinion, organising Chinatown has both advantages and disadvantages; there are many aspects. Well, we could create a livelier city atmosphere, concentrate more Chinese [businesses]. But I'm afraid of the bad side. If Chinatown prospers, there'll

be other interests involved, then these ganglords (dalao) will move in and contend each others' territories. I'm afraid of the complications they'll bring with them. At this time, now, the cleanest place is [this city], [this city] is the quietest place [among Chinatowns in Britain], there are no ganglords doing anything here. Little, anyway. In other places there are lots of them.

(059//171)

Keeping a low profile is good for the local businesses, for they do not have to pay protection money or shoulder the burden of other organised crime. The concern is that if the Chinatown area becomes too attractive, is targeted for city planning and beautification of the public space, and begins to give better earnings, not only will the rents in the area go up, but the enterprises will also be taxed by gangland elements. In that case, the net outcome for the individual restaurateur and shopkeeper may be negative. The price of being 'clean' is to be situated in derelict surroundings.

Only few places share these reservations. The pressure is to develop Chinatown, for it makes sense. Politically, it gives collective strength and recognition; economically, it generates good incomes; and in terms of the community, it provides a focus.

Antwerp

In Antwerp, the Chinatown consists of some shops, restaurants, meeting rooms of Chinese associations and offices in two streets near the railway station; the general impression in 1996 was poorly maintained houses in a drab area. A handful of Chinese shopkeepers and restaurateurs got together in the mid 1990s to form a Chinatown association.

The development of the Antwerp Chinatown in the 1990s, as it can be described with reference to our few interviews with some of the people involved, was a dynamic interplay between overseas Chinese, local authorities, and authorities in China. Different interests came together to create a momentum that had apparently been lacking in earlier times.

At the core of the new initiatives we may identify an overseas Chinese originating in the Shunde City of Guangdong. A restaurateur and trader in Antwerp, he was doing long-distance business with enterprises in his 'home' region, and gained fame as a dynamic businessman and a community mobiliser. He had facilitated his business contacts in Guangdong through an association of natives from Shunde and Nanhai cities, of which he was a member.[7] He helped a couple of Chinese associations to get together in 1995 around a 'Chinese festival' sponsored by the city council, a festival he described as 'very successful' (029//014).

On the back of this festival, he convinced the authorities in Nanhai to donate a dragon to the Chinese in Antwerp.[8] The plan was to perform a 'dragon dance' at the next festival in October 1996. The organiser was not to be the city council, but the newly organised 'neighbourhood association' of Antwerp's Chinatown, an organisation that 'not only included Chinese, but also Africans, Thai people and local Belgians' (029//014).

This community leader juggled the various factors; Antwerp's city council and Nanhai City were catalysts for the bringing together of the Chinese community in the Chinatown setting. As the nascent Chinatown area included shop owners and restaurateurs of a different origin, the Chinatown Association also included non-Chinese. The dragon was a symbolic centre of Chinatown Association: Nanhai City donated the dragon to the Chinatown Association:

> In the future, we will build an arch. During the first year [1995], we had no dragon. We are the descendants of the dragon, here in Belgium, well, we had got a kung-fu band, but we had only got dancing lions and dancing unicorns, so we would have to dance without a dragon. Therefore, last year, I went to Holland to Master Fei Yuliang and borrowed two dragons that came here to dance. But for the second festival this year, our Nanhai will send us a dragon; I think it will be here in September. We perform in October. There's time for the kung-fu people to train, they're very friendly with us.[9] It's good for the overseas Chinese and it's good for the hometown. It's the People's Government of Nanhai City that's donated the dragon, so it's good for both sides. Often, if we need something, they can help us. If I ask for something, within reason, it's for the sake of fellow-villagers, it's based on doing something for the overseas Chinese.
>
> (029//015)

The systematic exploitation of Chinese cultural symbols is at work here. The dragon (and the necessity to have one) is a rallying point. It symbolises good will of the people in Nanhai towards the overseas Chinese in Antwerp, it makes a formal voluntary association necessary, and it brings together overseas Chinese businessmen in a Chinatown association. A Chinese festival is attractive and useful for the Antwerp city council. A positive and inclusive role awarded to the non-Chinese business people in the Chinatown area and a cultural role and purpose to kung-fu clubs ensure friendly relations and collaboration.

Once activated, these cultural symbols gain their own momentum, spawning not only ethnic identification, but also all the political and economic processes that go into the construction of a Chinatown. The above quote from the interview may seem rather disjointed, but resonates with implied meanings. The interviewee states one aim, which is to erect a Chinatown arch; he then explains the process by which he was going about achieving the aim. The first argument is ethnic and cultural. Rallying the Chinese is done by referring to the emblem of common heritage, the dragon, for the Chinese are the descendants of the dragon (long de zisun). Lacking a formal structure among the Chinese, he gained the support from the city council and was thus able to involve a couple of Chinese associations. They did have some symbols of Chineseness, like dancing lions and unicorns, but he made the lack of a dragon an important point, and personally went to Holland to borrow one. That, of course, was a one-off solution, and it was necessary to get one's own dragon. When he related this problem to the local government of Nanhai, it promised to donate one. However, who was going to receive it? The only proper solution was to create a Chinatown association. Having a Chinatown association and a number of Chinese businesses concentrated on two small streets at the centre of Antwerp, the next step would be to build an arch and make sure that Chinatown could become an inner city regeneration project.

The interviewee, in order to create a common cause among the overseas Chinese in Antwerp, played down his particular, personal affiliation with Nanhai and Shunde and refrained from assuming a leadership position in the native-place association. He thought that retreating one step and not participating in the leadership election would 'better accommodate everybody' (029//063). He was in other words positioning himself to be a general representative of the Chinese in Antwerp.

The city council, so he claimed, had got European funding to the tune of 120 million BEF (or almost 3 million euros) to plan a Chinatown development, including two streets and a triangular park. He explained that the urban development plan involved a large shopping centre, pedestrian areas and roads with limited access for cars. Although the project was only on the drawing board, it was clear that Chinatown development aimed at securing European funding. The ethnic background of the project was, according the interviewee, to lift the part of the city upwards and to use the Chinese to create an up-market area, where black immigrants would be gradually pushed out.

Within the context of Flanders and Antwerp, the issue of ethnic exclusion is particularly sensitive due to the relative success of Vlaams Blok, a party of xenophobic populism. Using the development of Chinatown to push back the presence of blacks in the city centre (as suggested by one of our interviewees) would appear to be a rather contentious race-relations strategy. Chinatown development, of course, does not embody such a strategy, but arguments of this nature may have been used privately to make the plans more palatable to certain political players. The aim to improve Chinatown was (as also suggested by the interviewee) motivated by the need to give Antwerp the status of an up-market tourist destination. Antwerp had in the past been famous for its expensive, lifestyle-related trade, and had lost its status as the world's most important diamond city to Amsterdam. This was blamed on the fact that overseas tourists preferred Amsterdam to Antwerp. Chinatown, in that strategy, would help provide an attractive environment for eating out and a backdrop for staging events attracting tourists. Together with posh shopping opportunities, the nearby Zoological Garden, and the large railway station, Chinatown was designed to become a diverse and colourful metropolitan city centre. The plans included parking lots for tourist buses and considerations on how to attract local people back to the city centre from suburban multiplex cinemas (029//072...076).

How does this affect the individual Chinatown investor? An interviewee said:

> I feel that there is a large potential for tourism which the city council and the overseas Chinese haven't exploited yet. If tourism grows, the investors will come here. No investor is coming along, investing money, waiting for the tourists to come and for the business to start. You must get some people together here first, and then they'll consider those people's consumption. So at the moment,

I'm in contact with the city council and the tourist board to see how we can put tourism on track, for example people passing the border and spending a day or half a day in this area.[10] Erecting a [Chinatown] arch is one feature of this. They come to Belgium, take a picture in front of the arch, spend half a day here, have something to eat or buy a couple of souvenirs, that is also a form of consumption, a non-smokestack industry.

(030//043)

Cultural icons, economic ambitions and political functions together engender Chinatown community-building. The interests involved are far flung and the processes almost intractable, going beyond those directly involving overseas Chinese people.

Having or not having a Chinatown

In Britain there are Chinatowns, in the Netherlands they've got Chinatowns, but there are none in Germany. That's because the history is not very long. Furthermore, here because of the geographic distribution, in each place, at one or two hours' [driving distance], there are only one or two restaurants. There is no close contact between them. In catering we rely on ourselves. You'll have to do some of the work yourself and employ some waiters. If you don't do some of the work yourself, the restaurant can hardly make a profit. Work is from ten in the morning to twelve midnight, and many restaurateurs are not able to take any vacations.

(015//039)

The absence of Chinatowns in some European countries like Germany and the Scandinavian countries reflects the relative scarcity of the ethnic Chinese population and the scattered nature of their settlement. There is no reason to believe that it reflects a political and cultural adversity to ghetto formation in these countries, for in spite of explicit dispersal policies there are residential concentrations of other (non-Chinese) immigrant and refugee groups both in Germany and in the Scandinavian countries. Neither is it due to management of urban space in terms of business licences, city planning, and development preferences.

The business advantage of and local council interest in Chinatowns in Britain, the Netherlands, Belgium and France seem striking, when one considers the contrast that major conurbations like Berlin, Frankfurt, Hamburg, Munich, Düsseldorf, Cologne, Copenhagen, Stockholm, Oslo, Helsinki and Gothenburg lack even small Chinatowns. It makes sense if we consider that at the beginning of the 1950s the numbers of overseas Chinese in Germany and the Scandinavian countries were very low, and that the early Chinese catering industry was up-market. Chinese restaurants were scarce and situated in prime locations and their clientele was largely non-Chinese. Chinese immigration during the 1960s and 1970s was slow and gradual. The immigrants arrived from many different places and had different skills. They were therefore integrated in the 'host' economy in more diverse ways than in Britain and France where large groups of Chinese with similar backgrounds immigrated in a brief time span (in the early 1960s to Britain, and in the early 1980s to France). When the rapid increase of immigration to Germany and the Scandinavian countries took place in the 1980s and 1990s, the catering sector fanned out, establishing itself in smaller towns and scattering into low-market areas, but was unable to form Chinatowns.

The formation of Chinatowns in Britain, France and the Netherlands reflects different dynamics.

In Britain, the surge of relatively unskilled immigrants from Hong Kong was funnelled into the catering sector, which expanded spatially across the whole country. The influx of migrants coincided with the availability of inner city areas where concentrated development could take place, especially in London's Soho district, in Liverpool and in central Manchester. The mass influx of migrants created an ethnic Chinese market of a certain scale. In France, the formation of Chinatowns was much more an issue of Chinese immigrants taking advantage of scarce housing resources through personal networks.

The three major 'Chinatowns' of Paris inside the ring-road were formed in this way (although the one around Rue du Temple is largely devoid of Chinatown symbols and is only rarely referred to as a Chinatown):

- the area around Rue du Temple in the 3rd arrondissement before the Second World War already housed Chinese artisan workshops and lodgings and, with the immigration immediately after the war, the number of Chinese residents grew. As other groups left, the Chinese were able to expand in the area.
- the 13th arrondissement (in the area between Place d'Italie and Porte de Choisy) had large tower flats built in the 1960s and 1970s; these tower flats formed one of the few available areas of rented accommodation in Paris during the early 1980s when the Chinese refugees from Southeast Asia arrived in France in large numbers (White, Winchester and Guillon 1987; Costa-Lascoux and Live 1995, 27–34). Many settled there and, whenever a flat became available, Chinese were able to help co-natives obtain a lease. The area soon had a substantial Chinese population and a large variety of Chinese businesses and restaurants, becoming the most visible Chinatown of Paris.
- the area around Belleville emerged as a Chinatown in the 1980s and 1990s, mainly because it was a derelict area with a high proportion of immigrants from North Africa with low rents in which new Chinese migrants found it easy to open shops and restaurants. It is not primarily a residential area for the Chinese, but a commercial centre; adjacent areas provide relatively cheap accommodation for new Chinese immigrants.

The interesting point is that the Parisian Chinatowns emerged as primary residence areas for new immigrants, and developed to be major Chinese business areas, while retaining a residence function (in the case of Belleville in the larger region surrounding the quarter) for immigrants. That means that while the population was transient (earlier migrants moving to other parts), the ethnic character was retained.

In Amsterdam the Chinatown area expanded from the areas originally used by the overseas Chinese between the 1910s and the late 1930s. The expansion of Amsterdam in the 1950s, 1960s and 1970s provided modern and more sanitary housing in the outskirts and made small town-centre shops less viable. It thus opened up space for some Chinese residence and small ethnic enterprises in the Wallen area, coinciding with various streams of immigration. However, the administration of the Amsterdam housing stock has prevented the area from becoming a major residential area for overseas Chinese, as all rented property (public and private) is firmly controlled by a local administration – Gemeentelijke Herhuisvesting – that distributes rented living space on the basis of entitlement (based on previous residence in Amsterdam), waiting lists and specific social needs. That means that residential concentration of Chinese immigrants by word of mouth and through personal connections (like in the case of the Chinatown in Paris's 13th arrondissement) did not occur in Amsterdam. Of course, some residence in Amsterdam's Chinatown during earlier years violated official rules, but with amnesty to illegal immigrants in the 1960s and later great improvements of incomes and social status of the Chinese, they have entered the mainstream property market. The Amsterdam Chinatown, therefore, is mainly a commercial area with little ethnic Chinese residence.

In general terms, post-World War Two Chinatowns in Britain, France and the Netherlands are not prime residential areas. Only in France did the major Parisian Chinatowns have a residential function. Until the late 1990s, one can claim that the 'Chinatown' of Rue du Temple was not a Chinatown, for it was only a place of residence and work of many Chinese and totally lacked the symbolism and public functions of a Chinatown. The Belleville Chinatown mainly serves as a business district for a Chinese population that lives widely scattered across the north-eastern arrondissements of Paris, and only the Choisy Chinatown seems to combine residence, business, work, social functions and public symbolism. White, Winchester and Guillon (1987, 54), however, commented more than a decade ago:

> It is commerce that is at the heart of the Chinese presence today, and although the popular perception is of the area as being a Chinese residential district, its true function to the broader Chinese community of the Paris region, and indeed France as a whole, is commercial: it has become the centre for Chinese wholesaling and retailing activities for the whole country.[11]

The areas in Europe that come closest to the idea of a classical Chinatown are found near Florence (in Prato, San Donnino and Campi Bisenzio) in Italy, where large communities of relatively recent migrants work, live and fill their social space. Although these areas are not territorially bonded like a ghetto, and although they lack extensive display of Chinatown symbolism, they do concentrate functions of ethnic community within a relatively confined area that combines residence, work and services. Ironically, these areas are in the eyes of many people not Chinatowns,[12] for they do not provide the commercialised ambience of the Chinatowns of London, Liverpool, Manchester, the 13th arrondissement, Belleville, or Amsterdam. The area around Rue du Temple in Paris seems to have much in common with the Florentine settlements.

Having or not having a Chinatown, hence, is a question of specific historical circumstances and of popular perceptions of what a Chinatown is. In Europe it is a commercial centre with some shops, catering outlets, some ethnic services and institutions, a 'Chinatown association', and public display of Chinese symbols (arches, decorated shop-fronts and Chinese characters). When Taiwanese expatriates in the Netherlands talk about their suburban 'Chinatowns' in Amstelveen or Capelle aan den IJssel (meaning that several handfuls of Taiwanese families live in the same middle-class neighbourhood), they do so with tongue in cheek.

The many layers of meaning that go into the concept of Chinatown make it wonderfully elusive; it does not lend itself to strict definitions and formal comparisons. Each existing Chinatown in Europe has a separate background, function and history. They share the symbolic reference to an imaginary archetypal Chinatown that is manifest in names, rituals and decoration. For those involved, the symbolic reference is an important asset that defines their social and political interaction. It also functions as a trade emblem that attracts customers. In Chapter 7 I will discuss how Chinatown functions as a trade emblem. In the following I will focus on how Chinatown symbols, rituals and functions are assets within the circle of overseas Chinese leaders.

Building an arch

In Antwerp they have a dream of building a Chinatown arch. Manchester, London and Liverpool have an arch. There is none in Amsterdam or Paris (except for a small one that serves as the entrance to the Chinese-owned conference centre Chinagora). There may only be few Chinatown arches in Europe, but there are many in North America and in East and Southeast Asia, in places like New York, Boston, Philadelphia, San Francisco, Washington, Victoria, Yokohama and Penang to name a few places. Vancouver raised money for one in 2000, and even the Santo Domingo Chinatown in the Dominican Republic plans to get one. These arches are invariably linked to prestige, and having the 'first' and/or the 'largest' is an important asset for a Chinatown. An arch built of parts produced in China and assembled *in situ* is more authentic than one built from local materials. The amount raised by overseas Chinese for its construction is a measure of the collective prowess of the community.

The origin of the arch (pailou or paifang in Chinese) as a symbol of Chinatown in Europe in the 1980s gives us some food for thought. It is universally taken to express cultural and historical authenticity, but it is, in reality, recent. Is it just a gimmick to lure tourists? Or does it have a deeper significance? The examples of London and Manchester indicate that the arches have significance both as tourist attractions and as levers for Chinatown politics; they are considered barometers of the prowess of the people who created them. The Chinatown arch in Manchester also symbolises the Chinese authorities' interest in securing the support of the divided British overseas Chinese community in the period before Hong Kong's reunification with China in 1997.

The Chinatown arches of London and Manchester

An interviewee in London told us:

> If you want to develop Chinatown, you need the help from the city council. If
> they don't help, there are so many things we can't achieve. For example, the
> arch. At that time I was the chairman of the Chinatown Association, and I
> suggested to the city council to build an arch, but because the street is too
> narrow and because there are all sorts of gas and water pipes and electrical
> cables in the ground, we couldn't dig very deep, so the arch has got its present
> shape for that reason. If the place had been somewhat broader, we could have
> added some granite blocks to give it more character, but that's not possible at
> the moment. In addition there are lots of cars around it, if one hits it, it might
> collapse, so we haven't done that. As for the small pavilion – that was in 1986
> or 1987 – I myself spent more than £10,000 on it. I went to China to order
> the materials and got specialists over to build it. We got the city council to do
> the arch, but we, the Chinese, built the pavilion ourselves. I had a plaque
> inscribed[13] with the names of all those who contributed money. Some contri-
> buted a few hundred pounds each; the total cost was over £30,000.
>
> (006//040)

The London Chinatown arch was the second arch to be built in Europe, the first
being the Manchester Chinatown arch. It is small and unimpressive, but it is an
icon of London's Chinatown. The interviewee's formulation indicates that it does
not compare well to other arches in terms of being the first, largest or most authentic; being realised with the main contribution originating in the city council, it
does not reflect the prowess of the London Chinatown. The Soho Chinatown
began gradually in the 1960s when the area was, in the words of the interviewee,
'filthy' due both to rubbish in the streets, and to the mixture of strip-tease businesses
and street prostitution. There had been the odd Chinese restaurant in the area
since perhaps the 1930s, but when three or four businesses opened in the mid-
1960s, Chinatown began to take shape, and by the 1970s it was already firmly
established and prosperous. Westminster City Council promoted the development
of Chinatown to suppress the 'vice character' of the area. With the general rise in
the 1980s of environmental consciousness aimed at limiting traffic congestion and
improving public spaces, it was easy to make a case for improving the Chinatown
area. So when our interviewee became the chairman of the Chinatown association
in 1986, he began to work for erecting a Chinatown arch, took the lead in building
a pavilion, pushed for turning Gerrard Street into a pedestrian street, and rallied
Chinatown businesses behind him in order to achieve improvements in the area.

   Manchester Chinatown at that time was a smaller and poorer place, situated in
three narrow streets (George Street, Faulkner Street and Nicholas Street) in a dark
and derelict area dominated by abandoned textile warehouses where Chinese
entrepreneurs moved in during the late 1960s because the properties could be had
for a pittance. Chinatown in Manchester developed fast in the 1980s, especially

when derelict buildings were pulled down to create an open space between the three streets. This became a much-needed parking lot. Once these buildings had disappeared, the light and space suddenly gave a new feeling to the place. One interviewee in Manchester told the story of the arch like this:

> After these old buildings had been demolished, well that was the beginning. We had a Chinatown Association, and Mr M, an elderly gentleman in that association who had been an officer of the Hong Kong constabulary, made a proposal. He said, why is San Francisco so rich? Why is their Chinatown so rich? There are some monuments of old Chinese architecture there, that's how they could attract tourists. If we look across Europe there are no classical Chinese buildings anywhere, so we hope that the British and Chinese governments may expend some resources and efforts to erect an arch there. Everybody agreed, and applications were made to the Chinese embassy and through the city council to the British government. When it came together, the Chinese community finally discussed the matter.
>
> (058//037)

The effort of this old gentleman was timely, for the political situation of the time made it an attractive option for the Chinese and British governments to regard such a project with great sympathy. In the early days of the negotiations between China and Britain over Hong Kong in 1983–4 there was an idea within the British or Hong Kong government that the Hong Kong population would be part of the decision-making through some sort of referendum, and while it very soon became clear that this was not going to materialise, there had grown a momentum for this among Hong Kong elites and overseas Chinese in Britain of Hong Kong origin. Activism for and against such a measure soon created tensions within the overseas Chinese community in Britain. While some people with a background in Hong Kong's civil service and strong resentment against the CCP used any opportunity to discredit the Mainland, others representing a patriotic, anti-colonialist attitude were unofficially encouraged by the PRC Embassy to support Hong Kong's return to China. This unhappy situation became a dominant issue, which also impinged on all sorts of other relationships among the overseas Chinese. In the early and mid-1980s, both the Chinese and British authorities were keen to strengthen their ties with the overseas Chinese communities, for their support had moral significance and influenced public opinion on the intricate Hong Kong issue. The Chinese authorities were, furthermore, very keen to reinforce the budding Chinatown in Manchester, for a large overseas Chinese presence there was an excellent argument for establishing a Consulate-General in Manchester, the centre of the second-largest conurbation in England after London.

The Chinese government, accordingly, saw the support of a Chinatown arch as an ideal gesture that could reinforce patriotic sentiments. Such support could not easily be construed to be undue interference in a sensitive political situation, but would send a strong symbolic message to overseas Chinese in Britain.

Several of our interviewees told us of some of the unpleasant animosities that had emerged within the community. When the Manchester Chinatown arch plans began to take shape, the local Chinatown Association had split into two over several issues, each side accusing the other of monopolising public money and transgressing their rights. Both associations sought to capture the Chinatown arch; at first, one of the associations did all in its might to sabotage the project, and when it saw that the other association went ahead with great momentum, it took over the project. This move (if we are to believe our interviewees) was a mere formality, for the city council would only give planning permission to a legal entity, and leading members of one association hurriedly formed a limited company that was to be responsible for the construction, thereby preventing their opponents from sharing in the prestige. Although the trusted friends of the PRC thus lost out, one can only imagine the pleasure experienced by Chinese diplomats who entered into a working relationship with their opponents. Unfortunately most details of the Manchester Chinatown controversies are unknown to us, and there exist many different versions in the memories of the people who took part in them. However, they resulted in Europe's first Chinatown arch, for more than a decade the largest and most authentic (because it was built by Chinese workmen using materials imported directly from China).

The London Chinatown Association did not have the same determined and generous support from the Chinese authorities, and the problems and concerns in London were different, even when the community was able to raise a substantial sum of money to build a pavilion to complement the officially-sponsored arch.

The institutions of Chinatown

How are European Chinatowns organised? Chinatowns are mainly business districts; that means that they generally consist of a small or large number of businesses (shanghao), depending on the size of the Chinatown. Within the area considered to belong to the Chinatown, there will often be meeting places and offices of voluntary ethnic associations that serve the wider Chinese community. In large Chinatowns there may be community, arts, culture, health or activity centres that aim at serving the Chinese community. In some British Chinatowns (London, Manchester, Nottingham and Birmingham) there are also Chinatown Lions Clubs.

Chinatown businesses are in most cases organised in a Chinatown association (jiefanghui) that joins together the business people operating within Chinatown. All businesses in a region, including those in the Chinatown, will often be organised in a chamber of commerce (shanghui) or similar organisation. If a Chinatown is very small, the local Chinatown association or chamber of commerce may *de facto* be one body. Generally, however, the distinction between Chinatown business and other businesses is kept clear. The Chinatown association is normally an interest organisation that liaises with city councils and the public on mundane issues like town planning, security, parking, sanitation and so on, and thus exerts some influence on the public space of Chinatown.

In most parts, the Chinese have a number of voluntary associations that represent different groups among the Chinese living in a broader region. Their offices or meeting places are often situated near or in Chinatowns because the location is convenient, but they have little to do with Chinatown affairs; insofar as their leading members also have businesses in Chinatown, they are integrated into the Chinatown association. Some associations run Chinese language schools or provide other services situated in or near Chinatown, and so draw the wider Chinese community into Chinatown. Typical services may include Mah-jongg and reading rooms with Chinese newspapers.

Local government in many cities provide services directed at the Chinese in locations within Chinatown, including drop-in health clinics with Chinese-speaking staff, community centres aimed at supporting activities among young people, homes for elderly Chinese with Chinese-speaking staff and so on. Such projects may have a board where Chinese community leaders are represented, thus providing some institutional integration into the community.

In addition to such structures of integration, a small number of Chinatowns in the UK have Chinatown Lions Clubs, which are part of a global structure of clubs in which local business and other middle-class elites gather around general aims of social charity. As Lions Clubs in general are social clubs for local elites that promote integration across segments of local community, the 'Chinatown' variety seems to be an anomaly. Where other Lions Clubs are strictly regional within a city or a district, their Chinatown counterparts represent a form of non-regional segregation, unless one upholds the illusion of Chinatown as a regional unit in its own right.

The local casino may be a major social meeting place. In some places it doubles up as a board room for Chinatown associations and other voluntary organisations. Some casinos are even major financial supporters of local Chinese associations (006//046). The interviewees had strongly conflicting views on the role of the casino within the community. Some thought of it as a convenient place, offering leisure in an environment that had little else to offer, and as comparable to or even better than the 'sparrow houses' (maqueguan), the Chinese gambling dens offering Mah-jongg and other games (006//045–46; 058//028). Others saw them as the lesser alternative to participation in community association activities (059//045). In some places, voluntary associations ran their own Mah-jongg clubs in order to keep overseas Chinese away from the casino (060//189–191), and some older leaders encourage the 'younger people between 25 and 50' to 'open their eyes and look further, not to gamble, go less to the casino' (065//007).

In many parts of Europe, the overseas Chinese communities are good customers of the local casinos, for gambling is a preferred leisure activity for many. Voluntary associations, cultural centres or activity centres in many European countries cannot legally allow their members to play Mah-jongg, lest they break tough gambling laws or incur prejudice from the local population; casinos provide such services and in some parts bend over backwards to set up afternoon Mah-jongg tables for the ladies, while the gentlemen conduct association meetings in the board-room. In one place, we heard of an arrangement where the elderly would politely turn up for two weekly lunches offered cheaply by two different factions of a voluntary association with financial support from the city council. After lunch, they would reassemble around Mah-jongg tables in the local casino. As our informant indicated, nobody needed free or cheap lunches, but the elderly tended to see the lunches and excursions to the casino as an important pattern of their social life. The activity also gave purpose to the overseas Chinese association and created some activity in its otherwise sparsely used premises.

The two dimensions of delimited urban space and social interaction are thus intertwined in European Chinatowns. While the community exists outside and independently from Chinatown, it is drawn into it through the physical location of its organisations' meeting places and public services, as clients of public services supplied to them, and as customers in the Chinatown businesses. The Chinatown association, which is the only institution linking Chinatown space and ethnic community, indirectly gives shape to Chinatown, for it is drawn into city council decisions on town planning as a civil society organisation representing a particular interest.

Chinatown and the wider Chinese community are linked through community leaders' overlapping membership of ethnic voluntary and Chinatown associations. This means that the otherwise dispersed community (whose residence and work are mainly outside the Chinatown area) has a 'stake' in Chinatown, even though it is only weakly represented.

The Chinatown Lions Clubs – as social clubs for the business elite from a wider geographical area than the Chinatown – project an image of Chinatown as a social community through high-profile community events and charity.

Dividing Chinatowns

Chinatowns are different from place to place, and their conditions cannot easily be summarised. Yet one can see in major cities that have a Chinatown, that large ethnic Chinese businesses are established outside the Chinatown area. Combined wholesale and retail outlets with ample parking space (and the advantage of economy of scale) attract Chinese customers to out-of-town industrial or retail parks.

Building these large shops outside Chinatowns often evokes resistance among established Chinatown enterprises, for they create unwanted competition and draw customers away. When a successful Chinese businessman who had built a combined wholesale-retail-catering complex with good car park conditions at a distance of approximately three kilometres from Manchester Chinatown wanted to repeat his success in Liverpool in the mid-1990s, he encountered obstructions in the process of purchasing a piece of land to build on, presumably due to pressure from people in Liverpool Chinatown who put pressure on the relevant departments under Liverpool city council.[14] The case, although discussed in the Chinese community media, appears to have been characterised by behind-the-scenes dealings and complex negotiations. The public argument brought forward to protest against the new cash-and-carry initiative was that it was 'a secret scheme to build a new Chinatown' (*Siyu Chinese Times*, no. 78, Oct. 1995, p. 24). A campaign was set on track to collect signatures under a protest note against the plan; the wording was:

Liverpool Chinatown Association, all major [overseas Chinese] associations [in Liverpool], proprietors in Liverpool Chinatown and local councillors strongly oppose the [plan of] W. H. Lung in Manchester to build a new Chinatown in Liverpool with a restaurant and 15 shops.[15]

The Chinatowns of Europe like in other parts of the world unite competing businesses in a common purpose, namely to uphold a critical mass of business that allows the individual business to take advantage of the ethnic label. For the individual businessperson, however, the need to expand business and to respond to market demand may call for investment outside the Chinatown area. We saw in the case of Amsterdam the lack of space for Chinatown businesses to expand and the problems faced by potential new investors due to the geographical constraint of Chinatowns. Chinatowns rely on efficient suppliers of wholesale goods and services from companies based outside Chinatown in order to survive; but these outside companies also provide competition. Many conflicts that came to our knowledge during our research originated in this paradoxical problem of the Chinatowns. Fierce competition exists within the context of the need to cooperate. Chinatown associations are no better or worse at solving such issues than other professional or business associations.

Ethnic symbol

Chinatown's role as a symbol has deep roots in the business interests of both the Chinese community and the local authorities in European states. Interestingly, the notion of Chinatown in Europe is of a business district with a particular mix of retail and catering adorned with Chinese characters and decorations, serving both a non-Chinese and a Chinese community market. A Chinatown does provide some specialist services for the Chinese community, but is only rarely based on residence and work (except in the retail, catering and service businesses of Chinatown). European Chinese typically do not live in a Chinatown, do not work there, and only do some of their shopping there. This differs from the 'classical' image of Chinatown as a ghetto-like area dominated by vice and danger, where Chinese lived and worked in ethnic seclusion, following their own patterns of life.

Chinatown consists of ethnic icons that are useful in generating business and forging cooperation among the overseas Chinese. Cultural patterns and institutions of Chinatowns form a spine that allows political integration in local affairs and brings advantage to the business people of Chinatown. Arches, dragon and lion dances as well as public festivals with public processions and fireworks are valuable elements of the processes that create Chinatowns and hold them together.

4 Formation of sub-ethnic identities

Siyi and Qingtian

Observers often see the Chinese in Europe as one homogenous group. Most Chinese would agree that they share characteristics with other Chinese and relate to them in various ways – social, political and economic. Even so, closer scrutiny reveals that the Chinese are divided among themselves, and that their divisions are largely based on speech and local provenance. These divisions result in the differentiation of the larger Chinese category in to various sub-ethnic groups.

This chapter traces the history of two such groups (out of the many available), and examines the shifting importance of sub-ethnic divisions over time. It demonstrates how sub-ethnic groups maintain, reinvent, and make use of their identities. The two cases, Siyi and Qingtian, differ strikingly. Siyi identity was originally strong, but lost ground after World War Two; in the 1990s it has slowly begun to revive. Qingtian identity was slight until the 1980s and 1990s, but was nourished by the new links with China following Deng Xiaoping's open-door policy.

The Siyi and Qingtian identities, each in their own way, illustrate the volatility and political nature of sub-ethnic identification.

The Siyinese in Europe

The place

Siyi (or See Yip in Cantonese) means 'the four counties'. The original four counties are today part of the jurisdiction of Jiangmen City; they were Taishan (until 1914 called Xinning), Kaiping, Enping and Xinhui Counties. When the old Heshan County (which between 1959 and 1981 had been merged with neighbouring Gaoming County and as a part of Gaoming been subordinated to Foshan City) was restored as a county in its own right in 1981 under Jiangmen's jurisdiction, it again became associated with Siyi. In spite of this and many other changes in the jurisdiction borders, Siyi became entrenched as a popular name for the region. In the 1980s, however, after Heshan had been restored as a separate county, the name Wuyi, 'the five counties' (Ng Yip in Cantonese), emerged as an alternative name for the region. Today, the two names are used interchangeably among overseas Chinese.[1] Jiangmen City, the region's prefecture, was established in 1904 as a steamship landing and trading place in Xinhui County. Although it had city status for several years in the 1920s, it has been Siyi's prefecture only since the early 1970s. The areas that Jiangmen then comprised included some felt not to belong to Siyi. Its present, narrower jurisdiction over Siyi dates back only to 1988. When Taishan, Xinhui, Heshan, Kaiping, and Enping became county-level cities in 1994, they came directly under the province for all administrative purposes. Jiangmen City's jurisdiction as a prefecture is therefore only nominal.[2]

The people

Many overseas Chinese all over the world have their roots in Siyi. Official estimates from the early 1990s indicate that there are about 1.8 million overseas Chinese from Siyi, and that another 1.1 million live in Taiwan, Hong Kong, and Macau. Such statistics are almost certainly underestimates. Compared with the present population of 3.6 million in Siyi, they are nonetheless considerable.

Siyi is, and has been for more than a century, one of China's main sources of overseas migration. Yet few Siyi migrants went to Europe, save for some in the early years; after the early 1950s, hardly anyone left Siyi for Europe. The vestigial Siyi communities today comprise just a few thousand people.[3] Siyinese tend to emphasise their local cultural bonds. The native place, and its special identity, are prominent focal points among overseas Chinese from Siyi. Knowledge of each village, its lineages, and its prominent figures is surprisingly alive among people abroad hailing from Siyi.

Forging Siyi identity

How does the Siyi community manage to juggle its dual dimensions of locality and global community? How did the Siyinese community in Europe emerge and how does it maintain multiple relationships within Europe, within China, within the world, and within Siyi?

Table 4.1 Overseas Chinese from Siyi

	In Siyi	Overseas	T-H-M
Enping	433,417	113,000	110,000
Kaiping	648,633	420,000	118,000
Heshan	337,062	118,000	139,000
Taishan	996,600	785,000	350,000
Xinhui	879,186	245,000	323,000
Counties	**3,294,898**	**1,681,000**	**930,110**
City Districts	309,897	116,000	142,890
Jiangmen City	**3,604,795**	**1,797,000**	**1,073,000**

Source: Ministry of Public Security of the People's Republic of China (1993, 139); and Liu Nanwei (1994, 201–30).

Note: T-H-M means residents in Taiwan, Hong Kong and Macau of Siyi origin.

Siyi is not a strongly unified community joined together around one power centre. Formal authority in the 1990s is to a certain extent vested in Jiangmen City and incidentally overlaps with the concept of Siyi, but does not shape and unify Siyi as a community. Given the fluctuating and weak nature of the intermediate level of administration in the region between the relatively stable layers of the province and the county (or county-level city), people have no cause to make Jiangmen City the object of their affection. Their 'ancestral place' remains Siyi.

The university in Jiangmen, established in 1985 as Wuyi University, deliberately plays upon such sentiments. The university is not just a product of government policy, which upgraded colleges to universities and set up new universities in the 1980s. The university was a joint effort funded by overseas Chinese, local industry, and local government. Apart from a few million yuan invested by Jiangmen, Xinhui, and Taishan, much of the funding came from large enterprises in Jiangmen, Kaiping, and Enping that probably expected to receive some of the graduates. Whereas this public and semi-public investment amounted to just 4–5 million yuan, donations from overseas Chinese individuals totalled around 90 to 100 million Hong Kong dollars.[4] (The four largest donors gave a total of 43 million HK$.) Corporate overseas Chinese donations were in the order of about 20 million HK$. These donations were mainly from companies associated with native-place organisations in Hong Kong and Macau, or linked with Siyi in some way.[5] Wuyi University was thus funded mainly from overseas Chinese sources; the function of local investment was to attract such overseas donations. Throughout the twentieth century, educational donations have flowed into the region, to support or found primary and middle schools and libraries. The 1985 venture was the first opportunity for overseas donors to invest in higher education.

Many overseas Chinese communities of Siyi origin represent the whole region rather than its parts. They therefore look to Jiangmen as a level of government that reflects their membership's geographic background in its broadest sense. They find it easier to donate to inclusive Siyi projects, headed by Jiangmen, than to invest in smaller, regional projects. By encouraging the development of a Siyi identity, the Chinese authorities can, for their part, better draw on overseas Chinese resources.

Overseas Chinese with close ties to a native village do not abandon local ties by donating to or investing in the broader region. On the contrary, such donations and investment gain them prestige, for they are seen to hobnob with high officials. An informant told me:

> A friend of mine said he hoped to go to North America, own a car, and buy a large house, preferably with a large swimming-pool. He hoped to earn enough to go back to Taishan and donate a school or something similar, to leave a trace in the old home. I never thought of this as odd; actually, it sounded natural, like a dream that most people have. His ambition never struck me as something special. But now, on reflection, it strikes me as typical of Siyinese to want to demonstrate their prowess by donating to their hometown.

Jiangmen's role is to stimulate overseas Chinese to altruism and to provide them with frameworks within which to practise this altruism. Siyi identity is based on speech and cultural commonalties and a suspicion of outsiders rather than on some administrative reality. The new stress on Jiangmen City is an attempt on the part of the authorities to create an administrative focus for such feelings.

In the late 1980s and early 1990s, this project took on a historiographic dimension, when Jiangmen's Association for Overseas Chinese History started publishing the journal *Wuyi Qiaoshi* (*Overseas Chinese History of Wuyi*). The conventional practice in Chinese local history writing is to write about the counties. The same practice was, until recently, followed in Siyi. The introduction in the late 1980s of local history managed at the prefectural city level, way above that of the separate counties, is not unheard of in China, but the construction of a collective overseas Chinese historiography for the whole of the region is a remarkable step towards a new official historiography on the basis of a 'tradition' that lives more in the minds of overseas Chinese and ambitious regional authorities than in the ancestral villages and counties.

Historically, there is no evidence of a common regional authority that could claim the loyalty of the inhabitants of Siyi as a whole;[6] Jiangmen's role as a prefecture is recent. Its present status is a response to overseas Chinese demands for an administrative focus in China for organisations representing overseas Chinese from the different parts of Siyi.

Speech links the people of Siyi together and sets them off against other populations in the region. The dominant local speech (save in the urban districts of Jiangmen, where Cantonese is spoken) is Toysanese, a subdialect of Yue, to which also Cantonese (the speech of Guangzhou and Hong Kong) belongs. Toysanese (Taishanhua in Mandarin) is the language spoken in Taishan and other parts of Siyi. Cantonese and Toysanese speakers can communicate only with great difficulty, but identify as fellow-speakers of the dialects of the Guang–Zhao area (which covers the old Guangzhou and Zhaoqing Prefectures of dynastic times), as distinct from the Teochiu speakers of northeastern Guangdong (who speak a subdialect of Hokkien, or Minnanhua). Within Siyi, the varieties of Toysanese are close. This linguistic affinity enables the region to cohere socially and culturally.

Siyi has a substantial Hakka-speaking minority; this causes social and cultural segregation between speakers of Hakka and Toysanese, and reinforces cohesion among Toysanese speakers. This linguistic division is an important element in the construction of Siyi identity, as I shall show shortly.

In July 1993, the Jiangmen People's Congress adopted a Jiangmen City Anthem, praising the 'fresh flowers of reform that blossom in Wuyi (i.e. Siyi)' and explicitly linking Siyi with the overseas Chinese and the 'people of Jiangmen' (Zhang Danian 1996, 4).

Each of the five county-level cities within Siyi also pursues links on their own account with overseas Chinese. One example is Taishan City's establishment in September 1997 of an Association of People from Taishan in Guangdong (Guangdong Taishanren Lianyihui). At a meeting held on 18 October 1997 to 'cultivate [village] relatives' (kenqin), the Association expressed its determination to reinvigorate links with overseas Chinese from Taishan.[7]

Historical conflicts: shaping the identity

Siyi's strong local identity is a product of many influences. A main element in its construction was the conflict in past times between Toysanese speakers and Hakkas over land and markets. Zheng Dehua and Cheng Luxi (1991, 4) estimates that by the mid-nineteenth century 300,000 Hakka had immigrated to Taishan (at that time still called Xinning), where they mainly occupied poor, hilly areas. Between 1867 and 1953, Chixi County (populated mainly by Hakkas) was separated from Xinning (Taishan) due to warfare between Toysanese speakers (also known as Punti, a more general sub-ethnic classification of Yue dialect speakers in opposition to Hakkas) and the Hakkas (Liu Nanwei 1994, 213). According to Luo Xianglin's (1933, 93–124) survey of Hakka settlements, Chixi was a 'pure Hakka county'. The Qing and Nationalist governments acknowledged this Hakka majority by appointing Hakka county magistrates in Chixi (Wu Daorong 1920, 120–2).[8]

Siyi identity became stronger partly as a result of conflicts between the Puntis and the Hakkas. The region's early settlers (Toysanese-speaking Punti) had colonised the area before the Ming Dynasty (1368–1644). During the Qing Dynasty, in 1662, the coastal population was moved inland, resulting in the depopulation of a swathe of coastal territory 25 kilometres deep. This policy greatly alienated the Punti settlers, who lost their property. However, they complied, allowing their old farms to lie fallow. There was land enough in the region – so much so that the government later began to use large areas of uncultivated land to resettle poor people from outside the region. In 1733, for example, paupers from Huizhou and Chaozhou were resettled on the northeastern fringes of Kaiping County. According to the local history of Kaiping for 1733, 'The immigration of Hakkas within the boundaries of this county began at this time' (Anonymous 1933, 165). In the 1930s, more than 10 per cent of the inhabitants of Kaiping county were Hakkas (Luo Xianglin 1933, 102). The government-sponsored settlement of Hakkas in the 1730s set off a Hakka chain migration, not only in the remote hilly areas but also in the richer, previously abandoned stretches along the coast. Punti resentment and the resulting conflicts never ended. The Hakkas were a low-status group with different speech and traditions who 'usurped' land that the earlier settlers had been forced to abandon or saw as places for their own lineages to expand into.

This conflict was exacerbated by the Red Turban revolt in 1854. Mei (1979, 472–3) cites the violence and killings associated with the revolt as a push-factor for international migration away from Siyi – more than one million people killed throughout Guangdong Province, and 70,000 executed in Guangzhou alone. The Red Turban revolt created in Siyi a state of perpetual factional terrorism, whose main division was between Hakkas and Puntis.

Triads killed some Hakkas in Kaiping County. The Hakkas retaliated with ambushes, and the local authorities began to use the Hakkas against the Puntis. The Hakkas asserted themselves in areas that had previously been Puntis'. Punti gangs responded with even more violence. The deeper issues at stake included the control of markets and rents and the extraction of protection money. Hakka and Punti gangs fought a war of attrition that lasted for more than a decade.[9]

The Red Turban revolt reinforced the control of the large lineages in Siyi. According to Zheng Dehua and Cheng Luxi (1991), the lineages set up armed militias and gained greater control over lineage members. The heads of the larger lineages took local power and defied local officials.

Some 150,000 people are said to have perished in fighting between the Hakkas and Puntis in Guangdong between 1864 and 1866.[10]

Many people fled abroad, at a time when the coolie trade was in full swing.[11] Most Red Turbans who escaped execution were lured by crimps to go to the Americas (USA, Peru and Cuba), while others joined earlier migrants in Southeast Asia (Mei 1979, 465 and 473). *The History of Taishan County Native Place* (Chen Tianjun, Huang Renfu and Huan Zhongji 1985) chronicles how Puntis and Hakkas took each other prisoner in their wars and sold them to crimps in Macau or Hong Kong. Many of the migrants from Siyi were therefore political exiles who joined together overseas in the Hongmen (branches of the Heaven and Earth Society). They had been raised in an environment suspicious of intruders and strongly attached to their local speech and customs, which they saw threatened by the Hakkas.

The Siyinese also considered themselves to be in competition with the flourishing, Cantonese-speaking Sanyi region, whose economy developed early and which included Guangzhou, Guangdong's political centre.[12] Siyi, in contrast, was a mountainous enclave, far poorer than the well-endowed Sanyi. The Sanyi counties of Nanhai, Panyu and Shunde were flat and fertile, criss-crossed by arms of the Pearl River Delta that eased transport and trade, unlike the small rivers and streams of the Siyi counties, which were unsuitable for any but the smallest vessels. The proximity of these so differently endowed areas led to their social segregation. The rich Sanyinese looked down upon the backward Siyinese with their funny accents, coarse manners and parochial habits.

In the early and mid-nineteenth century, the Qing authorities unwittingly created another source of tension between Siyi and Sanyi. The policy of using local braves and the support of the local gentry to create a strong local militia brought the lineage leaders of Panyu, Shunde and Nanhai into close cooperation with the imperial authorities (Wakeman 1966). The distrust and insularity of the Siyi lineages was reinforced by the gravitation of local military control as well as wealth into the hands of the Sanyinese.

The Siyinese closed ranks, politically and economically, in self-defence. They failed to control access to the nearby conduits into the world market in Guangzhou, Macau, and Hong Kong. They were directly exposed to fluctuations in world trade, and at the same time faced fierce competition from the Sanyi, who were more favourably placed to take advantage of such openings. Linguistically, they put a far stronger emphasis than before on Toysanese, which, though divided into sub-dialects, stands in general opposition to Cantonese. In social and cultural interaction, too, they stressed the features that distinguished them from the Sanyinese.

They strengthened their lineages and adopted an increasingly independent stance in relation to the imperial authorities.[13] Lineage leaders tightened their grip on local power by a combination of employing violence and forming coalitions. Secret societies provided a further dimension of political cohesion. They created supra-regional political links for strong leaders and helped them control local communities.

The Toysanese dialect spoken in Siyi emerged from the same roots as Cantonese and would probably have remained more similar to it, had it not been for the great influx of Hakkas, which reinforced the identity of the Toysanese-speaking Puntis, in opposition not only to the Hakkas but also to the Cantonese-speaking Puntis. If trade, social interaction, intermarriage, and open attitudes had prevailed among Siyinese and Sanyinese, the difference in their speech-forms would have been much smaller. However, Toysanese dominance in the Chinatowns of pre-war America reinforced its status at home and exerted a conservative influence on it:

> Since most of the Chinese in New York City were from Toysan, it was natural that Toysanese became the lingua franca of this community, even though the Toysan dialect is only a variation of the standard Cantonese dialect spoken in Kwangtung Province. In fact, Cantonese and Toysanese are so different that they are unintelligible to each other. Thus, in order to be accepted into the community in those days, a Cantonese had to learn the Toysan dialect.
>
> (Wong 1982, 8)

In exile, Siyinese maintained lineage-style ties embodied in surname and native-place organisations. Over the centuries, they ganged up where necessary against other regional groups such as the Teochiunese, the Hainanese, the Hakkas and the Cantonese, and formed brotherhoods against the Qing.

Siyi's large overseas communities reinforced the home community, the lineages, and local traditions and social practices. The Siyinese in Europe were marginal to the migration from Siyi, playing little part in shaping Siyi's migrant community. Instead, they were shaped in turn by the patterns of Siyi economy and culture that emerged among overseas Siyinese in the USA, Peru, Southeast Asia, and the South Pacific.[14] Siyi's clannishness, lineage orientation, and emphasis on native-place ties emerged from a historical process of conflicts over resources and of social segregation, combined with the impact of a culture of migration that helped reinforce the region's cultural distinctiveness.

The early Siyinese in Europe

The early Siyi migrants to Europe were seamen working on steamships, mainly as stokers, who went ashore in European ports waiting for new hire. They were not coolies recruited by crimps or forced into exile by poor harvests or social conflict. However, in many ways there was little difference between the recruitment of coolies and of seamen. The recruiting agents used by the European steamship lines were little better than crimps, labour conditions on the ships were equally little better than those in the mines and plantations, and the contracts were unfair and made the seamen dependent on their gangers.

Chinese sailors had plied the European ports ever since the main trading nations set up freight lines to the Far East in the seventeenth and eighteenth centuries. However, their numbers jumped between the 1870s and the 1890s, when the steamship companies entered a period of cut-throat competition. Excessive capacity depressed freight rates, so the companies sought to cut costs (Hyde 1956, 88).

Liverpool's Blue Funnel Line began to recruit Chinese seamen in large numbers in 1892. At the beginning of the twentieth century, it employed approximately 300 Chinese seamen, rising to more than 2,500 after World War One. In the 1910s, a report counted 224 'Resident Chinamen', 132 'Chinamen in Boarding Houses', one Chinese woman, and 100 'Chinamen aboard ship' in Liverpool (Wong 1989, 4). In the early decades of the twentieth century, most Chinese seamen in Liverpool, Cardiff, and London were Siyinese. When Liverpool became the home of the Chinese Merchant Seamen's Pool in the 1940s, between 8,000 and 20,000 Chinese seamen lived in Liverpool at any given time, from all over China.

These seamen were recruited (by agents in Hong Kong) from a small number of counties in Guangdong, notably in Siyi, Baoan County (the northern part of former Xin'an, to which Kowloon, the New Territories and Shenzhen originally belonged), and Dongguan. Agents specialised in supplying crews of stokers, usually from the same village or group of villages. As a result, the recruitment base remained far narrower than that of the coolie trade.

The recruitment agents (or 'shipping masters') entered into group contracts with the steamship lines and handled the seamen's money. They retained the 'advance hire' that should rightfully have been paid to the seamen. Boarding-house masters in European ports were empowered to pay out wages from which boarding costs had already been deducted. This and similar practices, not unlike indentured labour arrangements, were effective mechanisms of control. However, the most effective means of control was the gangers' ability to exert pressure on the seamen's relatives in their home villages.

Paths of migration

Most seamen recruited by British lines were from Siyi, whereas those recruited by the Dutch lines were mainly from Baoan and Dongguan. Wubben (1986) describes the fate of the Baoan seamen hired by Baoan and Dongguan shipping masters, and indicates only sporadic competition from other organisations (Wubben 1986, 62). Wubben's observations tally with the recollections of relatives of Chinese who lived in the Netherlands in the early twentieth century. Most Chinese in the Netherlands before the deportations and exclusions of 1936–9 were from Dapeng in Baoan County, and the rest were from Shunde in Guangdong and Wenzhou in Zhejiang; there were probably none from Siyi.[15] In contrast, an interviewee in Manchester claims that the Siyinese were the largest group of Chinese in Britain until the early 1950s and that most arrived as seamen (060//001). It is possible that this difference reflects biased recollection by our interviewees.

Taishan historians in the 1980s who tried to estimate where Taishan's overseas migrants had settled were faced with a difficult task. The census figures from the 1950s were notoriously biased, but the census returns did contain information on the settlement of overseas relatives. In the returns, however, there were two main problems regarding information on the overseas Chinese. At the time of the census, Taishan people often had not been in contact with relatives overseas for many years and could only provide the last known details. Also, there seems to have been confusion about whether or not relatives were in the European metropoles or in their colonies. Based on their best judgement, the historians in the 1980s arrived at the revised numbers of overseas Taishanese listed in Table 4.2.

The revised numbers suggest that there were equal numbers of Taishanese in Britain and the Netherlands in the early 1950s. According to the 1953 population census, 4,250 Taishanese had been resident in Britain and 3,341 in the Netherlands. It may seem arbitrary that they were brought back to 365 and 341 respectively, but we do not have access to the exact criteria for reassessing the statistics. All we can conclude from the 1953 census (which was, in any case, incomplete and unreliable) and its subsequent reworking by local historians is that probably several hundred Taishanese people lived in Europe in the 1950s.

These Siyinese in Europe formed an important part of the European overseas Chinese community before the World War Two, even though their numbers remained small. After World War Two, there was further direct migration from Siyi to Europe, due to the small but steady stream of Siyi women who married overseas Chinese men.

There was also some secondary migration to Europe after the de-colonisation of the Dutch East Indies, French Indochina, Malaya, and other places, but it is impossible to to say how much. Europe was never the first choice for Siyinese. Most went, if they could, to North America.

At the beginning of the twentieth century, large numbers of Taishanese from Haiyan, a cluster of villages, were recruited to work in the phosphate mines on the South Pacific island of Nauru (063//004–005). During the nineteenth century, Haiyan suffered greatly during the Hakka wars and was preyed upon by pirates (He Fulai 1893), and in the twentieth century suffered heavy taxation and military

Table 4.2 People from Taishan County in Europe

Country		Country	
Britain	365	The Netherlands	341
France	53	Germany	18
Portugal	13	Belgium	6
Soviet Union	3	Switzerland	2
Denmark	2	Austria	1
Romania	1		
Total			**805**

Source: Original Compilation Group of the History of Taishan County (1985).

conscription at the hands of Nationalist officials. Haiyan had a tradition of emigration, and the continuous pressure on it resulted in the large-scale local recruitment of contract labour overseas. Nauru, a tropical island made of phosphate dug out by miners as the raw material for gunpowder and chemical fertilisers, was a hell on earth, a United Nations trust territory administrated by Australia on behalf of itself and of Britain and New Zealand until 1968 (when it became independent). Secondary migration of Haiyan people from Nauru to Britain took place between 1945 and 1968.

Other Siyinese migrated to Britain from Hong Kong. There had been a large Siyi community in Hong Kong since the mid-nineteenth century. Many of its members have, like other Hong Kong residents, come to Britain.

After World War Two, Hong Kong became a conduit for direct migration from Siyi to Britain. According to one interviewee (061//059–065), the Siyinese in postwar Britain began to ask their relatives over. Those relatives with a Hong Kong birth certificate had the right to settle in Britain, while others overcame this problem by buying birth certificates and by other subterfuges. Many Haiyanese arrived in Britain between 1947 and the mid-1950s, thus boosting Liverpool's Siyi population. Not until the late 1940s did the overseas Chinese community in Liverpool begin to stabilise. Before then, the Chinese had mainly been sailors waiting for a ship, including some who had gone ashore to open restaurants or laundries or had married English women. Not until the 1950s and 1960s did Chinese men bring wives over from China or go to China to marry.

Migrant mentality and global reality

For the Siyinese, Europe is a relatively unimportant corner of the world. Few live in Europe, their remittances to China are scant, and they never produced any great entrepreneurs or pillars of society. Siyi is an abstract place comprising the four (now five) counties in Guangdong Province together with Hong Kong, Macau and bits of North America. Just as Siyinese who have lived abroad for decades are still conversant with village lanes and lineage relations in their place of origin, so those in Siyi know about San Francisco, New York, Toronto and other places in North America. Social obligation and relative lineage position are still factors in the lives of those abroad – perhaps more so than their immediate social ties abroad.

Who is a Siyinese? A life that oscillates between the global Siyi and the reality of this or that specific place constitutes a complex mental process largely beyond the researcher's grasp. The two realities are not likely to conflict, and may not even be seen as separate or discrete. The global Siyi reality is dormant: it awakens only when needed. For the Siyinese, the determining factor is the ancestral village origin rather than proficiency in Toysanese, or some other cultural marker. To be born (or descend from someone born) in Siyi is sufficient basis for membership of the global Siyi.

There are no reliable frameworks for grasping the emergence of such a global reality, and this is not the place to attempt to establish one. The literature on Siyi provides insufficient data on the impact of massive emigration on social relations and on the evolution of social and behavioural norms. How does a village in an area dominated by lineages and ancestor worship cope when a high proportion of the population lives or dies abroad? How do women in such places deal with being alone, with farming, and with bearing and raising children? How are children prepared for a life overseas? When split families, depleted lineages, and departures for distant lands are as normal as giving birth, there must exist a special social order. Works by Hua and Thireau (1996) and Hsu (2000) explore the transnationality of Taishan in a historical perspective; while they perhaps do not answer the questions about how such a dispersed society functions, they do present us with a deep understanding of the historical changes in the structures of Taishan.

The European Siyi communities: the organisations of Siyi

Siyi organisations in Europe form a complex network. The oldest and most prestigious is the Che Kung Tong,[16] a formerly secret society in Liverpool, now described as a 'righteous' (zhengyi) rather than a native-place organisation. In other words, it is a traditional political body supposedly open to any (male) group in society, irrespective of race, creed and so on. The Che Kung Tong in Liverpool originated as an organisation by means of which Siyi leaders exerted social influence over the Chinese community, and it remains dominated by the Siyinese. It was already active in Liverpool in the 1880s (062//012), so it probably emerged at the same time as the Blue Funnel line began using Chinese seamen.

According to the history of the See Yip Chinese Association of England,[17] Yue Chun (Yu Jin) was the founder of the Chinese community in Liverpool:

> At the end of the 19th[18] Century, the first Chinese person to arrive in England was Mr. Yue Chun of Toi Shan [Taishan] County. He arrived in London and worked hard for a shipping company for a considerable period, until he had saved enough money to start a laundry in Liverpool where he eventually retired. During his time in Liverpool he was very diligent and always had a love for his own people. After 1900, more Chinese people came to England to look for a living. As the majority grew, they realised that they had to unite together in order to achieve more themselves. They called themselves the See Yip [Siyi] Chinese Association of England with Yue Chun leading the executive members.

Yue Chun was among the initiators in 1906 of the See Yip Chinese Association of England (in Liverpool), but never became its leader; his authority lay, we must surmise, in the Che Kung Tong. The Che Kung Tong had been present in Liverpool since the 1880s and had for 20-odd years organised the few hundred Chinese in Liverpool, most of them from Siyi. The number of Chinese rose after 1900, and included people from other parts of China. The Che Kung Tong now had to deal with Chinese of non-Siyi background. Presumably to safeguard the interests of the Siyinese, Yue Chun and others set up the Siyi Association in 1906 as a non-political and non-religious body under the leadership of Wong Kau (Huang Qiu).

The local police chief probably sensed the shifting power balance in Liverpool's Chinatown, but he was in the dark about what was going on (May 1978, 114). The establishment of the Siyi Association marked the start of a tradition in Liverpool of multiple organisations with interlocking leaderships initially aimed at securing Siyi hegemony over the Chinese community. Although the Che Kung Tong was supposedly above regional, speech, and clan interests and gradually began to include non-Siyi members in Liverpool, the Siyinese continued to dominate it.

The Che Kung Tong in London also changed in 1906, when it renamed itself the Chun Yee Association (Lundun Zhengyi Gongshanghui), ceased to be secret, and became a mixture of a trade union and social organisation for the Chinese in London. Hereafter, the Che Kung Tong existed only in Liverpool. Why these changes? In the British elections in 1906, Chinese indentured labour became an issue for the first time due to the large-scale importation of Chinese to the Transvaal Province in South Africa under conditions equal to those of slaves. At around the same time, British trade unions began a racist campaign against the 'Yellow Peril'. 'Concerned' citizens and officials had already begun to enquire into public health issues and the alleged seduction of young girls by Chinese. By forming public associations, the Chinese were in a better position to defend their interests and avoid discrimination.

In August 1905, the United League of China (Zhongguo Tongmenghui) was established in Tokyo. Branch offices were soon established in Paris, Berlin and Brussels, the site of its European headquarters. Previously, the Che Kung Tong had been Sun Yat-sen's representative in Europe. Now, his United League, a modern organisation of younger, nationalist revolutionaries, allowed him to dispense with former allies like the Che Kung Tong. As a result, the Chinese in London and Liverpool were cut off from Sun's revolutionary project in China, and no longer needed to keep their work secret.

One can only speculate why the Che Kung Tong in Liverpool has continued to exist right up to the present. The main reason is probably that it has allowed the Siyinese to dominate the Chinese community in Liverpool to a degree not possible in London.

Three elements shaped the way in which Chinese in Britain saw themselves: rising racist hostility; the influx of Chinese from places other than Siyi with the surge in freight between the turn of the century and World War One; and the gradual depoliticisation of the Hongmen organisations as the new nationalism rendered the arcane ways of the secret societies outdated. Tensions among overseas Chinese in response to these changes meant that community leaders in Liverpool could retain their domination only by rallying the Toysanese speech group. In London, the Siyinese were becoming a minority and influential Chinese were more responsive to the new nationalism. Abandoning the political mysticism of the Che Kung Tong and taking the lead in a public organisation like London's Chun Yee Association presumably encompassed a generation shift.

For the next 80-odd years, Siyi identity in London played little or no role in Chinese affairs. The Siyinese who remained were part of the Chinese community without any separate body to represent them.

Meanwhile, in Liverpool's Chinatown, the See Yip Chinese Association (Yinglun Siyi Zonghuiguan) formed a closed, elitist network of Siyinese. The (still secret) Che Kung Tong included increasing numbers of other Chinese, but the interlocking of the leaderships of the See Yip Association and the Che Kung Tong ensured Siyinese dominance until World War Two, when bombings (which affected the Pitt Street area where the Chinese were concentrated) and the enormous influx of people from other parts of China as part of the wartime Chinese Merchant Sea-men's Pool threw the Chinese community into disarray.

In the immediate postwar period, the community revived under the Siyinese Chan Kwon Charn (Chen Guangcan), who was apparently leader of both the Che Kung Tong and the See Yip Association. In 1954 Chan made 22 Nelson Street available for these bodies. In 1948 or 1949, the arrival of young people from the Haiyan area of Taishan together with internal disagreements over the leadership of the See Yip Organisation, led to the establishment of the Hoy Yin [Haiyan] Association (Lü Ying Haiyan Tongxianghui); most Siyinese in Liverpool were, in any case, from Haiyan. Eventually, the three organisations – the Che Kung Tong, the See Yip Association, and the Hoy Yin Association – became closely interlinked, with a high degree of overlapping membership and interlocking leaderships.

The main functions of these organisations was to care and provide lodgings for elderly, frail Chinese seafarers, to administrate the 'Past Chinese Friends' (Zhonghua Xianyou) section of Liverpool's Anfield Cemetery, and to celebrate Chinese festivals. Within the Chinese community in Liverpool, Siyinese dominance was formalised; such organisations provided an arena for the use of Toysanese and the communal practice of ancestor worship and geomancy. In the early period the organisations provided credit through the rocca (yuehui), by which funds were pooled for specific projects. Membership provided security for short- and long-term loans without the need for collateral.

The arrival in the 1960s and 1970s of large numbers of Hakkas and Puntis from Hong Kong's New Territories challenged the dominance of the Liverpool Siyinese, who looked set to become marginalised. In the first two decades after World War Two, Chinese community organisations were on the way to becoming increasingly unimportant as elderly seamen passed away, the welfare state grew, and the children of Siyinese migrants came of age and entered mainstream occup-ations.[19] In the 1960s and 1970s, however, great numbers of new arrivals intensified the sub-ethnic identification and reinvigorated the See Yip Association, the Hoy Yin Association, and the Che Kung Tong. Political differences between the three groups were obvious – many of the new arrivals were radical and positively inclined towards communist China.

Liverpool's economic decline in the 1960s and 1970s made things far worse for the Siyinese. Dereliction, unemployment, and social destitution damaged the catering niches in which the Chinese were active and people began to leave for elsewhere in Britain. Some Siyinese went to Manchester around 1960 to take advantage of cheap buildings in the area around Faulkner Street, George Street and Nicholas Street (060//001...002). These pioneers were soon outnumbered by people from the New Territories. They maintained their links with Liverpool, but Manchester's other overseas Chinese gradually overwhelmed them. Toysanese was rapidly replaced by Cantonese, which became the sole language of public communication. Many post-war immigrants from Siyi had lived in Hong Kong and spoke fluent Cantonese. Siyinese who went 'home' in search of wives found it easier to marry in Hong Kong, where there was a large Siyi community. Children were often sent for education to schools in Hong Kong rather than in Siyi. Moreover, Cantonese was the language of Hong Kong, a major communication and transport hub in East Asia, the most important transit point to China, and the place whose culture, tastes, and media dominated overseas Chinese communities worldwide.

The Siyinese in Manchester (and in their few other European enclaves) were engulfed by the Cantonese and largely assimilated to them. In Liverpool, however, this process was delayed due to the group's stronger organisation. Yet Toysanese speech was declining and the younger generation acquired a British orientation and outlook, entered mainstream schools and careers identified with a syncretic, Hong Kong-inspired overseas Chinese culture, and entered into friendships and relationships with other second-generation Chinese and native Britons.

The 1980s, however, saw a sudden reinvigoration of Siyi identity. The trend started in Manchester, where the Chinese community's organisational structure remained simple until the 1980s. Apart from a 'secret' organisation promoting the Cultural Revolution, strongly supported by the Consulate-General, there had only been one organisation to serve all sections of the overseas Chinese community. In the early 1980s, however, the availability of 'ethnically' directed grants from the city council resulted in the emergence of divisions. These divisions followed lines of ancestral origin. More and more groups of Chinese began to lobby councillors for money and influence (06//*passim*).

Siyinese in London formed the Five Yip Chinese Association[20] in the 1990s with the support of the See Yip [Siyi] Association in Liverpool and the Ng Yip [Wuyi] Association in Manchester. Its chief purpose was to facilitate the hosting of delegations to London from Jiangmen. It would probably not have emerged but for this link to China.

For the outside observer, it is obvious that Siyi identity is of declining importance in Britain. It is probably kept going to serve the needs of Chinatown politicians. The Siyinese in Europe are few and scattered. Little is done to emphasise their culture and dialect; the president of the Ng Yip Association, for example, speaks no Toysanese.

The Che Kung Tong, which started out as an ostensibly supra-regional political body but was in reality a vehicle for Siyi dominance in Liverpool's Chinese community, has undergone important changes over the last few years. It is not as secretive as before and is now part of the freemasons' organisation. Moreover, the Che Kung Tong is open to membership by non-Chinese:

> We do not look at nationality. If a Westerner participates, we accept him, if a Negro (heigui) participates, we accept him; the only requirement is that he

must be for the Che Kung Tong, he must give his effort to Che Kung Tong. We unite, we exclude no one ... The British Government recognises our Che Kong Tong, as freemasons; it's not that they recognise us in the sense of 'official' or 'unofficial', they are not opposed to us. They know we are a progressive organisation ... In reality, Che Kung Tong is orthodox, very orthodox, it is a righteous organisation not involved in bad activities. We will accept no one who uses the Che Kung Tong for bad ends.[21]

The ideology of openness suggests a cultural switch towards Western forms of organisation. By emphasising the parallel with the freemasons, the Che Kung Tong claims to be part of a dynamic cosmopolitan, and hence 'modern' and transnational movement.

Although it is still important for the Liverpool Siyinese, the Che Kung Tong has accepted members from all parts of China ever since its founding. Its importance for the Siyinese lay in its ability to ensure them leadership of the broader community. Its leadership includes non-Siyinese, but not its top posts. Today, the Che Kung Tong has lost its top place in the Chinese community. New organisations have emerged in Liverpool over the last 30 years that have broken the oligarchic role of the Siyi leaders. They include the Wah Sing Chinese Community, the Merseyside Chinese Centre, and the Liverpool Chinatown Business Association.

The Qingtianese in Europe

Many Chinese Europeans originate in the mountainous county of Qingtian in Zhejiang Province. Among the first Chinese in Europe, today they continue to arrive in comparatively large numbers. Very few overseas Qingtianese live outside Europe. Some went to Taiwan after the Civil War (1945–9) and migrated onward to North America. Other tiny communities live in Japan and Brazil, and elsewhere the world.

The Qingtianese emerged as a sub-ethnic group in Europe in the 1980s and 1990s. Sub-ethnic segregation happens when a group actively sets itself off against other groups (that is, when ascription becomes important for the group), institutionalises this difference for the sake of competing for resources or protecting assets, has access to an organisation through which to manage its interaction with the other groups, and has its own history or myth of separate origin. These four conditions all apply to the Qingtianese in Europe.

The culmination of this process of sub-ethnic segregation was celebrated at a Qingtianese rally in Paris in 1996. *Guangdong Qiaobao* (12.03.1996, p. 3) reported the event:

The Association of Qingtian Compatriots in Europe has been established in Paris. The Association of Qingtian Compatriots in Europe, already under preparation for a long time, was yesterday inaugurated in Paris. More than 3,000 people representing associations of Qingtian compatriots in each

European country and [overseas Chinese] residents in France participated in the inauguration assembly.

The general purpose of the Association of Qingtian Compatriots in Europe is to unite the compatriots of Qingtian origin, to promote the national culture of the Chinese, to further the development of the cause of the home area, to develop friendship between the peoples of the countries of residence and the motherland and economic intercourse and trade, to foster a spirit of mutual help and mutual love, respect for the laws in the countries of residence, and active integration in local society, and to let the Qingtian townspeople in Europe have flourishing families, successful businesses, and prosperous lives.

The president of the Association of Qingtian Compatriots in Europe said in his inauguration speech that the Association of Qingtian Compatriots in Europe is an international organisation of overseas Chinese organisations and the organisation that unites associations of Qingtian compatriots in each European country, and that its establishment embodied the trend towards the unity, mutual love, and high-level development of overseas Chinese.

The history of Qingtianese's residence in Europe can be traced back to the seventeenth and eighteenth centuries. The early Qingtianese trudged over long distances carrying Qingtian stones on their back. They walked through Siberia to settle in Europe and experienced immense hardship. Their spirit of building their livelihood through hard toil has become a model for the struggle of overseas Chinese.

The cause of the Qingtianese in Europe develops fast. They not only have a certain economic strength but their educational level also incessantly rises. For example, the two sons and three daughters of Zhu Guang, a Qingtian compatriot in France, have all graduated from Paris University, one son with a doctorate in political science and the other in medicine.

The Overseas Chinese Affairs Office of the State Council, the Consular Affairs Section of the Ministry of Foreign Affairs, the Overseas Chinese Affairs Office of Zhejiang Province, and the City Government of Qingtian all sent congratulatory telegrams on the occasion of the establishment of the Association of Qingtian Compatriots in Europe.

The 'Artistic Ensemble of Chinese Stars', which had been specially invited from China, performed a colourful show for the participants in the meeting.

Among the themes illustrated by this report are the scale and sophistication of organisation-building, the political sanction of the Chinese authorities, and the myth of separate origin. The meeting had been preceded by a decade of organisation-building in Europe, starting in Belgium in 1985, and of a project to write the history of the Qingtianese in Europe.

The group of overseas Chinese in Europe from southern Zhejiang is traditionally divided into Qingtianese and Wenzhouese, a distinction that goes back to the 1930s. There was, for many years, little reason to regard this difference as sub-ethnic although the differences in speech and attachment that marked it bore the seeds of future division.

Qingtian migration to Europe

Many writings about the Qingtianese in Europe quote the English edition of the China Yearbook for 1935, which says that as early as in the seventeenth and eighteenth centuries a small number of Chinese went to Europe by way of Siberia to engage in trade. Most of the earliest migrants were said to be Qingtianese. I have been unable to locate the exact source of this story,[22] but it is probably spurious. Some accounts indicate that people walked to Europe along the track of the Siberian Railway (Jiang Jing 1984, 387), which opened in 1904. Small ornaments and utensils carved from Qingtian soapstone probably found their way into European homes alongside China-ware, tea, and spices bought by Europeans from peddlers in Chinese ports. Certainly, some Qingtianese did come to Europe to sell soapstone articles. In 1900, a Mr Zhu was hired by a British merchant to work in a Chinese arts shop in London, and in 1908, Chen Yuanfeng took his merchandise to France by ship. He was so successful that he was able to bring over friends and relatives to help him sell his goods.

Up to 1928, almost 500 coolies went from Qingtian to Japan, and up to 1937, substantial numbers went to Brazil, Chile, Argentina, and Ecuador. Qingtian's poverty and proximity to the treaty port of Wenzhou made coolie recruitment among the Qingtianese a thriving business.

The main occasion for Qingtian migration to Europe was provided by the scheme agreed by the Chinese, French and British governments in 1916 and 1917 to recruit Chinese to serve as battlefield ancillaries on the western front. A special campaign was conducted in Qingtian that resulted in more than 2,000 signing up. Unlike other Chinese wartime workers, the large majority of Qingtianese remained in Europe after the peace, including 1,000 in France alone (Chen Murong 1990, 642). The postwar Qingtian population of Paris consisted predominantly of such people (Archaimbault 1987). According to Chen Sanjing (1986, 153–6), however, it is hard to estimate the exact number who remained in France or arrived later from other battlefronts in Europe.

The earlier presence of small groups of Qingtian petty traders in Paris and elsewhere in Europe provided a foothold for the wartime newcomers from Qingtian. Early post-war France's expanding industry needed hands to make up for huge losses on the battlefield, a demand that did not diminish until the depression of the early 1930s. The 1920s were a 'flourishing period for the emigration of people from the county' (Chen Murong 1990, 642). There were 10,000 Qingtianese in Europe, including 3,000 in France, 1,000 in Holland, in Austria, and in Italy, 300 in Belgium and in Spain, and more than 200 in Portugal.

Shi Cheng (1987) does not mention the wartime workers, but claims that the great numbers were a result of the trade in Qingtian soapstone. He cites an early account of 20,000 Qingtianese in Europe, including 2,000 in Paris alone.[23] Shi Cheng wants to paint the Qingtianese as fundamentally different from other overseas Chinese migrants, who left because of the intervention of foreign powers. The Qingtian migrants' 'special characteristic' was that they left not as coolies, but as 'spontaneous' petty traders.

Shi Cheng's analysis broadly follows the account written in the mid-1930s by the socialist Zou Taofen, who rhetorically railed against the lives 'lived below those of beasts of burden' by these people cast out from their own country by 'poverty and warlord terror'. They lived in 'dirty, narrow lanes', where 'poverty and filth are often their inseparable friends', they were 'clad in rags', and so on. Zou Taofen reveals himself as a poor observer.

The soapstone peddlers and wartime workers laid the basis for chain migration into Europe. The main migration seems to have been by ship, either as stowaways or with proper papers. The interwar migration was handled by banks like Gonghechang, Gongdali, and Tongchang owned by Qingtianese that offered a full package, including passport, ticket, and credit. The main ports of entry were Marseilles and Naples.

Many hundreds of Qingtianese accompanied Chiang Kai-shek's army to Taiwan in 1949, and later remigrated to the United States. Between 1945 and 1949, others fled to Europe, mostly by way of Hong Kong and Macau, in the last big wave for almost 30 years. Between 1950 and 1976, the Qingtian authorities granted only 367 exit permits (Chen Murong 1990) and rejected most applications from people wanting to join their family in Europe. During this period, on average fewer than 20 Qingtianese a year reached Europe.

The great watershed in post-war Qingtian migration was the announcement of the opening of China's door to the world in 1978. Between 1979 and 1986, 10,948 passports were issued, 3,128 of them in 1987 alone. As of 1987, the official estimate of the number of Qingtianese in Europe was 17,750, or 88.6 per cent of all Qingtian's overseas Chinese (Chen Murong 1990, 646). The increase in migration from Qingtian to Europe continued in the late 1980s and early 1990s.

The large number of permanently resident or naturalised Qingtianese in France, Italy, Belgium, and Spain was responsible for the initial rise. They were for the first time able to invite their relatives to join them. They acted as guarantors, in many cases provided the fare, arranged work for the new migrants, and helped handle visa formalities. The rapid rise in the Qingtian population in Europe was at first concentrated in a few cities, but soon led to further migration after 'market saturation' had been reached. For example, the Qingtian population of Milan rose to more than 1,000 in the early 1980s, but later people started moving to Rome and other places.

Chain migration can grow almost exponentially because of its special nature. Normally, one family member goes first, thus creating conditions for the rest of the family to follow. At first, the brother was sent for, rather than wife and children. This migration based on brothers was not unusual, given the nature of the work skills needed in the first phase of consolidation, or the need for business partnership, perhaps related to the economics of dividing the family wealth in China. When brother brought brother, and the spouses and children of all the brothers then joined the migrants in the place of destination, the rate of human increment could be stunning. Chain migration created a rage in Qingtian for marrying into families of overseas Chinese, marrying returned overseas Chinese who had been resettled on special state farms, or marrying overseas Chinese who returned to find a wife. Shi Cheng (1987, 43) gives examples of how individual overseas Chinese managed to get large numbers of relatives over.

Sun Ming Chuan (Sun Mingquan) in Milan fetched around 200; the Wang brothers in Rome, about 100; a Mr Chen in northern Italy, about 100; and the Wu brothers in Pisa, about 70. The large numbers of Qingtianese already resident in France, Italy, Belgium, the Netherlands, Spain, and elsewhere in the 1970s and 1980s either had been naturalised or had permanent residence permits. Such people could summon close family members, who, once settled, summoned other relatives in their turn. Even poor Qingtianese in Europe came under great pressure to help relatives migrate, sometimes at great cost to themselves. Such migration normally requires proper documents and official approval from all sides. However, some people in China provide false passports and visas and provide the fare in credit form. The credit is returned either in instalments once the migrant has started earning or by relatives in Europe, who come under pressure to repay the debt.[24] The amnesties to illegal immigrants in Italy, France, Spain, and Portugal in the 1980s and 1990s enabled those who had entered illegally to obtain legal residence permits, and thus summon a further wave of relatives. These basic mechanisms of Qingtian migration are, of course, typical of most large-scale migration.

The Qingtianese were not the only people to migrate from southern Zhejiang. Others migrated from Wenzhou, Wencheng and Ruian. Qingtian is linked by the Ou River to the port of Wenzhou, open to foreign trade since the Opium Wars, and linked by regular sailings to Shanghai. Qingtian was therefore always closer to the world market than Wencheng upstream of coastal Ruian, a minor port.

Mainly for geographical reasons, Qingtian always gravitated towards Wenzhou. Its trade and cultural contacts relied on Wenzhou, and wealthy Qingtianese settled either there or in Shanghai. The Qingtianese were Wenzhou's poor cousins, living in the mountains and speaking an outlandish dialect. Wenzhou, only 60 km downstream from Qingtian, was a natural focus for Qingtian.

The symbiotic relationship between Qintian and Wenzhou contrasts strikingly with that between the Siyi and the Sanyi discussed in the previous section. The Siyi elites were aloof, conservative, organised in strong lineages and belligerent, whereas the Sanyi elites were far richer and more powerful; consequently, the Siyi and Sanyi elites shunned each other. The Qingtian elite, in contrast, was part of the Wenzhou elite; Qingtian was economically dependent on Wenzhou.

The unequal relationship and obvious social difference between Wenzhou and Qingtian created prejudice and resentment. Charles Archaimbault (1987, 23) cites traditional Wenzhou opinions about people from Qingtian – that they are tramps, 'seep in everywhere, just like water', and lack normal intellectual capacities. Yet the rise of new economic elites in both counties and their outward orientation through the ports of Wenzhou and Shanghai made local distinctions increasingly fuzzier in the twentieth century. Those who went to Europe naturally relied first of all on people from their own place of origin, but Qingtianese saw Wenzhouese as approachable and reliable, whereas Wenzhouese felt at ease with Qingtianese, despite some minor misgivings. In the 1980s and 1990s, stereotyping apparently experienced a revival in some settings, as discussed by Ceccagno (1998, 17–18) and as outlined in the following.

The process of segregation

Not until the mid-1980s did people of Qingtian origin institutionalise their differences from other Chinese groups. Traditionally, the Qingtianese in Europe leaned towards the Guomindang, and many held Taibei passports. Taibei's embassies used informal networks among them to disseminate policy and influence them. (Perhaps Qingtianese confidence in Chiang Kai-shek's regime had something to do with Chiang's close reliance on General Chen Cheng, a native of Qingtian.)

The ousting of Chiang Kai-shek's embassy from Paris after France's recognition of the People's Republic in 1964 severed many of the old links between Taibei and the Chinese in Europe. In 1970, however, Qingtianese in Taiwan joined together in the Taibei Association of Qingtian Compatriots (Taibei Shi Qingtian Tongxianghui), a non-political body with no formal links to the Guomindang. This organisation revived lines of communication between Taibei and the Qingtianese in Europe, appointed contact persons in each European country, and set up contact offices.

Many older-generation Qingtianese in Europe occupied influential positions in overseas Chinese organisations and tended to see themselves not primarily as Qingtianese, but as Chinese, as nationalists with a small 'n', loyal to the Chinese Republic and Sun Yat-sen but not necessarily to Chiang Kai-shek. The diplomatic relations established in the 1970s between the People's Republic and the last major European countries resulted in a changed situation. The informal networks and offices of the Taibei Association of Qingtian Compatriots remained part of the Qingtianese world in Europe, but the arrival of more and more young relatives from Qingtian created the need for direct dealing with the ancestral county. Some old-timers who went there on visits found local officials more caring and forgiving than they had hoped. At the same time, the overseas Chinese administration in Qingtian improved its organisation and began wooing the older generation of Qingtianese in Europe. Native-place nostalgia offered a way out of conflicts of political loyalty. In 1985 and 1986, Hu Xizhen, Sun Ming Chuan and one hundred others bankrolled the establishment of the Zhongshan Middle School in Qingtian.

The Qingtianese in Europe needed an organisation to match the overseas Chinese administration in Qingtian itself, to organise social 'get-togethers' and liaise with the home authorities.

According to a Qingtianese leader in Belgium, an organisation was needed because of the huge increase in the number of Qingtianese in Belgium, combined with the coming of age of the children of the older generation. Informal networks had been effective when numbers were small, but it became increasingly difficult to keep track of newcomers, and the kids would 'gradually scatter, and forget our home' (033//003). The old Qingtianese networks in Belgium had been strongly influenced by the Taibei association, and by the fact that Brussels is the main hub for Taibei's official overseas Chinese work in Europe.[25] The Beijing authorities encouraged the formation of a Qingtian association to break Taiwan's hold on the Qingtianese in Belgium.

The new organisational structure led inevitably to a realignment of relations with other groups. In France, this realignment chiefly affected relations with the Wenzhouese:[26]

[Talking of the Association des Chinois résidant en France.[27]] Early on, it was really a community organisation, representing all, so to say, including the overseas Chinese from Southeast Asia, Hong Kong, everywhere. Now we have a situation where it has become [an organisation] for almost exclusively Wenzhouese. Other communities, [people from] other places, have established their own organisations, like Chaozhou, the Descendants[28] and Guangzhou–Zhaoqing. Shanghai even has two organisations. The Wenchengese, from Wencheng County in Zhejiang, also established their own organisation. So we Qingtianese, that's the year before last, on September 15, 1994, established our Qingtian association. Now, the Association des Chinois résidant en France consists, in reality, almost exclusively of Wenzhouese, there are very few others.

(042//001)

The distinction between Qingtian and Wenzhou was signally important for the establishment of a separate French Qingtian association:

Then these delegations came, from China, they were all from Wenzhou. Originally, Qingtian belonged to Wenzhou prefecture, later we were put under Lishui. Now we belong to different prefectures, so those people who came [with the Wenzhou delegations] were irrelevant to me, I didn't know them. Of course, I don't know the ones from Lishui either, because I came here rather early. But because I came early, they encouraged me to set up this Qingtian association. Be the president of it, damn it.

(042//003)

In reality, Qingtian had always belonged to Lishui and never to Wenzhou, at least from an administrative point of view. However, the fact that Qingtian was not a part of Wenzhou suddenly became important in 1984, when Wenzhou became one of the 14 coastal cities granted preferential treatment and local decision-making powers, especially in relation to foreign investment. Now, Wenzhou had a significant edge over Qingtian. Qingtian, under the lethargic and poor Lishui prefecture, was marginalised, at least in the eyes of overseas Chinese in Europe from southern Zhejiang. Wenzhou had always been more prosperous than Qingtian. Now, it also had far greater political status and administrative power.

This leader, explaining why the Qingtian association in France emerged, focused strongly on Wenzhou:

Before 1950, the Qingtianese in France were in a majority. There were somewhat fewer people from Wenzhou. After Liberation, however, in the 1970s and 1980s, Wenzhou opened up earlier and it became rather easy to get out; permission was given faster. Qingtian lagged a couple of years behind. In the

1980s, Wencheng also opened more quickly. The government encouraged you to leave. In Qingtian, you had to go by the back door. The fact that [Qingtian] opened up a couple of years later was of no use, for the foreign [governments] closed, reined in. One couldn't get residence permits any more.

(042//018)

The fact that Wenzhouese were threatening to outnumber Qingtianese in Europe and the increased importance the native-place links as a result of the open door were all contributory factors to the emergence of Qingtian associations in Europe. Similar factors were at work in all the major countries of residence for the Qingtianese: Belgium, France, Spain, the Netherlands, Italy, and Portugal.

The new Qingtianese organisations in these countries made the 'ancestral place' far more important as an ascriptive factor. People comfortable in all camps began to feel the heat. In the summer of 1996, the annual meeting of the European Federation of Chinese Organisations, due to be held in Paris, was suddenly postponed because of the crisis among overseas Chinese from Zhejiang. Qingtianese and Wenzhouese leaders from all parts of Europe attended a large gathering in Paris, convened by them and the Zhejiang overseas Chinese authorities. One influential leader was vehemently challenged by other participants. Was he Qingtian, Wenzhou, or what? This voluntary association leader, an affable man fluent in Mandarin, Cantonese, Shanghainese, Qingtianese, Wenzhouese and (so he claims) eight other languages and Chinese dialects, ultimately had to admit that he is from Qingtian.[29]

Before the emergence of separate organisations in the 1990s, Qingtian and Wenzhou were considered to be much the same. In a dual interview, a Qingtianese leader (C) and a Wenzhouese leader (H) in Brussels, illustrated this point with their comments:

H:	I am Wenzhouese.
Question:	How is it between Wenzhou and Qingtian?
H:	Very close, neighbours. Wenzhou is a city, Qingtian a county, some dozen kilometres [apart]. The dialects are different but similar. We can basically understand each other.
Question:	Are there more Wenzhouese or more Qingtianese here [in Belgium]?
H:	There are more Qingtianese, he [points at C] is from Qingtian. I am from Wenzhou.
C:	There are more than one hundred restaurants run by Qingtianese in Belgium.
Question:	What about Wenzhouese?
H:	I am not so sure. Some dozen, I should say.
Question:	Are you a member of the Qingtian Association?
H:	Yes, I am. The Wenzhouese and Qingtianese are relatives. There are so many relations. Qingtian and Wenzhou are totally mixed up with one another.

Question: So Qingtianese are members of the Wenzhou Association and vice versa?

H and C: Yes.

(032//026...034)

Qingtian identity has unfolded as a sub-ethnic identity in its own right largely since the mid-1980s. The newly established formal frameworks, the drawing of clear distinctions with other groups, and rigid management of sub-ethnic ascription all have contributed to that process. Finally, as is often the case in instances of ethno-genesis, a 'myth of origins' was constructed to validate the new European Qingtianese identity.

The Qingtian myth

The 'enigmatic people' is what their self-appointed chronicler calls them. In a series of articles, a European Qingtianese sought to define the roots and special characteristics of his fellow migrants. His was to record the history of the Qingtianese and thus legitimate the new emphasis on their separate identity. The titles of his articles include 'the enigmatic people', 'the resplendent legend', 'the sudden rise of the first Qingtianese', 'the virtues of the Qingtianese', and 'the Qingtianese's spirit of mutual help'. His writings are more concerned with a psycho-social invention than with the critical exploration of historical sources.

An amateur historian and writer, he replenishes the few available historical sources with the reminiscences of the older generation of Qingtianese. His other writings (mainly in a European Chinese-language newspaper) show him to be a person intensely preoccupied with the theme of ethnic belonging and the idea of unity among Chinese. The portrayal of Qingtian as separate and special does not, in his view, stand in the way of national unity and patriotic feeling. His writing is not simply a glorification of Qingtian. He is, for example, one of the few Chinese to have written about the immigrant-smuggling 'snakeheads', an issue relevant to the Qingtianese in Europe.

The writer's name is Ma Zhuomin. He lives in Barcelona, where he runs Gran Muralla (The Great Wall) restaurant. He writes in *Ouzhou Shibao – Nouvelles d'Europe*, a daily newspaper that leans towards Beijing and is published in Paris. A student of physics at Hangzhou University in 1973–6 in the last stages of the Cultural Revolution, and later a white-collar worker in a chemical factory, he has no formal training as a historian or writer. His interest in the Qingtianese is a hobby. He writes their story in order to 'do something for the native place'.[30] Ma Zhuomin re-tells a story that European Qingtianese have heard in fragments.

The land

Qingtian is a poor county in a landscape of steep mountains, from which (says Ma) the people have derived an indomitable spirit that helps them overcome hardship, 'venture far overseas, gain a foothold and develop in foreign parts'.

The Ou River runs through all of Qingtian. Its source is at the northern foot of Mount Guomaojian on the border area between Longquan and Qingyuan, and it runs through Qingtian for more than 80 kilometres, its basin covering 1,000 square kilometres. On either bank, green fields abound in emerald splendour and tall bamboo groves alternate with thick forests. Against the green background, smoke from kitchen stoves curls upwards, white sails speckle on the river, and ripples glitter on the water. The Ou River is like a painting.

Ma's sudden shift in style reveals his determination to turn the trivial into poetic pathos. The tranquillity, the poetry, and the sense of timelessness bestow mystical significance on the river. Qingtian becomes myth.

The river water, limpid and cool, has nurtured generation upon generation of Qingtianese; it flows day and night, bringing forth the hopes of generation upon generation of Qingtianese. The Ou River is the mother river of the Qingtianese.

Such topographical imagery is common in the representation of nationalism in almost any culture. Metaphorically, the Qingtianese are not only born of the landscape but eat and drink it:

Living off Qingtian's mountains, drinking Qingtian's water, they speak the Qingtianese [dialect]. For several millennia the mountain regions were cut off and had little communication with the outside world; the independent economic life of the Qingtianese shaped their local speech.

Ma Zhuomin goes on to describe how the mountains and the river have produced excellent scholars and officials, including General Chen Cheng and Chen Muhua, the former State Councillor, Minister of Foreign Trade and bank director.

The history of the Qingtianese overseas is obscure. Like other writers, Ma Zhuomin claims that they were already in Europe in the seventeenth and eighteenth centuries, and recites all the usual anecdotes.

First story

One day in the Hague, Lin Zicai came past a large building. The guards outside were busy chatting with somebody, so he entered a porch and knocked. A servant woman led him to a reception room where an elegant, middle-aged lady sat with an interpreter. The interpreter said: 'Sir, this is the Hague Palace. Why do you seek an audience with her Majesty the Queen?' Lin explained: 'I am from Qingtian in Zhejiang, my name is Lin Zicai. I have come to your honoured country to sell a special Chinese product, stone carvings from Qingtian. I am honoured to have come to the Royal Palace. I beg you to excuse me'. He unwrapped his stones, and the Queen was impressed. She asked him to return next day and personally wrote him a pass stamped with her own jade seal. With this market advantage, Lin soon became rich.

True or not, the story depicts the Qingtianese as polite, unimpressed by grandeur, and good traders. Westerners were quick to spot the artistic value of their merchandise. Ma uses this fairy-tale about the pauper and the queen with its rags-to-riches theme to paint a picture of the supposed character of the Qingtianese and their magic passage into European society.

Second story

This anecdote is taken word for word from Zou Taofen's essay about the Qingtianese in France. A man called Mou Jia left home to escape poverty. He took some soapstone carvings with him to Wenzhou and to Shanghai, but he failed to get rich. From Shanghai he strayed to Europe. Once ashore, he displayed at the roadside the various Qingtian soapstones he had brought with him. When the Europeans saw these things, some were seized by a strange feeling. Asked the price, Mou Jia who had not the faintest understanding of foreign languages, lifted some fingers in response. Sometimes he lifted two fingers, meaning two dimes, but the silly foreigners[31] gave him two dollars instead. He soon amassed a small fortune. The news reached his home village. Gradually, more and more people ventured overseas and within a decade had spread all over Europe.

Third story

According to Ma, representing the Qingtianese view on European Chinese history, in 1931, an unemployed Qingtianese in Amsterdam began selling candied peanut (pindakoekjes in Dutch) during the depression. However, other groups, including the Cantonese, also claim to have invented this trade (Li Minghuan 1989; Wubben 1986). Ma Zhuomin's aim is to claim responsibility on behalf of his own people for thinking up this practice, a celebrated episode in the history of Dutch Chinatowns. He wants to demonstrate Qingtianese ingenuity in coping with poverty, and their model role for other Chinese in Europe. Although the trade did happen, there is no firm evidence to support Ma's claim about its origins.

The dilemma of sub-ethnic identity

It is in the nature of things that most national-identity rhetoric bluntly juxtaposes the 'We' with the 'Other'. Ma Zhuomin, on the other hand, entirely avoids mentioning the 'Other' in his construction of Qingtian identity. 'We' in Ma Zhuomin's stories excludes any Chinese not directly from Qingtian. However, the Qingtianese are also part of the larger Chinese national collective, with which Ma cannot help but identify. He avoids saying anything at all about general Chinese identity but instead concentrates on building up Qingtian identity. So who exactly is Ma's 'Other'? Ma's 'Other' is actually Wenzhou, though he never says so in as many words.

Another Qingtian writer, Yu Mingren (1996), nicely illustrates this point. His story 'The Maidens of Qingtian' starts off by noting 'a great difference in the temperament of women in Qingtian and in Wenzhou'. The rest of Yu's story is a eulogy of Qingtian women in which Wenzhou women merit no mention. Qingtian women can withstand hardship, are mainly delightfully small (though some are tall), and are hard-working, frugal, and modest (they do not dress up in fancy clothes). 'In the old society, they were rather conservative, confining themselves to the private sphere'. The men worked in the public sphere, while the women 'stood sweetly behind their husbands in business and in the creation of family wealth and honour'. Their 'beauty is born of the fairy mountains and noble streams of Qingtian', so theirs is a 'natural grace'. Qingtian women do not wish to marry foreigners. Only one's imagination sets a limit to the appraisal of Wenzhou women *ex negativo*, as mirrored in this hymn to Qingtian women.

In identity-building in Qingtian, the 'Other' is missing from the text, but the reader intuitively knows. Yu Mingren's fleeting comparison with Wenzhou women creates the necessary contrast. Yu, writing in the journal of the Qingtian native-place organisation in Taibei, needs to highlight the distinction to be understood. Ma, writing in a European Chinese newspaper for an audience of Qingtianese who see the Wenzhouese as their main rivals, needs not even hint at it.

The character profile of modern Qingtianese in Europe

Ma Zhuomin's stories infer the special status of the Qingtianese from their 'special' character. He depicts them both as particularly successful and as possessing collective traits different from other Chinese groups:

> In the last decade or more, Qingtianese businesses have developed rapidly. In Spain, for example, restaurants run by Qingtianese have sprouted like bamboo after a spring rain. Rough estimates by people with some knowledge of the Qingtian business situation indicate that in the last eight years, Qingtianese have opened nearly 2,000 restaurants. At around the time of the Olympic Games in 1992, Qingtianese flooded Barcelona, and within approximately one year, the number of Qingtianese's restaurants had risen by a few hundred. This caused many compatriots from other places to gape in bewilderment and incredulity: 'Where do the Qingtianese get their money?' or 'How come that they can open restaurants so easily?'
>
> This is perhaps the greatest difference between Qingtianese and people from other parts. The Chinese spirit of enduring hardship seems to be a common characteristic, but the Qingtianese spirit of mutual aid is truly exceptional.
>
> A Sichuanese who once worked in a Qingtianese restaurant told me that he had seen with his own eyes how the Qingtianese he worked with had pooled unhesitatingly the several hundred thousand pesetas they had earned through hard graft and given it to another Qingtianese to open a restaurant. He said 'washing dishes for a month earns you 30,000 to 40,000 pesetas, saving several hundred thousand isn't easy! If I hadn't seen it with my own eyes, I wouldn't have believed it'.

Virtually all Qingtianese who have opened businesses in Europe borrow money in this way, without contracts, go-betweens, time limits, or the payment of interest. If money lent is not returned, the borrower is deemed to have run out of luck, and there the matter rests.

Ma believes, however, that Qingtianese infighting, mutual killings, and cut-throat competition are one unfortunate by-product of the overly cohesive nature of Qingtian society. Qingtianese may stick together as a people, but they also sometimes gang up against one another. According to Ma, this clannishness explains why they failed to establish a Qingtian organisation until the 1980s and why they have a difficult relationship with other Chinese groups. Qingtianese, says Ma in a great crescendo of purple prose, have created havoc in Spain by consistently undercutting their Qingtianese competitors in a 'civil war on a scale never seen before' and a 'slaughter that darkened the heavens and plunged mankind into chaos'.

Sub-ethnic divisions in flux

Sub-ethnic identities built on regional attachment and sentiments of mutual belonging emerge in response to needs and opportunities. The wish on the part of local authorities in China to forge links with Chinese overseas and the need of overseas Chinese leaders in Europe to maintain or gain influence in overseas Chinese associations are two important factors in that emergence. Sub-ethnic leaders use affinities of speech, sentimental stereotypes, and mythology to underpin formal organisational frameworks in the pursuit of political power and economic interest.

The concept of sub-ethnic identity based on local attachment has been questioned in research on China. Emily Honig (1992, 10), in her study on the Subei people in Shanghai, calls such local attachments ethnic rather than sub-ethnic, on the grounds that there can be no presumption of a 'more authentic type of ethnicity to which native place identities are subordinate'. It is true, at first sight, that each of the sub-ethnic groups analysed in this chapter sets itself off in practice from other such groups and occasionally interacts with them. However, that does not mean to say that it is not useful and necessary to posit a higher pan-Chinese level of identity that subsumes these lower levels. A sub-ethnic group positions itself in relation to other sub-ethnic groups within a framework of rules provided by the wider identity. Moreover, its members can switch between the two different registers, one 'national' and one 'local'. The cases discussed in this chapter support that view.

Localist attachments are not necessarily framed as native-place sentiment or sub-ethnic divisions. The patriotic policies of the Chinese government have provided local governments with the opportunities to elicit donations from Chinese overseas even where no direct ancestral tie obtains. Typical channels are the Hope Project (aimed at providing schools for China's poor) and programmes for improving healthcare provision and raising the living standards in poor areas. Inland provinces that have few overseas migrants have raked in donations from Chinese whose ancestral places are in distant parts of China. Chinese originating in Hong Kong's

New Territories have donated schools and clinics to the inland provinces of Sichuan and Shanxi, and Qingtianese have donated schools to Ningxia. That such affective bonds are possible even where there is no 'blood tie' illustrates the pliable nature of these attachments. The overseas Chinese, in return for their donations, are appointed to positions on 'representative' bodies of the provinces, become honorary citizens, and get moral and political support from their adopted beneficiaries for their work in the overseas Chinese communities. So sub-ethnic identities remain relevant, but they must be seen in the context of a wide range of identifications that Chinese can mobilise when necessary and opportune.

5 Ethnic politics

European Chinese organisations and their leaders

The first aim of establishing the European Federation of Chinese Organisations [EFCO] is that we intend to use it to raise the status of the overseas Chinese vis-à-vis the European Communities;[1] the second is to claim the benefits and infrastructure due to us overseas Chinese from the European Communities. Since there are more than a million overseas Chinese in Europe … as an overseas Chinese association, of course we will protect the benefits and other interests of the overseas Chinese in all of Europe.

(–/001/030)

The European Federation of Chinese Organisations claims to represent more than one million Chinese in Europe. The civil society of migrant groups plays an important role, and has done so as long as there have been migrants, in 'protecting' and 'representing' them. The scale of 'representation' depends on the role these organisations are afforded by authorities, and there is no doubt that the claim to represent all Chinese in Europe represents the degree to which the European institutions have developed and seek to define their own roles. It, of course, also reflects the ways in which Chinese organisation leaders seek to gain status and justify their role in society.

Organisational diversity

There are many different types of overseas Chinese organisations in Europe. Their great variety and density (in some European countries their number runs into the hundreds) reveals some interesting features of how the overseas Chinese community is organised.

The general Chinese term for the civil society organisations, shetuan (voluntary organisation), is a widely used technical and legal term; the frequency with which it features in overseas Chinese newspapers and media may indicate a strong preoccupation in some circles with the formalities of such organisations. At the other end of the scale is the common, informal, and traditional word used for any type of meeting and organisation, hui.

In between these two extremes the names of organisations give the impression that they are very specialised and divided. The most general and neutral term is probably xiehui (association), followed by lianhehui (federation), lianyihui (friendly association), and zonghui (general association). The words reveal an effort to distinguish levels and functions of organisation, but there is little difference in reality – a 'general association' or a 'federation' rarely federates lower levels or organisations in any rigorous way, and while a 'friendly association' by its name may seem to be concerned with leisure, in most cases its function does not differ from that of other types of organisation.

The term xuehui (scholarly association) is functionally separate, for it is largely used in names of associations of academics. I have come across three major types of scholarly associations among the overseas Chinese. The first organises Chinese academics in universities and colleges in European states, with organisations of Chinese sinologists and language teachers in such institutions, or of Chinese students and scholars in a university or a city; this type is the oldest in Europe. The second joins Chinese scholars by branches of science and furthers their professional liaison through conferences and formal links with parent organisations in China. The third promotes ideology, like the Zhongshan Xuehui that propagates Sun Yat-sen's ideas with the support of the Nationalist Party in Taiwan. The number of scholarly associations in Europe grew rapidly in the 1990s when the Mainland authorities sought to integrate Chinese scholars overseas in global networks of specialised associations, at a time when Mainland scholars on a larger scale found academic careers in Europe.

Tongxianghui (fellow-villager associations) include people who originate in one area in China, be it a village, a city or a province; such organisations also encompass the chongzhenghui (Tsung Chin associations) of Hakka dialect speakers (which are not *regional* in a strict sense). In previous chapters, we have already discussed the roles performed by sub-national (regional and dialect) groups; their associations provide some structure to and promote their identities.

Zongqinhui (clan associations) reflect the patterns of lineage organisation in China. Those existing in Europe mainly originate in the migration from the New Territories in Hong Hong, where lineages gained a strong political and economic function, and where it seemed useful to establish civil society organisations to cater for these large groups of migrants whose main characteristic is that they share the surname, be it Man, Tang or Cheung. Chain migration of Chinese to Europe is often based on family links, and in many cases kinship groups form small communities locally in Europe without any formal organisation.

There are several types of professional and business associations, like gong-shanghui (chambers of commerce) and jiefanghui (Chinatown associations), as well as interest organisations of people in the same trade, called tongyehui or gonghui, the latter literally meaning trade union, but normally not organised in that way. Chinese business people in some areas may also be members of charitable organisations like Chinatown Lions Clubs.

A 'traditional' type of organisation is the huiguan, a term sometimes misleadingly translated as 'guild'. Huiguans used to be organisations of Chinese from one area in China living in other parts of China, and among their various functions throughout history served the interests of business people and imperial examination candidates, providing practical assistance, lodgings and formal representation before local authorities. Many early Chinese migrant organisations abroad were, accordingly, called huiguans due to the similarity of their functions; they were considered organisations of people from a region in China living abroad; in Europe, the term was in the early twentieth century used to indicate organisations of all Chinese living in an area in Europe, like the Hanbao Zhonghua Huiguan (Chinesischer Verein in Hamburg). Later, in the 1980s and 1990s, immigrants from French Indochina reassembled into new huiguans in France, following the patterns of regional representations in Vietnam, Cambodia and Laos, like the Faguo Chaozhou Huiguan (Amicale des Teochew en France). The huiguan in the early twentieth century stood out as a modern organisation of public representation, as opposed to the secret societies (as discussed in the case of Liverpool in Chapter 4).

In addition to these types or organisation, there are Chinese churches, temples (some of which are subsidiaries of global Buddhist organisations), and sects (including Falun Gong); there are Chinese community centres and official and semi-official organisations where members of Chinese society in Europe are appointed to represent their fellow Chinese.

In particular in France, Britain and the Netherlands there are many organisations. Why? This chapter will examine the dynamics of migrant civil society.

Communities, the 'home' country and the local authorities are linked together through many channels, many of which are private and particular. However, in the public sphere the organisations provide officially recognised fora for contact, ethnic identity-building and political participation. Official recognition gives strength and vigour to overseas Chinese associations, both by providing the leaders of overseas Chinese organisations with status and power, and by allowing them to 'represent' overseas Chinese interests vis-à-vis China or the host society.

Even where overseas Chinese associations may in reality *not* represent the overseas Chinese community, they therefore have a public influence that works on the communities.

Representing or not representing the Chinese

Younger-generation Chinese, for example, often regard overseas Chinese associations as irrelevant and the resort of old men – a theme in many interviews was exactly the worry that so few young wished to participate in these organisations, and that they faced a continuous succession crisis. Chinese in 'non-ethnic' professions may find them unrepresentative of their interests, and so on. There are no mechanisms in any part of Europe that in any meaningful way ensure representativeness; even the 'Foreigners' Committees' (Ausländerbeiräte) in Germany (elected bodies) are woefully arbitrary in this respect. The diverse composition of the Chinese communities, one could argue, means that anybody who endeavours to 'represent' the Chinese community must do so on the basis of the smallest common denominator, which essentially is the assertion of shared ethnicity. We have already seen in previous chapters how flexible and negotiable

Chinese ethnicity is, and any claim to represent ethnicity is likely to be met by fellow Chinese with rejection or counterclaims about the nature of ethnicity.

It is, of course, true that virtually no Chinese association leaders directly claim to represent the Chinese, for the claim would seem absurd and open them to criticism. The claim is made indirectly, in several ways. As a reason for establishing new associations, leaders claim that they (or people of their sub-group) did not feel represented by an existing association. Others claim that they 'protect the legitimate interests of' the overseas Chinese, and even those whose association is based on a sub-group identity claim to be 'even-handed' in the treatment of overseas Chinese, without regard for their origin, 'for we are all Chinese'. 'Service to the community' is an important way of indirectly claiming a representative status. Overseas Chinese leaders can also claim to 'represent' the overseas Chinese community because European host societies invite them to sit on race relations committees or to advise on issues relating to the overseas Chinese community. In a similar way, Chinese consuls tend to liaise with association leaders on matters that are of importance for the community as a whole.

'Representation', in that sense, is a function of government intervention, of status afforded to individuals emerging from associations as purported leaders of communities. The claim to represent lies in the ethnic label, which therefore acquires a symbolic role in its own right. Ethnicity must both be visible (for separate representation is justified through ethnic difference), and wide and inclusive (in order to gain some acceptance among those 'represented'); a suitable common denominator is thus the cultural stereotype – the narrow range of symbolic activities that accomplish this: Chinese New Year celebrations, assertions of Confucian family, business and other values, and mother tongue education. Add to this the idea that Chinese citizens in Europe form a 'cultural bridge' to China, and the picture is complete: the colourful display, the moral distinctiveness, the organisational framework for inter-generational transmission (which normally involves local government and Chinese authorities), and the promise of economic utility.

Chinese community leaders, in consequence, see their role as custodians of these values, which they tend to phrase in the most general terms. In fact, in our interviews, the most prevalent expressions of 'Chinese values' were related to the practical tasks of running associations, where the activity in itself appeared more important than its purpose. One leader of a general association (021//094), for example, enumerated that each issue of their bulletin was printed in 5,000 copies, they worked hard to pull the National Day together with other associations, and being a general association, it gave direction to the associations on how to provide services for the overseas Chinese, and the association also spent energy supporting the Chinese sports association. These mundane and practical functions justified the more ephemeral ethnic character of which they were an expression.

Liang Xiujing (2001) discusses at length how overseas Chinese leaders develop a strong *discourse of altruism*. In the interview material, selfless behaviour and sacrifice for the overseas Chinese community stand out as a core theme. Community leaders – leaders of overseas Chinese ethnic associations of all types – indicate how they spend their own personal effort, time and money on the well-being of all Chinese.

Their authority, in the form of recognition and status, arises from their altruistic behaviour. Leaders tend to indicate the altruism of others and then mention their own, modest contributions. At the same time, bad leadership is phrased in terms of self-seeking behaviour by some other, yet unspecified, leaders.

The proliferation of overseas Chinese associations can be ascribed to a number of interrelated factors. On the one hand, it is attractive to become a leader of an association, for that gives a certain type of social status and influence. The threshold to set up an organisation is small, while the advantages so gained may be important and useful, but may vary from place to place in Europe.

The interviews indicated many and varied reasons why the overseas Chinese wanted to start their own overseas Chinese associations. One typical reason is groups of new migrants arriving in Europe, like Indochinese refugees arriving in France and setting up a 'Mekong' association in 1980, thereby signifying their origin in the several different Indochinese countries and China through which the Mekong river flows (036//017). Most overseas Chinese leaders cite the need for mutual help and practical aid among new immigrants, be they refugees or not, as an important task for associations. New associations emerge because groups among the overseas Chinese do not feel represented by the existing associations. In particular, the increase in migration and the different local origins of different generations of Chinese have helped bring about such a situation. One reason may be clique-formation, where some people dominate an association to the exclusion of others, thus provoking them to set up their own association to have their voice heard. A leader with strong ambitions, unable to get a sufficiently high position in an association, may establish a new one.

Leaders of new associations, however, often indicate that they do not act on their own initiative. They have often been approached by a Chinese consul or a local official in China with the request that they set up a specific association. Far from being a matter of seeking self-interest, most overseas Chinese leaders point to the fact that establishing a new association is a matter of sacrifice for a larger interest. In reality, most of them claim, they have invested much time and money in the process and gained little from it, except perhaps hostility from other associations.

In formal terms, the threshold for setting up new associations is very low. One only needs to gather together a few friends, fill in official registration forms as appropriate in the country of residence, and make one's existence as an association known; it takes little effort to argue for the specific and complementary role of a new association in relation to those that already exist.[2]

Interlocking leaderships

Overseas Chinese association leaders' business cards often reveal a high diversity of functions. Some carry several cards for different purposes – one card for business, one for roles in civil society, or several for different types of business and association activities. Some business cards are folded and list functions on four sides in order to accommodate them all. Having many functions and being keen to advertise them is an established practice among overseas Chinese leaders. Multiple leadership functions result from interlocking leaderships of overseas Chinese associations. Table 5.1 presents the distribution of leaders of British overseas Chinese associations as presented in a handbook for overseas Chinese in Britain. Due to the way the data were compiled, it may be inaccurate (whereby the trend would be an under-estimation of the cross-postings), but it does give an impression of how interlocking works.

Fifteen per cent of the leaders in the associations had leadership functions in several associations, and 4.6 per cent in three or more. The interlinking of associations indicates that somewhere between 50 and 100 out of around 2,100 leaders have a high prestige within the around 100 associations; close examination of the data reveals that the large majority of associations to some degree are drawn into this system.

These 50 to 100 people do not form a separate group – they emerge as an elite from the practice of the association system. Interviewees, discussing cross-posting in associations, indicated that it was an important aspect of association life. On the question of how many posts a particular leader held, he said, 'I don't want to name them all, but if you don't write about this, I can tell you'.[3] He went on to name five major associations, saying that he held posts in several more, and added:

> Sometimes, you have to accept. Sometimes, they don't particularly want you to do anything, they just want to put your name on [the list of leaders]. Many people don't understand that I don't like fishing for fame and honour. For example, really, I've got little money. When I give to charity, you rarely see my name in the papers, like XXX has donated so and so much, for when I give, I do so incognito. I think that if you give to good causes you should do just that and not let anybody know.

Table 5.1 Leaders in 103 British overseas Chinese associations

Leaders and posts	Number	Percentage
Number of posts	3,035	100.0
— leaders	2,158	100.0
— posts held by leaders with > 1 post	1,429	47.0
— leaders with > 1 post	560	26.0
— — with posts in > 1 organisation	957	32.0
— — — in 3 organisations	52	2.4
— — — in 4 organisations	21	1.0
— — — in 5 organisations	13	0.6
— — — in 6 organisations	8	0.4
— — — in 7 organisations	3	0.1
— — — in ≥ 8 organisations	3	0.1
— — — in ≥ 3 organisations	100	4.6

Source: You Hailong (1996, 150–76) The data have been corrected for inconsistencies.

He added that as an honorary chairman he did not take part in the management of the association. It normally meant that he had no influence on association matters, but was expected to give donations to good causes and to support activities financially. He claimed that he had repeatedly declined the offer of a post of deputy chairman in an organisation, but leaders of many associations had leaned upon him to take the post.

Some of the multiple postings of leaders, of course, arise from the diverse and complementary functions of associations, so that leaders of local associations will also be in regional and national associations. Business people may be in fellow-villager associations, Chinatown associations and also Chinatown Lions Clubs. Whereas membership of local associations is not formalised, there are much more established rules controlling local representation in federations. In particular, there are systems of leadership rotation and of balancing quotas reflecting the interests of the people involved.

A close look at the leadership posts in the various associations (You Hailong 1996) reveals a bloated range of functions. The same person often holds a variety of posts in one and the same association. The long lists of members make one wonder whether there is a leadership post for every single member of the organisation. In many associations it seems that individual membership only makes sense for listed leaders, or rather that only the prospect of being listed in a leadership function justifies membership. Whatever the reason, there is great inventiveness in creating leadership functions. In the case of core leaders, multiple posts within the same organisation reflect the logic of there being many posts in the first place – the functional diversity implied in the range of posts means that a core coordinating figure in an association will need to hold more than one post. The inflation in posts is also indicated in peculiar forms of duplication, where an organisation has both a president and a chairman, as well as a first deputy chairman and first vice president, plus several deputies of each sort.

Another striking feature is the number of honorary posts, honorary chairmen, presidents, advisers and so on in most of the associations, including titles like 'permanent honorary president'. The holders are often past chairmen or presidents who have retired from the front line activities and are held in esteem through such posts. Business cards reveal a similar aspect, namely the importance of *founders*. Having been the 'founding president' or a 'founding deputy chairman' of an association is a source of pride, and is listed alongside honorary chairmanships.

Associations gain links with each other through cross-postings. President X from association A becomes honorary chairman of association B, while Chairman Y from association B becomes honorary president of association C. The system does not work by simple reciprocity, for the associations are subtly ranked in relation to each other. A lower-ranking association seeks status and recognition by inviting a successful president of a higher-level organisation to be listed as a honorary chairman.

In some cases, leaders span several associations because they are functionally linked, like a set of local associations federated in regional and national hierarchies. A president of a national organisation normally also holds a high leadership post in lower-level organisations.

Concrete examples of five British overseas Chinese association leaders and their posts in 15 different associations (Table 5.2) show the intricacies of the system.

Each of these cases reflects a wider pattern. Mr A and Mr B, of course, only have positions in three or four associations and so differ from Mr C and Mr E who have posts in many more. The leaders' functions are spread over very diverse associations, ranging from clan associations to professional and sports organisations. The strengths and weaknesses of the individual leaders to a certain extent determine which functions they are in charge of. Mr D, for example, mainly functions as a financial specialist, and is also in charge of youth matters in an organisation, but at this level it seems that status, political acumen and influence are more important than specialist skills – the leaders take overall charge and delegate practical tasks to others.

We can from this piece together a picture of the associations as they function on practical and symbolic levels. In a simple sense they are vessels containing the ethnic identity, or rather, they are signified as such by outside institutions like 'host' and 'home' governments. For those people involved with them, they are a source of social status; participating in their functions, their leaders gain recognition by the 'home' and 'host' governments in some measure. Although associations implicitly purport to *represent* the overseas Chinese community, *ordinary membership* and *formal channels of representation* are of no or limited importance.[4] The ability of association leaders to uphold an ethnic emblem, therefore, is the prime source of legitimacy and status.

Table 5.2 Interlocking leadership: five persons and 15 associations

	Association type	Mr A	Mr B	Mr C	Mr D	Mr E
I	General	ii, iii, iv	i, iii, iv			
II	Clan	ii				
III	Professional	ii, iii, iii		hon.		
IV	Regional		i, iii			
V	Federation		iv	i	iii	ii
VI	Regional			i		
VII	Local			hon.		
VIII	Professional			ext.		rep.
IX	Dialect			ext.	ext.	ii
X	Sports		ii	hon.		ii
XI	Clan				i, iii, hon.	
XII	Commercial				iii	iii
XIII	Native				i	
XIV	Local					iii
XV	Lions Club					i

Source: You Hailong (1996, 150–76) and interviews.

Notes: i: chairmen, presidents and first deputies; ii: deputies; iii: functional officials; iv: committee and board members; hon.: honorary chairmen and advisers; ext.: external advisers and coopted board members; rep.: regional representative or delegate.

Regional and local associations, as well as federations refer to hierarchies of jurisdiction in Britain.

What makes a leader of an association? The attraction of becoming an association leader lies in the ability to derive social and political status as well as economic benefit from a leadership function.[5] Recognition derives from the degree to which a leader embodies the symbolic roles of the associations. Liang Xiujing (2001) has shown how leaders present themselves as selfless servants of the overseas Chinese community, and how their ethnic and cultural identity consists of a general reference to ethnic stereotypes. Gaining status is, in Liang's view, based on 'transfers of capital' – they invest time and money in the community and reap positions in overseas Chinese associations; having gained positions, they can gain benefits for the community from local government (be it money for a Chinese language school, solving an issue of a planning permission or persuading a mayor to come to a Chinese New Year's festival), thereby enhancing their perceived status among overseas Chinese and vis-à-vis the 'home' authorities, thus incrementing their status even further. According to Liang, association leaders tend to claim that their leadership roles do not enhance their business achievements, while in reality they do.

Interlocking leaderships among associations are partly a product of this; inviting an accomplished leader of another association to become honorary chairman of one's own association may reflect well on oneself, and the thus honoured leader also rises in esteem. The large number of people included in association leaderships gain status from their role. Being a deputy chairman of an association may not seem impressive when one is listed among the top 30 leaders of an association after chairmen, first deputy chairmen, presidents and vice-presidents of boards, plus various honorary posts, but it does have an impact if printed on a business card. The associations produce great opportunities for building up status and prestige.

The profusion of associations in some parts of Europe can be ascribed to a combination of factors. We have already discussed in Chapter 4 how regional identities are represented by separate associations, and we have seen some of the dynamics that lead to such differentiation. As long as representation of ethnic interest provides status and recognition, there will be competition for posts. The threshold for establishing new associations is small. One of our interviewees had, for example, established a native-place association for a city in Jiangsu, although the number of people hailing from that place was very small. Including his relatives, friends, and people hailing from other places willing to serve in some capacity in his association, he became a chairman and therefore also gained seats on a national federation, as well as within local business associations. These interlocking leadership posts mutually enhanced his status. In some situations, some overseas Chinese wishing to become leaders do not get recognition in line with their ambitions within existing associations, and therefore build up new ones.

Leader status and uniqueness are linked. To consolidate their status, the leaders define their role and status as *personal*. Although they may achieve status through donations of money to good causes and community projects, the real measure of their leadership role is the personal investment of time and effort and personal attributes that distinguish them from other leaders. Sub-ethnic identities belong to this set of personal attributes. The personal mixture of identity attributes is a crucial asset, for it allows leaders to gain *specific* statuses that distinguish them from other leaders and at the same time provides them with symbols legitimising their social status and leadership roles.

Being part of a sub-ethnic group, in other words, allows a leader to distinguish him- or herself from other leaders. The overall Chinese identity emblems are thus complemented with particular identity markers with which overseas Chinese leaders gain particular profiles. The effect is, of course, a fragmentation of the associations, for different leaders in Chinese associations together with their associations create a diversity of issues and dynamics that separate them from each other, and which at the same time allows integration across 'functional' differences – leaders emerge who have overlapping credentials in a native place, an ethnic economy sector, a region and so on, thereby giving the system of interlocking leaderships between associations significance.

Chinese ethnic organisations are thus able to moderate the intricate and changing interests of host and home authorities, as well as Chinese communities, by creating an arena for status-seeking and the ritualistic acting out of ethnic and sub-ethnic stereotypes. As we have discussed in Chapter 4, the associations have changed their meaning and functions over time. The aim of some associations like the secret societies may at the beginning have been to impose a secretive order in overseas Chinese communities, while their functions later changed to represent Chinese in a hostile environment, and to rally Chinese in relation to the Chinese authorities (be it in the Mainland or Taiwan). They have gained new significance as migrant organisations in European countries and in relation to the Chinese policies on overseas Chinese in the 1980s and 1990s.

The overseas Chinese and Europe

The European Union has sought to establish political links with migrant organisations, as already discussed.[6] The European Federation of Chinese Organisations was a direct response to such efforts. The Federation was long in the making, presumably due to disagreements and difficulties of coordination. One element that most likely has hampered the federation of Chinese across Europe is the fact that the European Union only had little of practical value to offer them. Involvement with the European Union through local government was an important way of gaining access to European development funds aimed at urban regeneration projects and specific schemes for combating racism. Institutionally, there seemed to be little to lobby for directly in Brussels, and the things dividing the Chinese were greater than those joining them.

Some factors, however, drew the Chinese associations across Europe together. Many Chinese associations in Europe worked across borders or maintained some links of interlocking leaderships with each other, and Chinese businesses operated in cross-border markets, in particular for Chinese foodstuffs, catering supplies, and various services; some entrepreneurs had enterprises in several countries, and there were tight family links between migrants in different European countries (Li Minghuan 1998a). Although most of these would not benefit in any specific way from a pan-European federation due to the limited lobbying opportunities at

European level, the increasing unification of Europe (especially with the Amsterdam and Maastricht Treaties of the 1990s) reinforced the feeling among the Chinese that Europe was of significance as a jurisdiction. More specifically, Hong Kong's retrocession threw Chinese language teaching in the United Kingdom, the Netherlands and Germany into a crisis. The Hong Kong government had given direct support to Cantonese classes, in particular by supplying text books. Winding down the functions of Hong Kong's official representation office in Britain, which had been in charge of coordinating aid to Cantonese language schools, meant that these schools lost an important source of support. Given the fact that Hong Kong migrants, especially from the New Territories, had settled in the Netherlands and Germany and had received help for their schools also, the crisis of the Chinese language schools gained pan-European significance.

The crisis was not simply in the lack of text books and other support, but also in changing attitudes to Mandarin both in the host societies and among the overseas Chinese. One purpose that could gather the overseas Chinese together, hence, was the issue of text books and Chinese language teaching – the balance shifted not only between Cantonese and Mandarin, but also between simplified and traditional characters, and the relation to Taiwan and the Mainland (in particular symbolised with the issue over phonetic transcription, where Hanyu Pinyin stood in opposition to the Zhuyin Zimu[7]). This reflected the rising demand among new migrants for Chinese language classes. Many interviewees cited the 'rise' of China as a world power after 1978 as an important factor increasing the importance of knowing Chinese. Given the few resources in terms of financing, text books, skilled teachers, and the urgency of action, the issue suddenly stood centre stage; across Europe, Chinese language schools were not only symbols of the 'continuation of Chinese culture', but they were also major sources of status and purpose for Chinese associations. Heads of Chinese associations gained significant status by contributing funds to schools and by facilitating local government contributions. Language schools were an ideal activity for ethnic associations, for they combined service to the community, links with local authorities, ethnic identity, and support from Chinese authorities.[8]

Another aspect that joined together the Chinese associations across Europe was the realisation from the Mainland side that the Taiwanese-leaning overseas Chinese in Europe had a strong network that since the mid-1970s had held annual meetings in major European cities with direct and indirect support from Taiwanese authorities and firms (Liang and Christiansen 1998). From the early 1990s, Taiwanese traders and professionals also entered Europe on a certain scale and met each other in a pan-European setting. Although these associations were never likely to gain official recognition for diplomatic reasons (no European state was likely to risk damaging the diplomatic relations with the Mainland), they created a platform for contact with politicians and business people and for putting across political messages that could be construed to represent 'all Chinese'. The existence of a successful 'competing' association had an impact on Mainland-inclined overseas Chinese leaders, who were, however, frustrated for a long time by the inability to find proper structures for their own pan-European association.

When EFCO was finally established, it used the crisis of the Chinese language schools as its first project. In the second period, it aimed, under the leadership of a Dutch overseas Chinese, to capture the issues of the migrant policy of the European Union, among other things by commissioning a report on the conditions of the Chinese in Europe (Li Minghuan 1998b) and by cooperating closely with a semi-official body in Amsterdam (Amsterdams Bureau Buitenlanders) that facilitated contacts in the European commission (see Liang Xiujing 2001). Unlike the Turkish migrant groups, the Chinese never gained a significant lobbying position within the European Union (Kastoryano, forthcoming), but their pan-European organisation did get off the ground.

EFCO's leadership structure was very competitive and the presidency would shift between European countries; as in most local and national organisations, legalistic power-balancing among leaders became a critical element; Liang Xiujing (2001) observed that intervention from Chinese representatives was crucial for maintaining the federation; the plan by some to boycott a meeting in Budapest in the late 1990s was foiled through pressure from Chinese embassies.

Associations as symbols and institutions

The Chinese ethnic associations, as we have seen, represent multiple interests, and are frameworks for interaction between ethnic leaders, Chinese 'home' authorities and 'host' governments. They embody ethnic stereotypes and use *symbolic* activities to signify ethnic difference. When asked about the meaning of 'Chinese culture', many interviewees named the range of *activities* their associations initiate.

The ethnic symbols used by the overseas Chinese associations, accordingly, include Chinese New Year and Mid-Autumn Festivals (the latter often coupled with the China's national day), Chinese food culture, calligraphy, music, and so on. The task of displaying ethnic culture in contrast to 'host' culture is an important raison d'être for the associations. (By contrast, private parties among overseas Chinese celebrating personal achievement or business success, and conventions where only overseas Chinese are invited, in many cases include Western brass bands, Scottish bagpipes, or Moulin Rouge-style chorus lines in their programme.) The display of ethnic distinctiveness through stereotypes on the one hand seeks to join the Chinese together in sentiments about 'our culture'.[9] On the other hand, it caters for the young overseas Chinese, attracting them away from the 'host' culture by arranging karaoke competitions, performances by Canto-pop stars, martial arts films from Hong Kong, as well as sinicised versions of Western culture. Overseas Chinese associations claim to be 'bridges' between cultures. Festival speeches by Chinese community leaders and invited local politicians often focus on this theme. Non-Chinese festival-goers can also have their names transcribed into Chinese and presented in calligraphy or their fates predicted according to Chinese horoscopes.

Deliberate and public use of ethnic symbols gives the ethnic associations meaning and purpose, as it creates activity and demands resources.

Ethnic symbols used in overseas Chinese communities *refer* to culture and tradition in China. Those involved in using them in overseas Chinese settings regard them as reflections of an imagined 'authentic' Chinese culture. Both the overseas Chinese and the non-Chinese participants in community events use them to act out the boundary between the two groups.

Overseas Chinese associations maintain ethnic symbols, provide help to co-natives and assert links with local and Chinese authorities. Juggling these different functions, the leaders of overseas Chinese associations tend to formulate ethnic stereotypes in simple and general terms, focusing on the activities involved in festivals and other public events. Social concern and public-spiritedness demonstrate their moral authority, and their political links are essential for perpetuating the role of the overseas Chinese associations.

6 European Chinese and Chinese patriotism

The Chinese word 'aiguozhuyi' literally means *love* for the country or the nation. The claim that the Chinese overseas are characterised by their love for the Chinese nation, however, has a political significance. It refers to the fact that overseas Chinese communities are drawn into the frameworks of official patriotism.

Patriotism is a framework that the Chinese leadership uses to control social movements and political groups that do not subscribe to communist ideology. Non-communist allies of the Chinese Communist Party are termed 'patriotic', for while they do not share the communist ideals, they are supposed to share the love of the fatherland and accept communist leadership.

Patriotism is part and parcel of the formal ideological vocabulary and is hardly ever used in any other meaning. For the Chinese Communist Party and the Chinese leadership, patriotism connotes inclusion and ideological tolerance, while for the targeted group it implies political subservience and dominance. In the context of overseas Chinese, patriotism signifies the willingness to be embraced by the political leadership of China. It includes an elaborate system of institutions and rituals aimed at cementing the alliance.

The formulations of one of our interviewees indicated the irony built into patriotism:

> The reason why there were only a dozen or so associations in the federation was that (a) there were only few overseas Chinese back then, and (b) because our demands and make-up were different. Why did we originally call it the federation of patriotic [Chinese] associations in Britain? What was the word patriotic good for? That's because the federation of overseas Chinese associations in Britain was very special, we emphasised quality above quantity. However, with the social changes, China's policy of opening up and the democratic trends nowadays, the association also underwent big changes ... Now our position is that we should unite the overseas Chinese, further Sino-British relations, promote Chinese language education and propagate Chinese culture.
>
> (001//020)

When the Chinese authorities had a policy of recruiting few, but highly reliable, patriots among the overseas Chinese, their voluntary organisations were called patriotic. The effort to cast the net wider, including broader, more diverse and politically less motivated groups in the patriotic cause, included *playing down* this terminology.

Our interviewees often used the terms patriot and patriotic to indicate their own relationship with China, a relationship of accepting Chinese government authority, of gaining recognition, and of playing out rituals of ethnic belonging. An interviewee indicated the complexity of this when talking about another overseas Chinese:

> China values his support for the state's education, for the Hope Programme,[1] so whether it is using him or whatever, it values his enthusiasm. But from another point of view this person is likely to have other motives, so the Embassy won't express anything special, they'll just say he's a patriotic compatriot (aiguo tongbao), patriotic like anybody else. But what do they think? Different people may see it differently. China has a policy, the united front policy, to unite and exploit, divide and disintegrate.[2] This is really fierce. So you won't be able to know what they really think about that person. Nobody knows and he doesn't know.
>
> (002//117)

Patriotism signifies overseas Chinese contributions of goodwill to China, and recognition by China of its overseas compatriots. In that sense it is a manifestation both of sentimental belonging and of political allegiance. The interviewee quoted above suggests that patriotism also implies calculation. Overseas Chinese ingratiate themselves with Chinese authorities to gain privileges, and Chinese authorities use patriotism to impose their will on the overseas Chinese or divide and rule them. The interviewee was a top leader of an association leaning towards the Mainland government and in other parts of the interview questioned the patriotic spirit of other leaders; he is known to speak his mind on contentious issues and his formulations about patriotism bluntly stated the mixed feelings involved in being a patriot.

This chapter examines the relations between the Chinese overseas and China as they are managed by both sides. The discourse of patriotism and the policy of the united front stand at the centre of the discussion. In Chapter 1, I have already discussed some aspects of how overseas Chinese are integrated constitutionally in Chinese statehood, and both in Chapter 1 and in Chapter 4 the relations between the overseas Chinese and their home villages have been analysed. The topic of this chapter is in between these two, seeking to explore the ways in which the Chinese state and the overseas Chinese relate to each other, and how that contributes to the formation of a Chinese identity.

Policies towards overseas Chinese compatriots: the Mainland

The relationship between the Chinese state and the overseas Chinese is the object of an elaborate policy area with its own administrative and political institutions,[3] spanning the Chinese Communist Party (the United Front Work Department),[4] the State Council (the Overseas Chinese Affairs Office), the National People's Congress (with it overseas Chinese affairs committee), the Chinese People's Political Consultative Conference (embodying the functions of the united front policy), the All-China Returned Overseas Chinese Association (a 'mass' organisation), and the Zhigongdang (one of the eight co-opted democratic parties; it is habitually associated with the representation of overseas Chinese interests). Some of these institutional frameworks are also present at provincial and city levels.

Overseas Chinese policy has changed much over the years, most radically during the Cultural Revolution 1966–76. The formal structures for overseas Chinese affairs came into being in the 1950s and were virtually suspended in 1966. They were resumed in 1976 and have undergone some changes in the 1980s and 1990s. I will mainly discuss the overseas Chinese policy of the 1980s and 1990s. In terms of budget and place in the national economy, overseas Chinese policy is of limited significance. Investments by overseas Chinese insofar as it is possible to gauge them through statistics and other economic reports only constituted between 5 and 10 per cent of all investments into the Mainland, and remittances and donations from overseas Chinese contribute moderately to China's balance of payments and foreign currency reserves.[5] In the overall picture of Chinese politics, overseas Chinese policy is dwarfed by the gigantic reform of the economic system, the rural reforms and the overhaul of state-owned enterprises, and it is not likely to take up much time on the central leadership's agenda. It is not the arena of major conflicts over issues and, since a couple of crucial meetings stipulated basic policy in 1977 and 1978, it has enjoyed a period of political calm.[6]

The formal position of overseas Chinese policy institutions within China's political and administrative system indicates a high prestige and importance, but they are in reality rather insignificant. For example, within the Chinese Communist Party top leadership it is functionally delinked from more important foreign policy and decision-making on the Taiwan Strait situation, yet in formal terms it ranks equal to them. In the State Council, the Overseas Chinese Affairs Office ranks as a ministry, yet is has few decisive powers (in particular, the Ministry of Foreign Affairs' consular department and not the overseas Chinese Affairs Office is in overall charge of the work abroad). The great involvement of overseas Chinese in the Chinese People's Political Consultative Conference is of great symbolic importance. While the CPPCC has virtually no power as an assembly, it has high social prestige. This constitutes a symbolic recognition of the overseas Chinese, while actual policy-making has a much lower priority.

1978–1983

The policies towards the overseas Chinese between 1978 and 1983 were aimed at restoring confidence.[7] During the Cultural Revolution, returned overseas Chinese (guiqiao) and dependents of overseas Chinese (qiaojuan) – both official classifications – had been exposed to abuse, confiscation of property and political persecution. The policy that took shape 1977–8 stipulated that these two groups 'on all fronts must be united with the people in the country in common struggle', and that 'actions and words not favourable for this must not be undertaken or spoken'. In return for becoming one with everybody else, they must share the 'sweet and the bitter' and make the 'spirit of assiduous struggle' their own, they must not emphasise their difference from other people or ask the authorities for excessive attention. Many had been deprived of education opportunities, and the policy aimed at providing full-scale entrance into all levels of education. This was partly done through special initiatives aimed at the two groups, through the re-opened Jinan University in Guangdong, the Overseas Chinese University, special middle schools and various preparation schools, as well as special political, cultural and science and technology evening schools and distance learning schools. The special education institutions were also aimed at absorbing young overseas Chinese directly from abroad, who wished to pursue an education in China.

The special state farms and factories established to employ returned overseas Chinese were to be reformed and improved, and the poor and inadequate treatment that Chinese authorities inflicted on overseas Chinese fleeing from Vietnam and Cambodia at the time when the new policy was being drafted was to be replaced with appropriate measures.

Most importantly, unjust verdicts were to be rescinded and confiscated property was to be restored to the original owners. This policy, part of which was based on a joint circular of the CCP Central Committee, the Overseas Chinese Affairs Commission, the Organisation Department of the Central Committee, and the Ministry for Public Security issued in May 1981, overturned 33,056 official cases from the Cultural Revolution, an unknown number of 'rogue struggle and criticism' (luan pi luan dou) cases, and 10,155 cases dating from before the Cultural Revolution; more than 2,000 cases were tested by political or judicial (rather than administrative) organs. A total of 322,987 personal files of overseas Chinese were cleared of prejudiced material, and the public security and state security authorities cleaned out in an unknown number of files.

The problem of overseas Chinese working in posts incommensurable with their educational level was solved through a variety of measures, among them the promotion of 17,781 people to leadership posts above county level.[8] People who had been deprived of pensions because they were demoted in the 1960s had their pension rights restored, and approximately 600 returned overseas Chinese who had been in penal camps were given jobs.

The return of confiscated property, in particular real estate, was an even greater operation. It was a policy based on a complex set of policy documents and rules issued between 1982 and 1987, which by 1991 had restored 3.1 million square metres of houses confiscated during the Cultural Revolution to their overseas Chinese owners; 22 million square metres of rural houses confiscated since 1949 had been returned, while 17 million square metres of town house cases remained unresolved. Cases of urban properties confiscated in the mid-1950s were only partly resolved, 12 million of 31 million square metres (or 40 per cent) of houses being transferred back to their original owners in terms of ownership, but only 20 per cent in terms of usufruct. Many cases dragged out due to complications and the involvement of many authorities with conflicting interests. The rules included different rules for different types of confiscation that had taken place in different timescales, and the status of individual claimants was often a crucial point for determining the handling of cases; there was much room for interpretation and local decision-making involving many authorities. Each case must have appeared a bureaucratic nightmare for both the claimants and for the overseas Chinese affairs authorities that were given the authority to oversee the work. In the late 1990s an official of the Overseas Chinese Affairs Commission, when asked what was the dominant part of the Commission's work, without hesitation answered, 'returning houses to their owners'.

These measures aimed not only to redress injustice, but also to build confidence. Any gesture to overseas Chinese outside the country would be pointless, unless those who had already returned were given better conditions. The Overseas Chinese Affairs Commission and its subordinate administrations were put in charge. In the following years, this administrative framework expanded rapidly.

The policy also provided for family visits by Chinese citizens living abroad, 'foreigners of Chinese blood', as well as Taiwan, Hong Kong and Macau compatriots. It also promoted 'contributions to the socialist construction of the fatherland', by allowing flexible forms for investment (through a national investment company, joint ventures, or forms of import substitution processing), as well as protection of the investment against currency fluctuations and ensuring favourable interest rates.

Both the domestic policies and those directed towards the overseas Chinese abroad were complicated, for they had to be carried out within the existing frameworks of the planned economy. Creating new education opportunities, the reform of 'returned overseas Chinese' state farms and factories, overturning old verdicts and returning confiscated property were much more complex than they seem in hindsight, for China's economy was still dominated by the state plan. Allowing overseas Chinese to travel into the country increased the need for acceptable tourist facilities. The lack of hotels, the poor transport infrastructure, and the inadequate training of personnel, it was felt, must be overcome, lest visiting overseas Chinese be disappointed. The Overseas Chinese Affairs Commission, therefore, established its own separate systems to deal with such visitors. Inward investment from overseas Chinese was difficult, due to the lack of rules and administrative experience, and the initiative was meant to leap ahead of general inward investment by foreigners. Special and more liberal rules for investment and economic management were introduced by overseas Chinese affairs authorities in the 'home' areas of overseas Chinese, allowing them to break red tape. Local authorities in these areas thus gained more power, and were able to do away with any institutional constraints on development; overseas Chinese 'home towns' (qiaoxiang), as a result, prospered and were able to take advantage of the reform policies much earlier than other areas.

1984–1988

China's policy towards overseas Chinese addressed Chinese citizens residing abroad, Chinese of foreign nationality, Hong Kong and Macau compatriots and Taiwanese compatriots.

The second phase of the policy starting in 1984 further encouraged overseas Chinese investments, donations and remittances. Preferential treatment and proper services were extended to investors and contributors. Returned overseas Chinese and dependents were encouraged to invest remittances and capital from abroad. The policy made it easier to remit and donate money. 'Overseas Chinese investment base areas' were the prime targets for investment in the 'economic construction' of the 'home areas'. The policy aimed at attracting talented overseas Chinese home. It promoted the 'great cause of the unity of the fatherland' and helped enterprises to be reformed with overseas Chinese participation, almost giving them free rein.

The policy designated overseas Chinese 'home' areas and established local administrations for overseas Chinese affairs in townships and small towns. This institutionalisation, combined with great flexibility in local affairs related to overseas Chinese, engendered local self-interest. Local authorities sought to capitalise on the links with overseas Chinese. Some local officials sought to attract donations for charity, education, infrastructure, health services and so on, and they facilitated joint ventures, direct investments and trade arrangements with overseas Chinese. Local institutional greed, so it seems, often took the upper hand, for government instructions to local officials repeatedly and consistently warned that such donations and investment must be spontaneous and voluntary: overseas Chinese were not to be exposed to inducement and pressure.[9]

Local officials, however, were not merely driven by money incentives. Visits from overseas Chinese, formal, ritual links with their organisations, and contacts with overseas Chinese dignitaries and notabilities, became symbols of local officials' political and administrative prowess. Their visits abroad allowed them to identify potential 'patriotic pillars of society'. Local governments soon found out how to build up notabilities and dignitaries. If you give them status in China, they will gain more status in the overseas Chinese community, and thereby more recognition by their 'host' society. Their enhanced status abroad, then, can be used as an argument for increasing their status in China. This game of implicit complicity between officials and overseas Chinese leaders aimed at putting the Chinese locality on the map, politically and culturally: a famous 'local' overseas Chinese was, in the warped logic of the planned economy, a target for 'plan fulfilment'. Entertaining links with a famous overseas Chinese was a political achievement that gave status to local officials. If fame was managed to the degree that the 'local' overseas Chinese was elevated from a status as, for example 'adviser' and 'honorary board member' in county contexts, to honorary functions at city or provincial level (ideally, the provincial Chinese People's Political Consultative Conference), not to speak of national level, his or her glory would shine on the locality.

'Home' areas with many Southeast Asian and North American overseas Chinese had higher status, and awarded European overseas Chinese (who were perceived to be less affluent and influential) lesser status, while places with fewer overseas Chinese abroad were able to grant higher status to their European overseas Chinese. Some overseas Chinese, whose 'home' areas were thus 'overcrowded', were 'adopted' by other 'home' areas hungry for overseas Chinese with some status. Association with inland counties, cities and provinces from where few Chinese had migrated, therefore, could provide higher formal status than places around the Pearl River Delta, Chaozhou and Xiamen.

Being a successful 'home' area gave more decision making-power, a licence to do things otherwise obstructed by policy. In the name of accommodating wishes from overseas Chinese, the creation of local heterodoxy became acceptable. Ancestral halls, folk religious practices, the influx of overseas norms and products, and emigration were condoned earlier in 'home' areas than in other parts of China.[10] More importantly, local initiative in the economy had freer rein, especially in the 1980s, so 'home' areas had more opportunities to 'get rich first'.

In Chapter 4, I mentioned how overseas Chinese leaders could negotiate on the restoration and maintenance of ancestral graves. Succeeding in protecting the graves earned them great status in their European communities. The graves became an issue of immense symbolic value, skilfully turned into power and influence by those involved. In Chapter 3, I discussed how Nanhai, a 'home' area, had donated a dancing dragon to Antwerp's Chinese community; the symbolism of this gift helped solve a problem of political organisation by forcing a Chinatown association into existence. There are thousands of examples and anecdotes on the importance of symbolic relations between overseas Chinese and their 'home' towns.

In the 1980s the overseas Chinese policy of the People's Republic of China created the foundation of a system of political and economic interaction among overseas Chinese and local authorities on a scale hitherto unheard of.

1989–2000

The huge expansion of local initiatives in the 1980s brought overseas Chinese affairs out of the tight central control that had previously characterised them. The central authorities still gave general direction. However, their power had declined by the early 1990s to the benefit of local governments who were expanding their direct links with 'their' overseas Chinese. This decline in central control was deliberate, for it served the purpose of attracting those overseas Chinese for whom 'love of the country' means 'state patriotism'.[11] Many overseas Chinese of the old generation whose allegiance was with the Republic of China (ROC) and the 'father of the Nation' Sun Yat-sen, and therefore had directed their loyalty to the Taibei authorities after 1949, did not accept patriotism as propagated by the Mainland authorities. Most of these 'old overseas Chinese' (laoqiao) did not originate in Taiwan, and few had lived there for any length of time; their ancestral places were in the Mainland. The devolution of overseas Chinese affairs policy in the Mainland aimed at creating a 'local place patriotism' (aixiang) acceptable to the large constituency of overseas Chinese still supporting the Taibei authorities. The affinity with one's own kin and co-natives was constructed as a bond more fundamental than politics. The Chinese terminology of patriotism during the 1980s and 1990s, accordingly, was expanded from 'aiguo' (love for the country) to 'aiguo, aixiang' (love for the country and love for the local place), a formula used with increasing frequency on ceremonial occasions.

Co-operation with overseas Chinese academics and scientists

The 1989 protest movement in China had a profound effect on overseas Chinese affairs policy. Tens of thousands Chinese intellectuals were studying or working abroad, or they were on scholarly exchanges and visits under various schemes, when the suppression of the protest movement occurred in early June 1989. Contact between the protesting students and networks of Chinese scholars and students living in foreign countries alerted the Chinese leadership to the great human resource spread across the globe.

The events in 1989 made foreign governments extend political asylum and other forms of residence permits to Chinese students and scholars, which allowed many to find work and settle abroad. The Chinese authorities in 1992 sent out reassuring signals to the students and scholars overseas that they were welcome home, that they had the automatic right of exit from China, and that any past political grievances, actions or attitudes would not prejudice them. (People against whom there were official indictments, who persisted in criticising the Chinese leadership, or sought to propagandise in China were not included in this grace.) The active cooperation included: (a) regional and national Chinese students and scholars' associations in countries of residence handled by the education sections of consulates and embassies, (b) national and international subject-specific scholarly associations including Chinese scholars with links to special associations in China, (c) subject-specific workshops and conferences in China with extensive participation by Chinese specialists abroad, (d) prizes and honours for foreign-based Chinese scholars, (e) alumni networks of prestigious Mainland universities, (f) participation of Chinese scholars living abroad in advisory committees and boards of governors in Chinese higher education and research institutions, and (g) high-profile research centres in China, often in cooperation with foreign universities and organisation, that could attract high-profile scholars to return home. Where possible, Taiwanese scholars residing abroad were drawn into various forms of cooperation. Although a distinction was upheld between those scholars who were Chinese citizens (huaqio), those who were ethnic Chinese with foreign nationality (huaren), and those who were Hong Kong, Macau, and Taiwanese compatriots (Gang Ao Tai tongbao), the policy aimed at furthering a broad cooperation between them.

The 'great cause of national unification'

The political presentation of Chinese history on ceremonial occasions was made inclusive with the aim to de-emphasise the Communist–Nationalist schism. Foreign affairs officials and diplomatic staff were encouraged to celebrate the anniversary of the 1911 Revolution on 10 October with Taiwan-leaning overseas Chinese who regard it as the 'national day'. They were, of course, not allowed to refer to the date as the 'national day', but could celebrate this as an important day in the common history. It was acceptable to honour Sun Yat-sen, whose historical role is recognised both in Taiwan and the Mainland; changing emphasis, the Mainland would stress the ideological common ground with the Nationalists. Mao Zedong's role was, on occasions like his 100th anniversary in 1993, presented as a continuation of the Nationalist ideas of Sun Yat-sen, while the animosity with Chiang Kai-shek's regime was de-emphasised. While Mao had been regarded in negative terms by many Chinese both in China and abroad, due to his repressive role during the 1960s and 1970s, his 100th anniversary was used as an opportunity to stress his positive role. He had made it possible for the Chinese people to 'stand up' and take their rightful place as an equal among the nations of the world; in that sense he had accomplished Sun Yat-sen's project. Respect for the Chinese nation in the eyes of the world had gained respect and status for the overseas Chinese. The staged, ceremonial shift of perspective, and the rhetorical inclusion of all compatriots into a common Chinese cause, was an important part of overseas Chinese policy.

Overseas Chinese affairs work sought to isolate and remove the rationale for overseas Chinese organisations in Europe inclined towards the Taibei government. Such organisations would, where they put official ROC systems on public display or involved the participation of politicians or senior officials representing the ROC government, be countered with official diplomatic protests to the host government. Where such organisations could be persuaded to shift side altogether or to move to a more neutral position, efforts to that end were tried. Prominent pro-Taiwan individuals were approached with much charm to explore how far they could or would move. Neutral or pro-Beijing associations received protests or 'friendly' suggestions where they inadvertently used or reflected official ROC or Nationalist Party symbolism and ideas. At the same time, personal and social contacts and friendships across the divide were regarded as positive. Repelling the political form and attracting the human and ethnic sentiments, Chinese officials hoped in the long term to tear Taiwan-leaning associations apart.

'Greater China'

The notion of 'greater China' was promoted by overseas Chinese scholars and some non-Chinese observers of China. It is a concept used with many meanings (or varying degrees of meaninglessness) to signify an economic sphere composed of people and territories characterised by Chinese ethnic background, or people across the world concerned with Chinese culture. Such notions of 'greater China' in the latter part of the 1980s became dynamic as fashionable reference points in academic debates, in conference and workshop titles, in executive and policy reports and in titles of airport lounge bestsellers.

The Chinese reforms had opened up intellectual debates on Chinese history, national destiny and identity. Democratisation in Taiwan and Hong Kong's and

Macau's impending retrocession also put debates on these issues on the agenda among Chinese outside the Chinese Mainland. Huge investments in the Mainland from Hong Kong and Taiwan not only integrated these economies, but also strengthened personal links and cultural convergence, thus giving substance to rethinking of what it meant to be Chinese.

The idea of 'greater China' and the redirection of the overseas Chinese affairs policy in the 1990s gave an impetus for people who had formerly let the Beijing–Taibei schism guide their own behaviour. An influential Dutch overseas Chinese declared:

> We are not separated from them, I tell you. Whenever the Taiwanese have an activity, I participate. I cannot represent in an official sense, that's the starting point, so I participate in all the non-official stuff. The issue is this and nothing else. From an official point of view, if you say 'Republic of China', that is no good. You can only say 'Taiwan'. We have to draw a clear line, if we hadn't got a line, it's impossible to achieve anything. As long as it is non-official, if you arrange a New Year's celebration, I'll go, but not on the 10th of October [the ROC's national day]. You have a karaoke competition, and I'll go, support it, donate money, no problem. But if you say, today an Overseas Chinese Affairs commissioner will attend a celebration, I won't go, you see, that's where we draw the line. They're our friends. Now the Cantonese Association , they're my friends, they are putting a karaoke competition together, I go there, donate money to them, no problem, for the sake of the overseas Chinese.
>
> (029//129)

The angst of previous eras still resonates in his description; for, in the past, any contact had been considered a transgression that would get one into trouble.

Another European overseas Chinese, a man of suavity and vision, said:

> Now we are doing some thinking, we have done it for some years now, on how to write the history of the overseas Chinese, a complete history. There are 30 million ethnic Chinese living abroad, 30 million people without direction, without common principle. Whether or not it is possible organise, write overseas Chinese, research overseas Chinese [history], will [determine] whether these 30 million overseas Chinese can become one body, can form a net; such a document would give direction to the overseas Chinese. Presently, the Chinese Communist Party, I feel, does not completely [fulfil this aim], it is not able to achieve this. I feel, that because there are different quarters in the Overseas Chinese Affairs Office and the Overseas Chinese Affairs Association, aren't there, during the last few years our China has emphasised patriotism. If we then add that since the [events of] the fourth of June, a small group went abroad and brought the [lack of common direction] to an extreme. They shout abuse, against the Communist Party, against the fatherland, indiscriminately, against their family, their father and mother. A small family

is composed of father, mother and their children, the big family is composed of the 1.3 billion people [of China]. Only the state can bring harmony.

(047//258)

He thinks that 'greater China' needs more positive direction under an all-encompassing patriotism, unified in one historical narrative. The Chinese authorities fail to give positive and unified direction, or rather their direction is not sufficient, and its agencies are divided amongst themselves. He does not seem to acknowledge the limited capacity of the Chinese authorities in dealing with 'greater China'.

Dealing with the new migrants

The nature of overseas Chinese policy changed during the 1990s as a consequence of the 'new migration' that began in the 1980s. Before then, overseas Chinese policy had mainly to do with the returned overseas Chinese and the dependents of Chinese abroad. In the 1980s, the policy focus shifted to restoring property confiscated during the Cultural Revolution, and to visits by and contacts with Chinese settled abroad. In the 1990s, the new migrants became a new policy area. The front line of contact was the consular service of the Ministry of Foreign Affairs. Both legal and illegal migrants caused the work load to increase, legal migrants because they needed more paperwork done, and illegal migrants because they, when found out, needed consular assistance. The real challenge created by new migrants, however, lay in integrating them in existing overseas Chinese communities.

Chinese officials encouraged able people among the new migrants and suitable leaders among established overseas Chinese to organise new migrants in voluntary associations. Several of our interviewees describe how they were approached with the request that they set up voluntary associations in order to meet the needs of new migrants, giving them advice and support. The initiative often came from consuls, concerned with particular local difficulties, but also often from local overseas Chinese affairs authorities in China seeking an organised counterpart in a European city or country. In our material, there are sporadic hints of consular annoyance at meddling by visiting officials from local overseas Chinese affairs authorities. In Hungary, the strategy for organisation along national as opposed to native-place lines became a major issue. In the mid-1990s this not only caused much disagreement among overseas Chinese in Hungary, but also revealed how central and local branches of the overseas Chinese affairs authorities pursued different interests.

Although authorities sought to expand their influence at each other's expense, they often worked together to dissipate animosities within the overseas Chinese communities. The large majority of overseas Chinese in Bologna, for example, are new migrants, many of whom seem to be in a troubled and unstable situation, living and working in semi-legality as street vendors and sweatshop workers. The few 'old' overseas Chinese in Bologna, a small group of well-off restaurateurs and merchants with long-standing bonds in Taibei, could easily have turned their back on their poorer and less educated co-natives, but did not do so. While they still maintained a high-profile Taiwan orientation, playing a prominent role in the ROC-oriented associations, they began to cooperate with the Zhejiang authorities in the cultural field, inviting Chinese artists to Bologna, and putting on activities to enhance the popular view of China among Italians. They organised Chinese language classes for the Mainland children, for as they said, 'our kids have grown up and do not need Chinese lessons any more', and they were concerned that the Mainland children might grow up without knowledge of the Chinese language. Their attitude was possible not only due to themselves, but also to coordinated efforts by Mainland Chinese officials.

The example from Bologna may be an extreme example of 'old' and 'new' Chinese immigrants dealing with each other across barriers of origin, social class, and political inclination. The ethnic bond does not obliterate these barriers, but mitigates them and gives them a different significance. In Bologna, the new migrants provide an opportunity for extending charity and demonstrating social responsibility towards co-ethnics. Such behaviour gives more social status and opportunities than rejection and isolation would. Overseas Chinese leaders across Europe gain from their social responsibility towards new migrants, for they act as intermediaries with local authorities, entertain meaningful contacts with local authorities in the places of origin of the migrants, and perform roles in relation to Chinese consulates and embassies. Building community among new migrants gives them standing in those communities as they mature. The role of overseas Chinese affairs policy has been to use and respond to these mechanisms. In that effort, playing the co-ethnic card has been of major importance.

Co-optation

Political inclusion of the overseas Chinese was revived after the Cultural Revolution. The revival was centred on two core institutions, the original Overseas Chinese Affairs Commission of the 1950s and 1960s, and the Chinese People's Political Consultative Conference (the state founding assembly of 1949, which had continued to exist until the Cultural Revolution).[12]

In 1977 it was clear that convening the Chinese People's Political Consultative Conference without restoring the overseas Chinese affairs work would be meaningless. A strong signal had to go out to overseas Chinese that things were changing, so reinstating overseas Chinese affairs work under Liao Chengzhi's leadership was a symbolic measure aimed at making the Chinese People's Political Consultative Conference credible and constitutionally legitimate. The overseas Chinese, in other words, were indispensable for the political effort to rebuild China after the Cultural Revolution.

The appointment of a few overseas Chinese members of the Chinese People's Political Consultative Conference gave all overseas Chinese a symbolic presence and recognition. Local levels of the Conference also included overseas Chinese.

The overseas Chinese members of the Chinese People's Political Consultative Conferences at national and local levels constituted a top selection of those who received official recognition by Chinese authorities. In addition to this, local authorities bestowed various honorific positions and titles on overseas Chinese, ranging from honorary citizens to advisers and board members of institutions and organisations. Such titles were mainly ceremonial, and recognised contributions made by overseas Chinese. The Overseas Chinese Affairs Office also invited overseas Chinese to participate in meetings and particular events. Overseas Chinese tend to regard such invitations as a great honour. Top overseas Chinese community leaders, for example, were invited to participate in Hong Kong's retrocession ceremony in 1997; the delegation of overseas Chinese from Europe may have included about 30 persons.

Co-optation does not give power, but status. Although there is a rough hierarchy of posts and honours, the variety and ad hoc nature of many of them make them difficult to compare and rank. Status is therefore open to interpretation and can be compared in many different ways.

Policies towards overseas Chinese: Taiwan

1950s–1970s

The Nationalist government that had been China's internationally recognised government since 1928, and had reconstituted itself in 1947–8 after a decade of warfare, lost the Civil War to the communists in 1949. When the government in early 1949 withdrew to Taiwan, it continued to rule as the only legitimate and internationally recognised government of China. When the People's Republic of China was proclaimed in October 1949, the new state was recognised by a number of countries in the Soviet sphere of influence and some Western countries, but many states continued to recognise the ROC government, now in Taibei, as the legitimate government of China.

Chiang Kai-shek's only claim to power was the Republic of China. While the Taiwanese rightly could regard the end of Japanese occupation in 1945 as a liberation, they soon found that being host to the rump of the Republic meant that Guomindang's version of pan-Chineseness was forced upon them. Society became split between around one million refugees from the Mainland and the 'real' Taiwanese, those who had lived in Taiwan before 1945 and their descendants.

For many overseas Chinese across the world, the Nationalist Party had a strong affective significance. During the Cold War and in particular the Cultural Revolution, the People's Republic of China on the Mainland alienated many overseas Chinese. The propaganda war between Taibei and Beijing was sustained by world public opinion that regarded everything 'behind the iron curtain' as inhumane and repressive. Pamphlets listing the people in overseas Chinese homelands killed during the Land Reform provided a macabre start to three decades of separation of overseas Chinese from the Mainland. The United Nations-imposed embargo that isolated the Mainland during the Korean War and after broke the direct contact between overseas Chinese and their families; letters and other forms of communication were interrupted for long periods.

Apart from the embargo, political pressure both in China and abroad meant that contacts were seen as high-risk. Not knowing the fate and whereabouts of relatives, overseas Chinese avoided contact in order not to add to any hardship their relatives might suffer. Holders of Chinese passports, i.e. Republic of China passports, in the 1950s found themselves represented by the government of Taibei in many western countries.

In this political context, Chiang Kai-shek's government in Taiwan continued to regard and promote itself as the guardian of all Chinese overseas. It also assumed the role of custodian of the Chinese historical and cultural heritage. It collated and edited classics, promoted classical studies, and edited rare sources on any topic related to China's history and culture. While language reform in China introduced simplified characters, the Taiwanese authorities maintained the 'authentic' traditional characters. Chiang's government was thus carried by a geopolitical context, and although it ideologically was a ruthlessly *modernising* regime, it legitimised itself by embracing the Chinese past. It also built upon Sun Yat-sen's 'Three People's Principles' (Sanminzhuyi) that provided the ideological glue of the Nationalist Party and the link to the overseas Chinese who still regarded Sun Yat-sen as their leader. Loyalty and identification of the overseas Chinese became one of the pillars of the political legitimacy of the Taibei government.

Some of our interviewees related how overseas Chinese communities in the 1950s, 1960s and 1970s had been influenced by the schism between Taibei and Beijing. Representatives of both governments met contacts across the divide with exclusion and pressure. The situation was different in various places in Europe: in Denmark and Britain, the Chiang government in Taibei had virtually no foothold, as these countries recognised the People's Republic early, while its impact in France before 1964, in Italy and in the Netherlands until the early 1970s, and so on, was considerable. The Cold War made direct contacts with the Mainland awkward and difficult for many overseas Chinese.

The forces working in the favour of the Taibei government were thus substantial and diverse. In order to consolidate its global position during the Cold War, it drew on the patriotic affiliation of the overseas Chinese and through the Overseas Chinese Affairs Commission included them in the structures of the Republic.

1970s–1990s

From the beginning of the 1970s the situation changed. The People's Republic of China took over the Chinese seat in the United Nations and ever more European states withdrew their recognition from the Republic of China government. Taiwan, accordingly, became isolated on the international scene. Overseas Chinese loyal to the Taiwan authorities, therefore, came under growing pressure, while those leaning towards the Mainland gained strength. Taiwan's problems grew when the reform policy and the new policy of the Mainland towards overseas Chinese gained momentum after 1978. Among the many developments that profoundly changed the conditions for the overseas Chinese work of the Taibei government in the 1980s, three merit special attention.

First, the Mainland gradually began to represent Chinese cultural authenticity and gained increasing international respect. We have already seen how overseas Chinese were actively attracted by the overseas Chinese policy of the Mainland. Taiwan's claim to represent the unspoilt Chinese tradition was undermined.

Second, the relation between the Mainland and Taiwan changed fundamentally in a short span of years. From outright hostilities and an acrimonious propaganda war, the two sides were drawn into closer cooperation. The opening of business opportunities in the Mainland attracted Taiwanese businesses, for Taiwan's economy experienced a transition from a low-technology manufacturing boom in the 1960s and 1970s to an economy based on a mixture of services and high technology. Relocation of industries to other parts of the Asia Pacific region took place, but the cheap labour markets and easily accessible structures for investment in the Mainland proved very attractive. Taiwanese businesses first began investing in the Mainland through indirect channels, flouting prohibition by their government, and by 1988 the ban on investment was lifted. Tourist travel by Taiwanese to the Mainland was allowed in 1986, although it had to pass through third countries or territories. The climate became favourable for non-official contacts, which were stimulated. Where overseas Chinese leaning to either side formerly had been encouraged to oppose each other, they were now in a position to forge friendships and engage in personal contacts.

Third, Taiwan's internal situation changed. The greater affluence that came with Taiwan's status as a 'newly industrialised country', and the democratisation process that began in the mid-1980s, strongly affected Taiwan's claim to represent all China. Although the façade of the Republic of China was upheld, it was clear that the political preoccupation in Taiwan was with the issues on the island itself. Issues of governance became centred on the livelihood of people in Taiwan. The Constitutional changes in the 1980s and 1990s did away with the administrative layer of Taiwan Province (retaining it in name and as an office of no significance), letting the Republic of China government be directly in charge of the province; as a consequence, politics became 'Taiwanised'. The rise of the Taiwanese computer industry in the 1990s created a need for direct government support on the international scene. Through Taiwanese representative offices and trade councils across the world, Taiwanese businessmen gained access to the world market; as their contribution to Taiwan's economy was significant, the Taiwanese traders operating abroad achieved much more attention than the overseas Chinese who had for decades sided with Taibei. This created strong tensions in the overseas Chinese groups inclined towards Taiwan. The trusted old guard felt pushed aside, and younger, Taiwan-born, higher educated and often better-off professionals and traders emerged.

Taibei's overseas Chinese affairs authorities use salaried posts of 'Secretary of Overseas Chinese Affairs' (qiaowu zhuanyuan) to employ overseas Chinese to co-ordinate regional activities. These secretaries are employed in the Taibei representative offices as civil servants (on contracts that limit their careers to the overseas Chinese affairs function). These functions are entrusted to overseas Chinese of considerable standing and as there are, to our knowledge, concurrently only one or two functions like these for Europe, they are coveted and regarded as important markers of social and political achievement.

Other posts to which the Taibei government appoints overseas Chinese include 'Commissioner of the Overseas Chinese Affairs Commission' (Qiaowu Weiyuanhui weiyuan), 'Consultant of the Overseas Chinese Affairs Commission' (Qiaowu guwen), 'Advancement Member of the Overseas Chinese Affairs Commission' (Qiaowu Cujin weiyuan) and so on. These are all, in reality, honorary posts. However, the commissioners have effected some policy changes and air their views on issues relating to the duration of the validity of ROC passports, excessive and intimidating customs controls directed at overseas Chinese returning, or problems relating to young overseas Chinese males returning on visits to Taiwan being drafted for national service (008//169; 008//177). In 1995, 15 posts as Commissioner in the 180-strong Overseas Chinese Affairs Commission were reserved for European overseas Chinese. The Nationalist Party also had posts aimed at including overseas Chinese. However, probably the most important aspect was the provision in the Republic of China Constitution that overseas Chinese are represented in the Legislative Yuan (parliament). The principle was retained during the constitutional reforms of the late 1980s and the 1990s. In the present model, the overseas Chinese legislators are elected from ranked lists of candidates nominated by the political parties; their seats are distributed in proportion to the votes won by the parties in the elections; due to the way the elections are conducted, there is no fixed proportion of seats for the overseas Chinese in Europe.

The institutional links between the overseas Chinese and the 'home base' in Taiwan are significant. They create focal points for the ambitions of some people, and imply official recognition and status. Due to the continuity of Taibei's relations with overseas Chinese throughout the 1950s, 1960s and 1970s and the fact that the Republic of China recognises dual citizenship, the distinction between overseas Chinese holding ROC passports and Chinese living permanently in Taiwan is not as sharp as the distinction between the various categories of overseas Chinese and Chinese living in the Mainland. Where the Mainland created a separate category of citizens called 'returned overseas Chinese', there is no formal distinction between an ROC citizen who has returned from an existence as overseas Chinese and somebody who has always lived permanently in Taiwan.

However, the rise of the new Taiwanese industrialists and traders with their global economic interests has driven a wedge into this system. The Taiwanese traders (Taishang) or 'new overseas Chinese' (xinqiao) have come to stand in some opposition to 'Chinese traders' (huashang) or 'old overseas Chinese' (laoqiao). Given their influence and prowess they are able to gain access to many of the functions previously held by 'old overseas Chinese'. They are more in tune with lifestyles in Taiwan and have direct access to social and political resources there, while 'old overseas Chinese' feel less catered for by the authorities. A 'new overseas Chinese' made the point in this way:

> Due to the difference [between people], everybody must try to get on with each other, not exclude each other, and it's important to avoid other clashes. The

problem isn't with the Taiwanese traders, but with the old overseas Chinese, they're dissatisfied with the Taiwanese traders because they think they've been too much in the limelight recently. Government bodies give them active support, participate in their activities ... Those old overseas Chinese think, before there weren't any Taiwanese traders organisations, you people from the Overseas Chinese Affairs Commission came to us, only supported us. Now there are Taiwanese traders, they think they've been ditched.

(017//020).

This 'new' overseas Chinese who had already been in Germany for more than ten years no longer perceived the distinction as sharply as before. He had social contacts among and went to meetings and conferences arranged by 'old' overseas Chinese. However,

if I go to your conference and the Taiwanese traders find out, they're not happy about it. So this year (1996) our Taiwanese trader organisation has decided to hold its congress – originally it was always held together with the Annual Meeting of Overseas Chinese in Europe, everybody getting together, you see – we have decided to hold it separately.

(017//021).

The Overseas Chinese Affairs Commission contributes funds to the Taiwanese traders, and the Taiwanese traders deliberately sever their links with the 'old' overseas Chinese. This causes tensions. The priorities of policy-making in Taibei created a problem of loyalty: 'When XXX convenes a meeting, YYY is not keen to participate' (017//056), where both were long-standing supporters of the Nationalist Party. The younger of the two, XXX, based his career on providing financial advice and political contacts for the Taiwanese traders (and operated with great political acumen in this function). Conversely, YYY had taken a Chinese law degree before 1949 and worked in government departments in China and Hong Kong before migrating to Britain. In Britain he worked first in restaurants doing odd jobs and later as a bank manager, and became deeply involved in Chinatown affairs as a community leader. YYY was for decades a major pillar among the Taiwan-leaning overseas Chinese in Britain until the early 1990s, after which XXX gained influence through his instrumental role in realising large Taiwanese investment projects in Britain. Even slight changes of policy emphasis exacerbate personal rivalries of this sort.

The split down the middle of the Taiwan-leaning community has to do with the greater focus on Taiwan itself and the identity of its own people. However, several of our interviewees went to great lengths to emphasise that Taiwanese traders were not exclusively Hokkien-speaking, Taiwan-born and -raised, and so on. They did not represent a political trend or sub-ethnic roots, but simply pursued shared economic interests that happened to coincide with the trade interests of Taiwan.

With the presidential elections in March 2000 ending in the victory of Chen Shuibian, the 'old' overseas Chinese in particular tended to find that the momentum

went against them. Their allegiance had been to the Republic of China as represented by the Nationalist Party, and in many cases had no or little affinity with
Taiwan as a place. The fact that the Nationalist Party lost a major election and
entered a deep internal crisis, while a leading member of the Democratic Progress
Party became president, was in itself a blow to the perception of the Republic as
coterminous with Nationalism and Chinese identity. Chen was seen as hostile to
overseas Chinese, having argued for dismantling the Overseas Chinese Affairs
Commission that pumped taxpayers' money out of the country without any good
reason. Although his victory led Chen to moderate his views on this, he had earned
much distrust among overseas Chinese. In the event, the Commission was maintained, and strong reassuring messages were sent out to the overseas Chinese. Of
course, the Taibei authorities could not afford to lose the support of the overseas
Chinese, who had been an essential part in the citizens' diplomacy (guomin waijiao).
These people had, generally speaking, lived in their countries of residence longer
than any of the Taiwan traders, and they represented the form of dual patriotic
allegiance to the 'host' and the 'home' countries that the traders could not. Being
seen as 'ordinary', hard-working people, they had people's sympathy, where the
image of the traders was that of slick businessmen.

While much of the division among the Taiwan-leaning overseas Chinese without
doubt reflects the dynamics of change in Taiwan, the Mainland government did
not fail to use the opportunity of widening such divisions. On 18 May 2001, the
Central News Agency in Taibei issued a telegram,[13] 'exposing' the Chinese Communist Party's effort to sow discord among overseas Chinese by spreading slogans
about 'opposing the proponents of [Taiwan's] independence and to support the
proponents of unification'. This news telegram was part of a well-orchestrated
attempt by Chen Shuibian to rally support among the overseas Chinese. He had
originally been regarded as a proponent of Taiwanese independence, but had
softened his stance before he was elected president, and so had to reassure the
overseas Chinese that he was on the side of the one-China principle. Chen Shuibian's presence at the 'Third Overseas Chinese Affairs Conference' in May 2001
aimed at eradicating the doubt that overseas Chinese had voiced about his stance
on 'unification' or 'independence'. His strategy was to point at the Mainland as
the source of the campaign against him, and to associate the doubt with the
Mainland's propaganda. His stance was that 'unless the Mainland makes a military
attack on China, he would not in his incumbency declare independence, change
the name of the republic or establish the two-country principle in the Constitution,
(*Ouzhou Shibao – Nouvelles d'Europe*, 19.05.2000, 10). Chen's effort to address meetings
with many overseas Chinese delegates personally and explain his change of stance
on overseas Chinese affairs publicly demonstrated how the cross-Straits issue is
deeply intertwined with overseas Chinese affairs policy.

Patriotism, nationalism and ethnic identity

Patriotism (aiguozhuyi), as we have seen it above, is highly politicised, interwoven
with the political legitimacy of governments and a core factor in the construction

of Chinese identity. The issue is complex, for should overseas Chinese simply accept being subject to 'home' governments' political impositions?

One of our interviewees reflected on this issue by claiming that the overseas Chinese in the world existed in their own right, had their own history, and that they in the future would constitute an integral unity, a network of their own. He felt that the Chinese authorities in the Mainland pursued their own separate interests; there was no question, he said, that 'we are all patriotic'. However, since the events of 4 June 1989, some 'extremists' have come out from China,

> cursing, cursing the Chinese Communist Party, cursing the fatherland. Abroad, you should protect your own, your own family, your own father and mother, a small family is a father and mother and their children, the big family is the 1.3 billion Chinese. When the country is blessed with fair weather and prospers, then all's well ... But these people, making such a fuss abroad, cursing their own fatherland all day, or even relying on the Nationalist Party, we think these people are ignorant.
>
> (047//258)

Political dependence on authorities in the Mainland promoting patriotism to boost their own interests clashes with feelings of national solidarity in the face of unfavourable publicity about the Mainland. The interviewee believes that Chinese 'extremists' criticising China abroad are immoral and 'ignorant'. The claim that they receive money and other support from the Nationalist Party (in Taiwan) proves their immorality. The interviewee does not see these people as sons and daughters of the Chinese nation who have been wronged, for their behaviour is in his perception wrong. It is also interesting to observe this interviewee's ambivalence when it comes to Taiwan, for in many other contexts he actively promotes dialogue and makes many positive formulations on how Taiwan is a part of China. Yet seeking the support of the authorities in Taiwan, Mainland protesters are morally wrong.

The patriotic affiliation with the Chinese state (in either guise) is not a constraint on inclusive nationalist identification of Mainlanders and Taiwanese. This ethnic nationalism goes beyond the political; it cannot ignore the political constraints, but it is seen as an inconvenient aspect of being Chinese. Living with this unfortunate schism is part of being a good ethnic nationalist. Using the political schism for the pursuit of separate interest or 'creating a fuss abroad', conversely, is immoral.[14]

Overseas Chinese on both sides of the divide seek confirmation and status through their relationship with the official systems in the Mainland and in Taiwan, but at the same time, they emphasise a fundamental moral cause of China's ethnic unity, and their ethnic relationship with other Chinese. They regard this as a consistent way of expressing their ethnicity.

> The two sides of the Strait are presently [1996] moving fast, many people from Taiwan are visiting the Mainland and investing there. However, overseas Chinese community associations are always closer either to the Mainland or to Taiwan; this isn't peculiar, why? You must see where the members come

from. We, for example, all come from the Mainland, we don't know Taiwan, we don't understand it, [we haven't got] the sentiments for the soil of the homeland [there], we don't have the feeling that we'll go there. We've only got this feeling for the soil of the homeland in Zhejiang, in our southeastern coastal region, that's only natural. Those people from Taiwan, their sentiments are in Taiwan. However, being abroad, it ought to be like this, everybody ought to abandon this political element and then realise that we have many common interests in our countries of residence, that we must unite, based on those common interests. Our community association, doesn't involve itself in any other politics, only patriotism. That's the first point. The second is, for the sake of patriotism, we promote unity, we do not hope that China splits. Division would neither be to our benefit, nor to China's or the Chinese nation's. We hope for unity across the Strait.

(048//079)

This pattern was present throughout the interviews. Overseas Chinese community leaders applied a complex moral standard to the issue of the nation. Patriotism involves political links with governments that provide status and recognition to the leaders of overseas Chinese; these links are morally validated by the adherence to the idea of Chinese national unity. Solidarity with other Chinese from either side of the divide is an essential part of this moral model. The existing difference between the two is construed simply to be an expression of localism or sub-ethnic affiliations.

Sub-ethnic affiliations do not properly explain the Mainland–Taiwan division among overseas Chinese associations (for many people originating in the Mainland lean towards the Nationalist Party), and the official links with government departments in the two places must be regarded as a major dividing factor, for overseas Chinese seeking promotion from one government are not likely to be actively recognised by the other government. More important is the relative disarray among the overseas Chinese leaning towards Taiwan. The issue of 'old' and 'new' overseas Chinese has grown more important, while assurances from Taiwan's leadership under Chen Shuibian have not been sufficient to allay fears of a 'two-China policy'.

7 Chinese business, ethnic business

Chinese immigrant communities seem to establish themselves in economic niches that symbolise Chinese ethnicity. The niches change over time, and differ locally due to various national regulations and global trends. The continued immigration of new groups not only keeps the niches alive, but also transforms them. Not all overseas Chinese are active in the niches; some earn their living within the mainstream economy. Earlier and later migrants tend to have different functions in the niches, and second- and third-generation are less likely than first-generation overseas Chinese to be active within Chinese economic niches.

The changing nature of the Chinese economic niches is well illustrated by the fate of the overseas Chinese laundry business. During the first 50 years of the twentieth century the laundry business was probably the most important Chinese economic niche in main European Chinatowns. But 50 years later, a laundry owned or managed by a Chinese was not considered a Chinese ethnic business.

The laundry business was, after the Second World War gradually replaced by the restaurant and fast food niches in Western Europe. Other important Chinese niches in Europe are production, wholesale and retail of Chinese groceries (in most parts of Europe), leather ware and clothing manufacture (mainly in Italy), and import-export business (in most parts of Europe, but on a particularly large scale in Hungary and France). In addition, ancillary services to the catering sector like furnishing and decoration; services to the Chinese community like herbal medicine, gambling, travel agencies, accounting and legal services, as well as haircutting; and services to inward investment projects from the Chinese Mainland, Taiwan and Hong Kong have emerged in response to demand.[1]

This changeability of the Chinese economic niches contrasts with the idea that they reflect an immutable Chinese cultural tradition or innate ethnic traits of the Chinese. One may explore their political and economic determinants, and how the Chinese who participate in their activities perceive them. The Chinese economic niches, however, are not mere functions of economic conjunctures. They exist in their own right, by virtue of how their participants act within them and how society and political forces interact with them. The niches do not reflect the primordial ethnic destiny of their participants; on the contrary, the ethnic Chinese collectively create their economic niches to pursue their own political and economic interests within the frameworks provided by their economic environment.

Chinese economic niches have been defined as 'connections and regular patterns of interaction among people sharing common national background or migration experiences'.[2] This definition is useful because it accurately delimits the scope of inquiry. The ideas implied in this formulation, namely (a) that niches are mainly constituted in terms of the interaction among co-natives; and (b) that 'common national background' is an uncomplicated given, however, imply that internal dynamics within the niches (rather than their interaction with external conditions and forces) constitute the main causality behind them, and that it is possible to infer people's behaviour from their national background *per se* (rather than from their social and economic roles).

How do overseas Chinese perceive their economic niches? Which political and economic dynamics created them? Immigration, market forces and the choices of the individual are at the centre of this exploration.

One case may illustrate the interaction of the individual and the market forces. In the early 1990s, a restaurateur with over 20 years of experience running Chinese restaurants opened an Italian restaurant in the heart of Copenhagen with an all-Chinese staff (including the cooks) and a run-of-the-mill Italian menu (–/010/044...054). As an experienced entrepreneur in the ethnic business sector, he calculated the market demand for an Italian to be higher than for a Chinese restaurant in the particular location. By which standards may he be regarded as a Chinese entrepreneur? Does his restaurant belong to the overseas Chinese niche economy? Is he as a Chinese predetermined to enter the ethnic catering sector, even if the food he serves is Italian? These questions boil down to the issue of the ethnic nature of the ethnic niche.[3]

Culture: a gloss on reality?

Overseas Chinese often emphasise that Chinese culture shapes their economic niches. The Chinese, in their view, have an ethic of hard work, self-reliance and mutual help.

Many of the interviewees referred to Chinese money clubs as typical examples of mutual help. These private credit arrangements are considered by overseas Chinese to be an exclusively Chinese tradition (043//108; 001:9). In immigrant communities it is always an issue how one can obtain loans. The failure of financial institutions of the 'host' society to provide credit to immigrants (for example due to prejudice, or their lack of collateral) forces them to enter into private loan arrangements. Usury and reliance on loan sharks create so much instability that they can normally not satisfy the need for business capital. Mutual reliance among relatives, co-villagers or friends on pooling resources provides an alternative. The Chinese money club (in Chinese biaohui, yuehui, yuelanhui, or simply hui) normally consists of several dozen members, each of whom commits an amount to a pool of money. The member who pledges to pay the highest interest is allowed to borrow the pool without collateral, normally for investment purposes.

The case of the money club is indicative of how overseas Chinese invent lore of unique Chinese values. The money club arrangement is a primitive economic institution, widely known in villages and immigrant communities in all parts of the world. The risk is lowered by limiting membership to friends, relatives, people who originate in the same village, or the fellows of a secret society. The function is to provide credit where it is not readily available from regular financial institutions, and to protect the members from the negative effects of usury and pawnbroking. The terminology of ethnic virtues of mutual help and mutual trust forms a collective rationalisation of the money club phenomenon. From the perspective of the participants, it is confined to the group itself and is experienced by the participants as something shared by those who have the same background, as something that can only be explained by their common cultural background. It is perhaps, as Benton and Gomez (2001) remind us, useful to note that the money club is *not* used where other sources of investment capital are available (like in the case of New Territory immigrants in Britain).

Interviewees also use cultural uniqueness to explain why the Chinese work in specific occupations. For example, the catering niche embodies 'Chinese culinary culture' (yinshi wenhua). Overseas Chinese who 'couldn't even fry an egg when they were in China' entered the Chinese restaurant business when they arrived in Europe because that was their ethnic destiny (025//138).

The invention of Chinese cultural qualities to account for the life of Chinese immigrant communities takes many forms, but can be summarised as follows: Confucianism and Chinese culture or tradition in a broader sense merge in an ethic of hard work, frugality, efficiency, flexibility, adaptability and pragmatism needed in the Chinese economic niches.

Overseas Chinese in Europe make a distinction between the Chinese economy (Huaren jingji) as opposed the 'local' (dangdi) or 'mainstream' (zhuliu) economy. General concepts of overseas Chinese economy are built around one or several economic niches that stand in a vague contrast to the 'mainstream'. The Chinese economy reflects the cultural uniqueness of the Chinese. A French overseas Chinese says:

> We Chinese all have this assiduous and indefatigable spirit. When we leave China we have no economic support. For example, when I came here, I had nobody to support me. I had to fight for myself, gradually, through unremitting work. Afterwards, all my friends were fine and helped me a bit, and we traded on our own and set up a restaurant. That's how I started ... and set up restaurants. One restaurant has been running for 26 years now.
>
> (041//073)

Another overseas Chinese, who migrated to France from Southeast Asia where his family had lived for several generations, claims that Chinese virtues of untiring toil are universal and account for the ubiquity of overseas Chinese:

> When we overseas Chinese go to foreign places, no matter where, we can always make a living. If there's only some smoke [from a chimney], we Chinese

will be there. We are hardworking and industrious, so if we go to China or back to Southeast Asia, our feelings will be just as deep.

(043//076)

He also ascribes the rapid development of Paris' Chinatown to the 'spirit of mutual love' (hu'ai jingshen) among the overseas Chinese and their assiduous work spirit (043//113).

On the whole, however, the interviewees tend to use culture as a superficial gloss on the economic reality. A British Chinese interviewee regards catering as 'a tradition of Chinese culture', but he thinks that the most important reason why many began to work in the restaurants was that they found odd jobs there on arrival and thus gained work experience within this low-skills sector (001//002).

An overseas Chinese in the Netherlands is ambivalent in his perception of the catering niche. He sees it as rooted in Chinese culture, but discusses it pragmatically in terms of business options and strategies for the community. It is even a burden that can be disposed of:

> The Chinese economy in the Netherlands has a niche, it is the restaurant business. This is our vantage ground, but also a drawback. The advantage is that in the restaurant business investment is small and the returns come fast, it is part our Chinese culture, the food culture, and the older generation of overseas Chinese has prepared the basis for us … The drawback is that it is small-scale trade; ultimately, the (Chinese) restaurant business in the Netherlands is a small enterprise. There are some large restaurants now, but there isn't a climate for them, so the overseas Chinese associations see it as their aim to help the restaurant business thrive, so that the (Chinese) economy may eventually leave the restaurant business and enter local society.

(025//138)

The next generation Chinese, according to this interviewee, are not likely to enter the catering niche but will join sectors where they are in real competition with non-Chinese. He favours a strategy of using the success of the catering niche to become part of mainstream Dutch economy (025//139).

Although the interviews abound in expressions of cultural uniqueness like the ones cited above, it is striking how few form a coherent view of Chinese business. The question is whether cultural uniqueness determines Chinese business structures or whether they serve to explain away the hard conditions and darker sides of immigrant economic activities, which are marginalised by mainstream society.

Immigrant community: economic constraints

Handicraft niches in Italy

An interviewee (051//002…005) relates how Italian women immediately after the defeat in the Second World War were keen to marry Chinese men because they were citizens of a victorious allied nation and so had privileged access to resources and opportunities. In Italy's poor economic climate that lasted until well into the 1960s, a handful of such mixed couples, like many other people in Italy, survived in labour-intensive handicrafts, for example manufacturing leather belts, purses, wallets, jackets, and other leather products. The interviewee regarded the activity of these Chinese–Italian couples as a precursor of the later rise in the overseas Chinese presence in the handicraft sector.

This small-scale handicraft sector relied on the self-exploitation of the owner-operators and their families. The sector declined in the 1980s, as incomes became increasingly uncompetitive with labour market salaries. Yet the sector was an ideal breeding ground for chain migration.

New Chinese immigrants, whether 'legal' or 'illegal', were easily accommodated as workers. Poorly educated and mainly from southern Zhejiang's countryside, they fitted into the low-skill leather handicraft sector and, even at remuneration and living conditions far below the normal Italian level, they experienced a distinct improvement above village life.

A treaty between Italy and China signed in January 1985 on the mutual protection of the citizens of the other state, their investments and other economic interests, created the basis for an expanded immigration of Chinese (Carchedi 1994, 50). Several amnesties (in 1987, in 1990 and later in the 1990s),[4] and various changes in immigration law (Carchedi 1994, 49–50) consolidated the small handicraft workshops' role as channels for chain migration. The number of Chinese-owned began to outnumber Italian-owned leatherware enterprises in the early 1990s (on the situation in Campi Bisenzio, see Bortolotti 1993).

Most of the Chinese enterprises in Tuscany seem to be registered and work above board (unlike the Chinese sweatshops in, for example, France). However, 'most of the fiscal obligations and labour protection legislations are still ignored, and the overlap of kinship and economic ties favour the emergence of informal labour practices' (Tomba 1999, 291).

This growth reflected the increasing migration and the need to employ new Chinese immigrants. Immigrants needed employment not only in order to earn a living, but also in order to be eligible for an amnesty; if they could prove *de facto* employment, they were more likely to have their residence status legalised. Although the Chinese in Italy locally dominate the leather sector, one may ask whether they are a 'Chinese niche' or a 'Chinese economic system'. The enterprises are highly specialised, have a small scale, only require low levels of investment and technology, and their existence is contingent on a system of supply enterprises producing fittings and accessories, of which many are Italian-owned. The rent from the workshops is also a source of income for Italian owners. One may speculate by which standards the Chinese workshops in Tuscany can be considered an 'ethnic business'. I do not think that any specific criterion suffices; they form an ethnic business because they are based on migration and reflect a combination of factors typical of an immigrant community that operates outside the 'mainstream' economy. In this respect Tomba's comparison of an immigrant Wenzhou community in Beijing with the one in Tuscany is highly illuminating (Tomba 1999).

The growth of the leather niche in the 1980s and 1990s was a function of the immigration laws that provide a ready availability of workers, flexible work hours and other work conditions, as well as low salaries, and also ensure the workers' almost total dependency on their bosses.

From the mid-1980s the trickle of Chinese immigrants to Italy began to grow into a steady flow. The immigrants had few options in the labour market. With few skills, lack of language proficiency in Italian, and in many cases obscure immigration status, they were largely excluded from employment in Italian firms and institutions. Many of the immigrants entered the large street vending circuit in Italy, which provides the wherewithal for thousands of African and Asian immigrants, selling electronic gadgets, leather belts, toys, cigarette lighters and other gimcrackery at tourist spots.

Relatives and co-natives in the restaurant, leather and clothes-making sectors could accommodate new hands; the employment of immigrants in these sectors was governed by the large, continuous supply of more immigrants and the need to press costs in production structures that had become uneconomical if measured by normal wage levels and demands for investments in work safety and environmental protection. The absence of wage competition with the rest of the economy (due to the fact that the Chinese workers were largely unemployable in mainstream enterprises), one can imagine, exacerbated the downwards pressures on pay and conditions.

The ability of Chinese entrepreneurs within this sector to expand suddenly, accounts for the rapid growth in number and size of leather and clothes-making enterprises (be they officially registered or not) at the beginning of the 1990s. Italian immigration law began to distinguish between independent labourers (lavoro autonomo) on the one hand and on the other dependent workers (lavoro subordinato) and family reunion, study, and so on. The residence status, once given, was almost impossible to change; only 'independents' were allowed to register enterprises. The effect was that one of the few ways in which first-generation immigrants are normally able to survive once their residence status is legalised did not apply in Italy: a couple of years of hard labour in a co-native's enterprise often provides experience and starting capital for one's own enterprise in the same branch. The lack of this opportunity in Italy during most of the 1990s made the immigrants highly dependent on their employers and helped isolate the sector from the mainstream economy.

The political economy created by immigration rules and historical circumstance may be formulated in terms of innate Chinese traits such as 'assiduous spirit', 'ability to work hard and to adapt', 'diligence', 'frugality', 'family bonds', 'mutual trust among co-natives' and so on. This is what many of our interviewees did. But such terms embellish the reality that the immigrants were excluded from the main labour market and worked under conditions very different from the rest of the Italian economy.

The ambivalence of the cultural interpretation shows in many interviews. One example:

> But in reality the Chinese have few difficulties. Because the Chinese have a very good habit, the several-thousand-years-old heritage of Confucian thinking,

even with so many immigrants, illegal immigrants coming in, there is not one who has begged for food, not one hustling in the streets. A Chinese is assiduous, you only need the faintest work opportunity, no matter how hard, no matter how poorly paid, and he does not want to beg for food. The Chinese coming here are relatives, tied by old bonds, kinsfolk summoned by kinsfolk, friends summoned by friends. On arrival, his food and accommodation are taken care of. It does not matter whether he eats well or not or stays in a good or poor place, the most basic is cared for. It's not like those people who come from the third world, who go to the municipal government, demanding housing and work. They say 'you Chinese give us the least trouble because you solve your own problems.' …This is a good side of the Chinese, as a Chinese you can't allow (another Chinese) to go hungry. 'Haven't you eaten yet?' No problem. But few foreigners are like that.

(051//046)

Chain migration, of course, means that migrants know each other or are obliged by convention to look after each other. The Chinese therefore consider 'solving their own problems' an extension of hospitality and friendliness. In Italian society, their labour market practices stand out as unsocial and exploitative, as a grey or black economy. Overseas Chinese regard the conflicting perception simply as a lack of understanding:

Our factories are in the basements of the houses they sleep in, so in the evenings we—, because there are many who immigrated illegally and spent a lot of money and want to earn it back here in Italy, when they want to earn money, the work day is sixteen hours, they are always very hard working. So the Italians turn this issue into—, they don't understand us Chinese, they even suspect that we are keeping slaves in this society, or that overseas Chinese are taking advantage of the Chinese. But we Chinese understand ourselves, whenever we go abroad, we are hard working, we all enjoy working for our (own upkeep), to gradually make our own fortune. … In '90 Italy had a large amnesty, in '87 it had a small one that incited many of our immigrants to come over. When they had arrived, they caused many social problems, so the Italians began organising demonstrations, protesting specifically again the problems the Chinese had created for them.

(053//004)

The overseas Chinese in Italy do not use the cultural language to sweep the issue of illegal immigration under the carpet (several interviewees talked bluntly about it), but it enables them to put words on a difficult situation, in which the individual has little choice. The hard toil and miserable conditions of the new immigrants now does not differ much from the situation that applied for earlier groups of immigrants. Earlier migrants (for example in the 1930s or the 1950s) were themselves able to gain a foothold through kindness and help from other Chinese. This does generate a basic empathy and urge to help, especially in an environment where it is impossible or deemed inadvisable to hand the social obligation on to the authorities. Feeding and accommodating illegal immigrants without asking compensation in the form of labour is in most cases harmful to one's own financial health, and so is employing people at 'fair' market rates in labour-intensive and low-skill sectors already on the decline and only surviving due to self-exploitation. Where the authorities, like in Italy, provoke further immigration (through large-scale amnesties), condone grey and black labour markets (see Segre 1991), and only intervene in the most extreme cases, the flow of new immigrants continues and so does the pressure on overseas Chinese entrepreneurs to accommodate them. It is understandable that overseas Chinese interpret this deplorable situation as 'mutual aid', 'assiduousness' and moral duty inherited from Chinese – or Confucian – tradition.

The influx of new migrants was furthered by 'snakeheads' (shetou) that arrange irregular immigration. The Zhou Yiping case (see Chapter 2) exemplifies the mechanisms at work. The fact that Zhou Yiping provided Chinese citizens with false Italian visas and other papers was only the extreme end of a broad spectrum of immigration practices, ranging from legal to illegal. Irregularity was not the result of migration, it was a cause and vehicle for it. The immigration from China was caused by the existence of a sector within the economy that gained from an abundant supply of cheap labour and by the 'pull' of a marginally better, albeit illegal or 'irregular', situation for the migrants.

The 'ethnic' labour market in France

The idea that Chinese ethnic businesses form a separate sector of the economy can be based in an examination of to what degree it employs 'its own' people, how much it trades with 'its own', how much it is directed towards trade with the 'home' country, and how much it relies on services (e.g. finance, maintenance, furnishing) from 'its own' people. If a large part of the 'ethnic' population works in 'ethnic' sector enterprises, one probably can argue that ethnic business is a prominent phenomenon. However, there is no way to measure these aspects due to the lack of satisfactory definitions and statistics. As we saw in the case of enterprises in Italy, they do exist in some autonomy from the mainstream system, at least in terms of their labour recruitment. But this autonomy is fragile, and the ethnic enterprises involved are critically dependent on market demand and immigration and welfare policy.

In France, the situation is more complex than in Italy because the overseas Chinese communities are much more composite. The main difference is in the mixture of Chinese descendants from Southeast Asia and Chinese from Zhejiang province. The ethnic labour market in France is characterised by the meshing of legal and illegal labourers in the leather, clothing and catering sectors. Like in Italy, the ethnic character is strengthened by illegality in part of the labour market, where wages are poor and work conditions dangerous. It is very difficult to draw a line between legal and illegal forms of labour management, as some workshops are run like family businesses in an informal way, and it is hard to distinguish between work space and living quarters (Ma Mung 1991).

The illegality of some labour activities surfaces every so often when a special branch of the police busts illegal Chinese workshops, like in May 1996 the arrest of 32 persons mainly of Zhejiang origin involved in running illegal workshops on all six floors in a house in the 12th arrondissement (*Le Monde* 18.05.1996, p. 9), or in May 1997 the arrest of 17 illegal Chinese workers in two workshops in the 3rd arrondissement producing leather handbags (*Le Monde* 07.05.1997, p. 11). Although the activities are organised along ethnic lines (Ma Mung, 1991), they can hardly be an ethnic issue limited to the Chinese. In France, a number of immigrant groups are considered to operate a large number of workshops illegally, including people of Turkish, Sri Lankan, Indian, Pakistani and Chinese origin (*Le Monde* 16.10.1996, p. 9). These workshops operate underground, in some cases with a registered firm as a façade, as a system of out-contracting to people who work at home, or avoiding long-term occupation of the same buildings. They produce clothing and leather goods for the mainstream market at low prices. Most women's fashion products in France are said to come from such sweatshop factories (*Le Monde* 16.10.1996, p. 9).

The availability of cheap workers who are willing to slog away 15 hours a day, seven days a week for between 450 and 600 euros a month and the greed of large fashion houses that subcontract their production to sweatshop factories through intermediaries combine to create a huge incentive for the entrepreneurs, whose profit greatly exceeds the risk of being caught and punished (*Le Monde* 16.10.1996, p. 9). The main difference from Italy is that the Italian authorities *de facto* condone illegal enterprises, while the French authorities adopt a harder line, clamping down on the sector.

The importance of clandestine labour in the Chinese ethnic labour market is most conspicuous in Italy and Spain, both countries which in spite of considerable domestic unemployment condone or even encourage the use of irregular labour resources in order to squeeze production costs. Zhang Jialin in an article in *Ouzhou Shibao – Nouvelles d'Europe* (10.02.1999, p. 5) bluntly states:

Compared with Spanish enterprises in the same sectors, the price of our commodities of the same quality only reaches 30 per cent of theirs. Only through the use of black labour, selling of smuggled goods, tax avoidance and tax evasion is it possible to achieve a meagre profit. This situation implies an enormous catastrophe for the overseas Chinese economy.

The ethnic labour market is a function of market demand and of the degree to which immigration and labour policies are implemented. To ignore this and to reduce this tragic state of affairs to Chinese culture, Confucian virtues or co-native compassion is unacceptable. But it is understandable that those who are most directly affected by the issues of black labour, illegal immigration and misery do use these stereotypes euphemistically to protect themselves from vilification.

Catering as an immigrant sector

The largest part of the Chinese economic niche is the catering sector. In the pre-war period Chinese restaurants were mainly diners for the all-male Chinese population. Very few had a non-Chinese clientele:

> Early on, forty or fifty years ago, the English didn't eat Chinese food, they scorned Chinatown and wouldn't know anything of it. After the Second World War the Americans who had been fighting in China against Japan came here; these soldiers carried along a taste for Chinese food, and introduced it to other people.
>
> (062:33)

> There were only one, two or perhaps three Chinese restaurants, in early times, at the time of the Anti-Japanese War (1937–1945), serving some Chinese–Western hotchpotch, like sausages, fried eggs, or meat-and-eggs, that sort of thing, calling it Chinese food. In reality it was chop-suey; there was no such thing as Cantonese style food then. After the War some people began to think, since our Chinese food is so famous, why don't we develop restaurants, so around 1950, there was one ... in Manchester.
>
> (061:114)

After the Second World War, the sector grew into a large sector serving a mainly non-Chinese public. Chinese restaurants in Europe have developed very differently in different countries. In the western parts of Europe the American taste for Chinese and other exotic foods in the post-war period was an important inspiration; post-war Europe followed American fashions closely, and Chinese were quick to respond to the demand in all parts west of the iron curtain.

In the beginning Chinese restaurants were rare and metropolitan. Post-colonial repatriation of Dutch citizens and former colonial civil servants in the late 1940s created a demand for the culinary fusion of Malay and Chinese food that the Dutch call 'Chineesch-Indisch'. Chinese cooks in Dutch Chinatowns took up the challenge, adapting their cooking to the palates of the Dutch customers.

Improving living standards in the 1960s and the huge immigration from Hong Kong to Britain started an explosive development of Chinese restaurants catering for the middle class. The steady flow of migrants both generated more customers for Chinese cuisine and created a demand for employment. Until the late 1950s, laundries had been the main business of the Chinese in Britain, but they could not absorb the large numbers of new immigrants:

> If you are in the laundry business, you'll need two or three people at most. You couldn't accommodate all the people who came, so gradually they went into the catering business
>
> (061:120)

The immigration rules that entitled people with a labour voucher to migrate were probably the strongest force behind the development of Chinese restaurants in Britain. Investment in the restaurant sector was easy, and immediately gave access to employing people directly from the New Territories.

In the rest of Europe the Chinese restaurant sector remained exclusive and small until the 1970s. In Spain, Germany, Italy, Denmark, Belgium and so on, some restaurants opened in large cities. Their development was impeded by lack of workers. The establishment in the 1970s of a pan-European labour market, and Britain's accession to the European Economic Community in 1973 changed this. The catering labour market in Britain was saturated with immigrants from the New Territories in Hong Kong, and workers fanned out over northern Europe, most of them holders of British passports. Also Dutch Chinatowns began to export Chinese cooks and waiters to Germany and Belgium. The restaurant business in these countries, however, remained more upmarket than in Britain.

The French situation was influenced by the arrival of overseas Chinese from French Indochina in the 1970s. There had been Chinese restaurants in France from the 1920s, but from the end of the 1970s, the sector grew, mainly because the Chinese immigrants from Laos, Cambodia and Vietnam formed a large new market:

> Chinese want to eat Chinese food, so this type of Chinese restaurant began to appear and the (13th) arrondissement (in Paris) became a bustling place. Originally it was a poor area, now it has become an upper middle-class area. The Chinese economy played an important role in this process.
>
> (106:25)

According to Emmanuel Ma Mung (1993), the number of Chinese restaurants in central Paris was 645 in 1985 and had grown to 863 three years later; by the early 1990s they comprised one-sixth of all restaurants in Paris.

The growth of the restaurant sector followed a pattern of local saturation followed by geographical dispersion, different in each country. In Britain for example, it grew first from the old Chinatowns like London and Liverpool, to new Chinatowns in other large cities, like Birmingham and Manchester; the next stage was towards single restaurants outside Chinatowns; the last stage was the large-scale entrance in the downmarket fast-food sector, where 'Chinese takeaways' replaced or complemented 'fish-and-chips' shops. The takeaways, catering for local needs, are spread evenly over the land, while restaurants are normally concentrated in downtown metropolitan locations with single restaurants in suburban and small-town settings. The market for Chinese catering follows the general pattern of the restaurant business; it is segmented into middle-class restaurants and fast-food outlets. Chinese catering changed constantly in response to the supply of labour, market demand and political climate. The economic calculus operates within narrow margins:

> Earlier on I ran a restaurant. Now restaurants have turned difficult, so I sold it and went into takeaways. Now that has become difficult, the rents are high.

> If you buy it yourself and can avoid the rent, it is different. We bought our
> own takeaway and do not pay rent. If we had to pay rent, it would be hard.
>
> (101:91)

An interviewee tells of the special situation in Belfast in Northern Ireland, where the terrorist attacks for a long time prevented the restaurant business from developing in the city centre. The atmosphere meant that there were only few customers. Chinese catering therefore developed 'in the outside', in the outskirts of Belfast. But the last '18 months of peace means that people are now flocking to the city centre, so that Chinese takeaways in the outside aren't that ideal any more'. But of course, a lasting peace will foster prosperity and growth, and will bring many customers (003//047).

In post-war Germany, the Chinese restaurant sector grew slowly in large cities (there were no Chinatowns); they gradually spread down a continuum of large and medium-sized cities, down to small towns.

After the war, the Rhineland rapidly gained a new Chinese population and a growing Chinese restaurant sector. The expansion, according to several of our interviewees, began with one Chinese restaurant in Essen in the late 1940s. Former Chinese shipping masters from the Netherlands introduced many former Chinese seamen to work in the restaurants in the Rhineland. Many entered Germany illegally and only much later had their status legalised. Most came from Dapeng in Baoan and from Shunde. At the beginning, they worked under miserable conditions for a pittance, from 9 o'clock in the morning to 2 o'clock in the night, and they lived in crammed quarters, but 'everything has now turned prosperous for that generation' (015//003–004).

Before the Second World War there had only been one or two restaurants in Hamburg (which had a transient population of Chinese seafarers and a small community serving them). In the early 1970s, Hamburg mustered a score of Chinese restaurants (–/012/007). By the mid-1990s, the restaurant sector in Hamburg proper had expanded to more than 250, according to semi-official estimates. If suburbs and satellite towns are included, an estimate from the trade is 'more than 500 outlets' (–/012/022) .

From the 1970s, the Chinese restaurant business in Germany developed steadily, mainly due to the influx of Hong Kong Chinese who came over from Britain, often after working some time in the Netherlands (–/012/010; 013:5). The boat refugees from Southeast Asia, conversely, did not enter the restaurant business when they first arrived. They were taken care of through government programmes aimed at integrating them in the mainstream economy. They received social benefit, housing and jobs in German enterprises. They did not want to work in Chinese restaurants for 'they feared them because they all knew that the working hours in Chinese restaurants was around 10 hours'.

Labour market competition and unemployment in the wake of German reunification, however, in the 1990s forced some of former boat refugees into the restaurant sector. They are now regarded critically as newcomers in the sector by the more established restaurateurs, who consider them government-subsidised (through starter schemes) and inexperienced (–/012/020).

The restaurant sector has turned downmarket in the 1990s. This is because reunification suddenly opened a new large market in the East, where investments were low (-/012/026). This enabled more people to invest, and skilled restaurant workers could realise their dream of opening their own place. This led to strong competition for workers with skills. The old-established restaurateurs tend to regard this development critically. They think that the new restaurants in the eastern parts of Germany cannot keep up standards. One even sniped, 'they even serve meals that are a bit off'. The sudden expansion of the whole Chinese restaurant sector in Germany made it almost impossible to hire skilled cooks and waiters (–/012/026).

The established restaurateurs who hope to develop their restaurants in scale, in quality of food and service and in market status see themselves hemmed in by this structural development of the Chinese catering sector. Not only are they unable to find new personnel, but the image of the whole sector is slumping.

The lack of skilled cooks is noted as a major constraint by interviewees. In earlier decades, cooks came from Hong Kong, Taiwan, Malaysia and other Southeast Asian countries. They came because the wages in Germany were high. In the 1960s and early 1970s, the wage was around 1,000 DM (equivalent to around 1,600 HKD) a month, while the wage was only between 500 and 600 HKD in Hong Kong. In the 1990s, a salary of 4,000 DM (equivalent to about 24,000 HKD) was considered very good, but a good cook could make more than 20,000 HKD a month in Hong Kong (–/012/031), so the incentive to move had decreased radically. Similar trends hold true for Taiwan and Southeast Asian countries. The only major source of new cooks is the Mainland, but frictions between restaurant owners and cooks hired directly from the Mainland have become a serious problem, especially due to attitudes and different dialects (–/012/031). Attempts are made to recruit directly from vocational schools in Guangdong that are supposed to train the best Cantonese style cooks, but immigration laws work against such efforts:

> In Germany, they used to practise a limitation on Chinese restaurants. You were only allowed to recruit two cooks from the outside (abroad). If you take a careful look at this behaviour … it was suffocating the Chinese restaurant business.
>
> (–/012/041)

The decline of the sector has also been visible in consumer expectations. Where Germans 20 years ago dressed up to go to the Chinese restaurant, behaving very dignified, they now look 'as if they were just having some fast food' (–/012/026). The dog meat scandal in the 1990s added to these problems, causing a trough in the Chinese catering market. This will be discussed in more detail in a later section.

In the Netherlands, restaurants spread out from the Chinatowns in a pattern similar to that in Britain; the popular 'Chineesch-Indisch' restaurants were gradually complemented with restaurants selling 'genuine' (mainly Cantonese-style) Chinese food. The interviews reveal that Chinese restaurants in the Netherlands follow roughly the same dynamics as they do in Britain and Germany. The pattern includes:

- restaurants as a first-generation immigrant institution, providing a livelihood at relatively low investment, long working hours and self-exploitation for people whose professional skills are not recognised by the 'host' society, and who have difficulty in language communication;
- their role as conduits of chain migration;
- their geographical spread;
- their sensitivity to market trends, immigration laws and social security legislation stands out.

Dutch Chinese interviewees pointed at the paradoxes of state policies: the Chinese pride themselves of being the 'good immigrants', and their unemployment rate was low:

> There was no unemployment. The Chinese knew no unemployment. I remember back then, if we were out of job, we didn't go on the dole, we thought it was a sort of stigma ... The Dutch government is really responsible for the fact that so many of our people claim unemployment benefit now. That's because some people had not collected their benefit, they still had some money left, they didn't go on the dole, for they had enough [money] to buy food and to live on. But then, when they opened a restaurant or something, the (authorities) found out that they hadn't worked for a long time, asking 'where have you been?' Then the (Chinese) said, 'I didn't work, I haven't been away' ... (The civil servant) says, 'If you didn't work, what did you live on?' He says, 'I had some money left over from previous work, so that's what I lived on' ... (The civil servant) says, 'No, you certainly must have done black work' ... He thought you must have done black work or stolen money, how else could you live?
>
> (–/038/060)

The behaviour of Dutch authorities meant that this practice had to stop; they virtually forced unemployed restaurant workers to join the dole queue. Rising unemployment among restaurant workers meant that the authorities enforced an embargo on the direct recruitment of people from China as long as there were any unemployed Chinese restaurant workers; this hampered the development of large and high-quality restaurants that needed highly skilled and specialised workers. The Dutch authorities did not discriminate sufficiently between unskilled and skilled restaurant workers, and so unemployment in the sector meant that it was impossible to develop it by recruiting skilled cooks in China. This labour market paradox takes different guises in different European countries, but perhaps it is most accentuated in Germany and the Netherlands.

The 'dog meat scandal' in Germany

The 'dog meat scandal' in Germany was a media campaign against Chinese restaurants. The scandal did not originate in the Chinese restaurants, for they never served dog meat. The scandalous behaviour was on the side of media deliberately fabricating untrue stories or uncritically transmitting them to the public. The event started in a trivial way. Official concern with black labour and tax evasion caused authorities near Berlin to check on ethnic food outlets, including some Chinese restaurants. Such clamp-downs occur often across Europe, and apart from the annoyance for restaurateurs and the intimidation of their customers, there is little to it. Occasionally an ethnic restaurant or two are closed down for some days, or somebody is fined for employing people without labour permits or for evading taxes.

But on this occasion in April 1995, a journalist from the large regional newspaper *Berliner Morgenpost* interviewed a local government functionary who had participated in the raids. Perhaps bored with the routine flavour, the official spiced up his account with a misplaced joke about having seen dog meat in Chinese restaurants, and allegedly claiming that he himself would never eat in such places. The journalist took the joke as a serious statement and rushed it to press, presumably adding a tinge of horror for effect.

A news story in a regional newspaper normally has little impact; after a couple of days it tends to fade into oblivion while new iniquities soil the front pages. But the story was not forgotten. *Berliner Morgenpost* is part of the Axel Springer media empire, whose newspaper flagship *Bildzeitung* in Hamburg has a constant hunger for bizarre and sordid tales for their banner headlines. *Bildzeitung* is often classified as part of the tabloid press, but unjustly so. *Bildzeitung* is a broadsheet and can blow the banner-lines up to unsurpassed proportions; where tabloids often cannot avoid some core of truth, no matter how irrelevant, behind their stories, *Bildzeitung* has cultivated the art of poetic licence to the acme of perfection. The story of stolen pet dogs served to unsuspecting restaurant-goers is the sort of staple *Bildzeitung* lives off.

One interviewee related the story as follows:

> Germany has a newspaper called *Bildzeitung* … This paper has the largest circulation of all newspapers in Europe, it sells more than five million copies a day. It is published by a trust, the Springer Konzern, that owns several television stations, magazines and so on, it is a very powerful factor in Germany. Why can it sell more than five million copies a day? Because it has local editorial offices and distribution centres in all German cities. To put it simply, all of Germany, most of the 89 million people read it, because it is the newspaper of the common man. So that day, on the 4th of April, that's last year (1995), on the front page there was a Pekinese dog with its head popping out and a large-letter title that simply said: 'The Chinese Sell Dog Meat'. The most pathetic is, even though the Germans belong to a high-level culture and a country with a high-level knowledge, these people are so stupid that – if you

look at these issues, you can't really describe it – they just have utter faith in (what they are told). Then everything changed. At the time it went as far as our kids in primary school and secondary school, even in kindergarten ... eh ... all the schoolmates went, 'I won't play with you, your mum and dad sell dog meat'. There were even some people who phoned Chinese restaurants, swearing. The Chinese restaurant business was already going downhill due to other things, but the events last year really made it tilt.

(011:59)

The original news came from Berlin, that's to say, the first newspaper report was from Berlin, on a Chinese restaurant ... What had really happened was that an official from the labour administration who had been checking black labour in a raid, for some reason later told a press conference, 'on this and this day I went to a Chinese restaurant to check, and there I saw a pot of something that looked like dog meat'. It was that simple. But the problem is, this *Berliner Morgenpost*, this small newspaper, was unable to see the twinkle in his eye, and within three days *Bildzeitung* had turned it into a huge news item, citing the classics where they say that the history of dog-eating among Chinese has distant origins ... This person knew a lot about Chinese things, and when he wrote about this, he was able to cite a treatise by Li Shizhen on traditional medicine where it states that eating dog meat can preserve your health, and even a classical novel telling a story about a monk who ate dog meat, he poured all this stuff into his article. So from our point of view it was not easy to stand up to the newspaper.

(011:73)

The event shook the overseas community in Germany. Trade in the Chinese catering sector slumped overnight, and the Chinese who had lived out of the public eye became the target of public vilification and personal distrust. The event instantaneously made the overseas Chinese in Germany join hands in protest:

When we at the Chinese Association read this news, we immediately wrote to the authority mentioned in the paper, demanding that they answer whether the facts reported in the article were true or not. Through these efforts on our side to establish the responsibility of the authorities, they provided formal responses from three departments, the police, the external affairs and the labour affairs departments, which all proved that it was defamation without any basis in the reality. In particular the deputy head of the labour affairs department wrote an official letter of apology to us.

(020//081)

On that same day when this happened, we organised our professional association for the first time. A total of one hundred restaurant owners drove from Hamburg to Berlin in a hired eighty-seat double-decker bus and eight small cars – there was an excited spirit – to support the press conference of the Chinese association in Berlin. The next thing was, because the headquarters of *Bildzeitung* are in Hamburg, that our professional association for the first time ever in Germany gathered between 500 and 600 Chinese in one place carrying placards and shouting slogans in Chinese and German, protesting against *Bildzeitung*. We had obtained permission from the police department, and afterwards we organised some youngsters to sweep the place clean. It was all tightly controlled by our professional association. We had contacted some German martial arts clubs, directly organising them to clamp down on any protest placards that went further than our protest target lest somebody for example shout that Germans are fascists or whatever. The racial stuff we did not want to raise because it's political. One can say the demonstration succeeded ... in the end the chief editor appeared and agreed to publish a brief correction the next day.

　　Looking at this rather dispassionately, after this protest right up till this day, they were not as arrogant as before. Before there were stories on and off, like Chinese heroin ravaging Hamburg and whatnot, and when you looked closely at it, it was based on several-years-old material – they didn't put a date on it – to which they added some pictures. Then there were some journalists who went to China and filmed some free markets, the things we Chinese can accept, but that Germans strongly oppose, like selling dog meat, game and so on.

(011:75)

The Chinese community in Germany had never been able to unite or cooperate on common issues. The dog meat scandal was a unifying issue, but it was isolated and in itself short-lived. The community was under many divisive pressures, and it is probably due to the political acumen of overseas Chinese leaders that the dog meat scandal did not end in disorder and grief. The determination to centre the protest on the dog meat allegations, merely insisting on a correction of the media's transgression and demanding an inquiry into how an official could be cited for false accusations, was an important aspect of the reaction.

　　Cleaning up after the demonstration and preventing the issue from being phrased in terms of racist discrimination served not only to deprive the media of additional attack points, but also to preserve internal unity on the issue. Citizens protesting against media defamation constituted a strategy of inclusion: the conflict was not set between the Chinese and the Germans, but between defamation and civic rights; the protesters were not ethnic extremists, but responsible citizens, cleaning up after themselves. A disorderly campaign based on anti-xenophobic slogans would have alienated not only the German public, but also large groups among the Chinese.

　　A complicating factor was that some Chinese participating in the demonstration hoped to use the event to promote the 'Democracy Movement' and to protest against the Mainland government for its handling of the Tiananmen incident in 1989 (011:107; 011:109). If they had succeeded, they would have split the overseas Chinese, and the Embassy of the People's Republic might have withdrawn its tacit support for the protests. This tacit support was an important unifying factor among the Chinese.[5] *Sing Tao Daily* had a journalist on the scene of the demonstration all day who made a lengthy report (011:109), and other Chinese newspapers across Europe gave the matter much attention. Sympathy across the continent gave further impetus to the feeling of unity. The Taiwanese-leaning *Ouzhou Ribao – Europe – Journal Quotidien* in Paris allegedly reported negatively on the 'repression' of the democracy activists' 'public will' (103//003). This instance of anti-Mainland expression did not accord with the positive evaluation of the significance of the demonstration by pro-Taiwan Chinese leaders in Germany.

This feeling of unity reinvigorated the drive towards institution-building. The restaurant business had been in a slump for some time, and Chinese restaurateurs in Germany had begun talks on building up a professional association (tongye gonghui), but nothing had come of it. The dog meat scandal put the efforts back on track for while. Several interviewees report that the incident gave them a sudden opportunity to get to know leaders of Chinese associations across Germany they had never heard of before. Within hours of deciding to start a demonstration in Hamburg, the local association was inundated with telephone calls and support from other cities.

Interviewees summed the situation up like this: 'From the dog meat incident of April '95 onwards, the overseas Chinese have begun to wake up, before they were just like a heap of sand' (–/024/050); and 'the dog meat incident united people. Every Chinese cares about our international reputation, and the incident directly impinged on it' (–/022/051). Most importantly, however, was the attitude that 'we Chinese cannot easily be unjustly treated, within the limits of the law we will seek to place the legal responsibility' (020//096).

The dog meat scandal was a turning point for the overseas Chinese community leaders in Germany. It gave them a foundation on which to forge unity, albeit narrow and short-lived. By using the language of inclusion in German society and by refusing to take the implications further than the question of the catering business, earning a meagre victory (in the form of a retraction by *Bildzeitung*), leaders sought to find new ground for cooperation between themselves in the area of the Chinese catering trade. The event was thus a catalyst for renewed efforts to organise the sector professionally, but it also reinforced the perception that Chinese catering was a sector apart. All Chinese restaurateurs had experienced a sudden decline in their business due to the dog meat allegations. Chinese catering in Germany, accordingly, is torn between inclusion in mainstream society and its convergence on its own problems. In the event, the impetus created by the scandal was lost, and no effective organisational framework has emerged. However, informal networks and mutual understanding were strengthened.

The allegation that the Chinese serve dog meat in their restaurants occasionally surfaces in the media in Europe, and few people tend to pay attention to it. Interviewees mentioned a number of examples of similar reporting, normally more general, like 'the Chinese eat dogs and snakes' rather than 'they sell dog meats in Chinese restaurants', and often also more distant cases, like reporting to the Italian public about 'sweet-and-sour dog ribs' sold in Chinese restaurants in Germany (057//161).

China as a trade emblem

Walking through Rue du Temple in Paris is different from walking through the streets of Belleville (also in Paris), George Street in Manchester or Gerrard Street in London. These areas all house overseas Chinese businesses. The difference lies in the abundance of Chinese ethnic emblems in Belleville, Gerrard Street and George Street, and their total absence in Rue du Temple. Rue du Temple stands out due to its sober dullness and half-anonymity of its import-export as well as its leather goods and clothes wholesaling businesses, whose names tend not to give away any ethnic link. One has to peer deep into the darkness at the bottom of the shops to distinguish the Chinese faces of the owners and their workers; there are few, if any, other clues to the ethnic character of the many businesses in Rue du Temple.

By contrast, Gerrard Street and George Street are adorned with Chinese arches, signposts in Chinese, shop-fronts boasting names in Chinese characters and all sorts of China-style kitsch, and huge Chinese neon signs. Westernised restaurant names, often written in brush-stroke letters, ranging from 'Asia House', 'Hong Kong' and 'Peking' to 'Laughing Buddha', 'Lucky Dragon', 'Happy Valley' and 'Great Wall', alternate with seemingly meaningless transcriptions like 'Ah Chau' (Asia) and 'Kwok Man' (Nation).

The Oriental ambience is a main emblem of the Chinese catering trade which is provided by firms specialised in furnishing and decorating restaurants or providing them with everything from chopsticks and rice bowls to printed menu cards, serviettes and paper covers for chopsticks. The Oriental atmosphere has become increasingly standardised as consumer expectations have grown more sophisticated. The style of each restaurant is signalled in the specific combination of ethnic props and symbols and in their richness. Carved rosewood furniture, Ming vases and silk dresses for the waitresses are not used anywhere, but their imitations are. Some restaurants will make do with a thick red carpet, red lamps and perhaps a Chinese-style picture on the wall, while others are decorated with bordered wallpaper, dark-lacquered wooden furniture, bronze strips, thick dark-red velvet curtains, simile Ming vases, a huge 'double happiness' sign on the wall behind the largest table, and large wall reliefs of junks at sea or rustic scenes with water buffaloes. The exotic is standardised in order to satisfy the customers' hopes of predictability. The ambience is like the menus, a mixture of strange sensations and reassuring explicitness, like the menu text that provides both an incomprehensible name of a dish and a simple, but still exotic, statement of its main ingredients, like 'beef and green pepper in oyster sauce' or 'spicy chicken and cashew nuts'. It is a world in which the customer can become an expert, learning the meaning of 'double happiness' and 'dim sum', and the difference between Cantonese and Sichuan food.

The 'Tai-Ji Restaurant' (Taiji Fanzhuang) in Uhlandstrasse, Berlin, takes its role of transmitting Chinese culture seriously to the extreme. Its floor plan is shaped like the taiji or yin- and yang-symbol, and large round tables have the same form and can be separated in yin and yang halves. Its menu provides an introduction to the history and culinary topography of the individual dishes, alongside their names in Chinese characters, Hanyu Pinyin transcription (with tone markers) and translations into German, as well as general, pedagogic introductions to Chinese culture, language and table manners. The restaurant's decoration reveals the clientele: it is simple and light, designed to cater for the academic middle class of the early or mid-1990s that was attracted to Italian-style cafés.

The Chinese restaurant business is an ethnic business sector because it manipulates and invents ethnic symbolism as a part of the business calculus. One interviewee, telling of his early venture into the restaurant business in the 1950s, reported:

> If it were to be like in Hong Kong, decorating (the restaurant) would cost several millions, and it would be a major expense. The overseas Chinese here (in Germany) did not have such money, they had no way of running a Chinese restaurant. But those who could open a restaurant, as the first calculation, did not decorate as richly. They hung some (red Chinese) lanterns (denglong), and put up a signboard.
>
> (–/024/035)

Chinese-style decoration is an investment and one important parameter for comparison between Chinese restaurants. Expensive decoration gives the restaurant status, but it must be matched with earning capacity to recoup the investment. The Chinese restaurant business operates with a set of variables that determine its feasibility. Like all other restaurants, the number of seats, location, repute, decoration and the quality of the cooks are the most important variables. Each of the variables can be improved so as to increase the earning capacity, but any improvement demands investments and higher operating costs. People in the trade assess the feasibility of a restaurant by comparing the gross investment or the monthly rent to the seating capacity. One restaurateur who took us in his car from one city to another remarked wryly, when we were passing a large house that had been turned into a Chinese restaurant, that the investment in the estate could not be carried by the number of seats, so it was possibly used to 'launder ill-gained money'.

Decoration, in other words, is a set of ethnic emblems that form part of a careful economic calculation. A suburban take-away will not be bothered with expensive decoration, and will often even dispense with Chinese characters on the facade. The customers are more attracted by accessibility, long opening hours, cheap prices and convenience than by the atmosphere.

At the other end of the spectrum are large restaurants in unique locations that have high-quality Chinese decoration. One of the more extreme cases in Europe is perhaps the 'Ocean Palace' (Haishang Huagong), a floating restaurant that was opened in the Oosterdok of Amsterdam in October 1984. The restaurant itself is a highly ornamented Chinese-style building with curved, green-tiled roofs built on a huge barge. It stands out as a landmark near the Central Station close to the parking lot assigned to tourist coaches and with ample parking opportunities in this otherwise congested city. It can accommodate several big banquets at the same time, and the internal decoration is exquisite. It has, over the years, built up a reputation of high-quality cuisine. It has become a tourist attraction in itself.

'Restaurant Sinostar' (Baitiane Da Jiujia) on Avenue de Fontainebleu in Paris combines huge size, high-quality Chinese-style decoration and accessibility. It is able to accommodate large business banquets of high culinary quality. 'Ocean Palace' and 'Restaurant Sinostar' reflect a business calculation, directed towards a specific market segment, in which the ethnic decoration is an important variable.

This ethnic symbolism gradually migrates from the catering business to other economic branches.

Chinese warehouses in Britain, like Wing Yip in Birmingham and Chi Yip in the Manchester area, are examples of the ethnic decoration rage. In these cases, the trade emblem at a first glance seems much less critical to the business. The warehouses in Britain, however, have become hybrid retail, wholesale and leisure centres aimed at the overseas Chinese community. They are wholesale businesses because they supply the goods needed in takeaways and restaurants. They are retail businesses because they provide daily utilities and high-quality Chinese foodstuffs and Chinese-style furniture; they also sell Chinese language magazines and papers, as well as films and karaoke on tapes and compact discs. They are leisure centres because they have Chinese restaurants and are aimed at whole families going on shopping tours. These businesses have developed a specific profile to take up competition in a specific market segment. They are situated on cheap land in industrial estates outside the city. They have sufficient space for their warehouse function (which was either too expensive or impossible to obtain in Chinatown locations), and they have as their customers both large businesses and small family businesses. Small family businesses are keen to cover both their private consumption needs and their commercial purchases in one place; private consumption is normally covered by crammed Chinatown supermarkets in locations with traffic congestion, so the incentive for customers to go to large out-of-town stores is great. The warehouses, however, find it useful to mimic the atmosphere, diversity of services and leisure element of the Chinatowns in order to make their customers feel welcome. Once the ethnic emblem has gained currency in the warehouse sector it is likely to spread.

Another example is the industrial building of Enta Technologies in Telford (Britain); its owner, who originates in Taiwan, built and decorated it in Chinese style. An exceptional profile may be very useful in the computer sector that is dominated by large international brands, faceless no-brand suppliers, and myriads of small businesses that are difficult to distinguish from each other. The publicity effect may be great. The owner of the enterprise is acutely aware of the ethnic image, playing on contrasts, and publicly discussing the need to promote Chinese culture. At the opening of his industrial building at a large ceremony in 1996, he spoke in English and had one of his British associates speak in Chinese. He makes donations to Chinese cultural and education initiatives in Britain. The stunning growth of his company from a basement workshop to a large enterprise within ten years has, of course, given him strong social credit. More importantly, the ethnic profile has reinforced his social recognition; President Lee Teng-hui has personally received him, while the first lady entertained his wife, and he has gained considerable standing in British political and business circles due to this.

The Danish Daloon Company (established in the 1950s by an overseas Chinese) produces Chinese-style frozen foods for European customers. The company uses synthesised Chinese symbolism in its TV advertisements, but this seems to be unique in Europe. Ethnic symbolism is mainly employed to create a Chinese atmosphere in physical locations like shops and restaurants or in print media advertisements for restaurants.

Overseas Chinese often explain ethnic symbolism as a sentimental heritage, as a time-honoured trait of the national psyche, as something happy and unproblematic. In the words of the Spanish overseas Chinese Ma Zhuomin:

> In early times it was difficult for overseas Chinese to open shop, and there was no way to decorate the restaurants properly, so some just hung a pair of red lanterns. Red lanterns, (signifying that the shop was) 'open for business', are something propitious, handed down through generations, they express joy. So it has been adopted to express the hope for business, wealth and happiness among our compatriots on foreign shores
>
> (*Ouzhou Shibao – Nouvelles d'Europe* 27.04.1994)

Others are of the opinion that ethnic symbols are ambiguous and have a darker side. An Italian Chinese interviewee told us that Chinese enterprises in Italy, no matter whether they are factories or shops, hang a Chinese lantern outside as a sort of symbol. He told us he had written a long essay in a local Chinese newspaper about this symbol not as one of ethnic pride, but more as a symbol of the sweat and hardship of those working under their light, both 'the legal and illegal (immigrants), those who earn and those who don't, those who own and those who eat bitterness' (052:81). Allowing for the exaggeration and pathos of social engagement and artistic allusion in the Chinese essayist tradition, he makes an important point: ethnic emblems have a strong affective value for immigrant groups that are concentrated socially, occupationally and geographically.

Such emblems signify the otherness, the pride and the misery of the group. However, this sweet-sour image probably attaches too much symbolic importance to the use of ethnic emblems. They are used because they are available and have been used before – they do not constitute a conscious act of signification, but are habitual and their users normally do not reflect upon them. Where membership of a group is contested or where leaders and other pillars of the community compete for legitimacy and authority within the group, ethnic symbolism may become an important instrument, and its use will become conscious.

Maurizio Berlincioni's photo reportage from 1994 and 1995 on the Chinese in Florence (Colombo, Marcetti, Omodeo and Solimano 1995, 96–190) provides a strong visual testimony of how the community uses ethnic emblems. Such emblems were apparently not prominent in daily life situations in 1995. However, collective public activities like New Year processions included banners, musical instruments, dragons and other emblems of Chineseness. Local overseas Chinese associations arrange such festivals in order to display community cohesion with the help of such emblems.

The boundaries between the deliberate, commercial use of ethnic emblems, their use to delimit the ethnic economy and their public use as social and cultural rallying points fluctuate. Reducing the use of ethnic emblems to marketing or to the conscious display of sentiment would ignore the elasticity of such symbolism. One example of such elasticity has to do with the 3rd arrondissement in Paris, the area of Rue du Temple that totally lacks ethnic signs. In 1997 and 1999, this area had large-scale public New Year celebrations. A report in *Ouzhou Shibao – Nouvelles d'Europe* (24.02.1999) talks about this area of people originating in Zhejiang, hanging red Chinese lanterns in the streets and adopting the Cantonese-Hongkongese tradition (Yue-Gang fengsu) of a New Year procession where the businesses en route provide offerings to the 'Dancing Lions', and receive symbolic money from the 'God of Wealth' and his companion. The fact that this community of Zhejiangese adopt Cantonese New Year rituals is not at all commented upon by the newspaper, but it is noted. The Cantonese-style New Year practices have become an ethnic symbol for all overseas Chinese irrespective of their origin. One may, as a French newspaper has, speculate that the 1998 amnesty that legalised the status of many Chinese of Zhejiang origin created a bolder and more open atmosphere in the area around Rue du Temple so that public manifestations like the Chinese New Year have become viable (*Le Monde*, 15.02.1999, 20). However, the festival may also give a higher profile to the Chinese business interests in the area and provide a suitable point of contact between the overseas Chinese leaders and the local politicians.

Chinese business as an exception?

It would probably be wrong to argue that Chinese business enterprises are just like any other enterprises. The argument I have put forward in this chapter does not sustain such a view. They operate under the same fundamental market conditions as all other enterprises, but are in the advantageous position that they can exploit a particular ethnic emblem. The Chinese business sectors are to a large extent a product of immigration laws and the difficulties that face all immigrant groups in labour markets. Chinese businesses may, therefore, seem particular, as structured differently from other enterprises. However, the widespread view that Chinese enterprises are fundamentally different from other enterprises in terms of organisation, 'spirit' of operation, and ideology does not seem to reflect the situation in Europe. The variety of forms of operation, the 'assiduous spirit' and so on seem best explained by the particular difficulties the Chinese enterprises labour under, as we have already seen in earlier parts of this chapter. The real test of the idea that Chinese enterprises are an exception by their very nature, would be to compare them with other enterprises throughout history, examining their particular functions in the wider economy. Ideas regarding familism as the structuring aspect of Chinese enterprises (e.g. Wong 1985) seem unable to explain Chinese business behaviour beyond what applies in similar non-Chinese enterprises. In particular, growth problems and generation shifts seem generic, and the structure of large family firms seems in most cases to be a function of the wider economic and fiscal environment. I shall not discuss this in detail, but only note that the overseas Chinese enterprises of different sizes in Europe I have examined appear to be similar in structure to non-Chinese enterprises. It may be possible to interpret the Daloon company in Denmark as a family enterprise (given the role of family members, and the fact that the eldest son has taken over daily business from his father, the company's ageing founder). In structure and functional respects, however, the company is not different from similar companies in Denmark, except for the fact that it uses Chinese symbols in marketing and donates money (through the Daloon foundation) to worthy causes that are related to China or Chinese culture. The contributions on individual European countries in Benton and Pieke (1998), where they discuss Chinese businesses, largely support this view. Where the contributors, like Teixera (1998, 244–55) in the case of Portuguese Chinese entrepreneurs, touch on the enterprise cluster, the role of the family and other business behaviour, they stand out as rational responses to both structural constraints and market opportunities.

Mette Thunø's (1997) analysis, in contrast, while understanding the ramifications of Chinese business activities as a function of their economic environment, regards the behaviour in Chinese entrepreneurial families in Denmark as based on forms of organisation and value systems particular to the Chinese, albeit interpreted in response to the environment:

> A shared ethnic culture is created by persons sharing experiences in social interaction, and consequently new behavioural guidelines and normative order are adapted and readapted.
>
> (Thunø 1997, 204)

Accordingly, she regards the dominant business practice as 'highly conservative, irrational (in an economic sense) and inflexible' (Thunø 1997, 204), and attributes that to cultural and ethnic characteristics, rather than examining how the general frameworks have changed in the Danish retail and catering sectors. Which are the rational and flexible arrangements that comparable 'ethnic Danish' entrepreneurs could enter into during the structural changes in the small shopkeeper economy during the last two decades of the twentieth century? Were these arrangements open to 'ethnic Chinese' entrepreneurs in the same forms? Are conservatism, irrationality and lack of flexibility a product of cultural characteristics or of belonging to a declining class of small-scale owner-operators? Is the failure to organise politically in ethnic terms (Thunø 1997, 221–36) due to an individualistic or family-centred strategy of getting accepted in wider society by not stressing the ethnic issue (as Thunø seems to suggest)? Is such a strategy 'irrational' (given 'racial attacks and economic pressure', Thunø 1997, 227) or is it a reflection of a generally exposed position under external conditions where ethnic solidarity in the collective experience among the Chinese has never offered any solution or justice? There is no doubt that familism is a core form in small Chinese businesses in Denmark (and in other parts of Europe), but it would appear to be a characteristic of the owner-operator (or in pseudo-Marxist terms 'self-exploitative') business organisation that for a large part relies on illegal immigrants as a source of cheap labour (Thunø 1997, 174–87; and discussions above on France and Italy).

The interpretation by Chinese of this situation and their use of ethnic stereotypes to rationalise their economic situation (that is mainly a product of ethnic exclusion and the pressure of migration) emphasise Chineseness and use ethnic and cultural explanations. Yet such interpretations and stereotypical explanations by the Chinese themselves may not provide a stringent and logical explanation of the causalities behind their business organisation and behaviour.

We may, however, consider the points where Chinese businesses do emphasise their separate nature at a symbolic level. In places with large Chinese communities, the maintenance of a ritual affinity with the community is an important aspect of business operation. Jean-Pierre Hassoun (1993) has discussed various social mechanisms invoked by Parisian Chinese entrepreneurs as frameworks for community interaction; he describes how the invocation of 'traditional' social norms of face, respect and reciprocity generates authenticity through its references to a presumed rustic or village ideal. Likewise, the use of religious symbolism signifies the return to local authenticity shared by all Chinese or Chinese within various sub-ethnic groups, thus creating a symbolic resource for the interpretation of business practices among co-ethnics (Hassoun 1992). My own observations among Chinese entrepreneurs indicate that such symbolism is important in various ways.

The order in which collective rituals are carried out indicates the rank of a business within the community. The consecration by a 'master' (shifu) of a Guanyin figurine, other deity, or ancestral tablet, or the performance of a fengshui ritual, constitutes a social acknowledgement of an entrepreneur and his or her business. The substantial expense of such rituals aims at consolidating the business among peers by paying respect to shared ideas. Starting the business on a day that is listed as propitious in the Chinese almanac belongs to the same category. By failing to act in such ways, one may lose face in the community, and, who knows? expose oneself to bad luck.

Absorption into the economic mainstream

The ideal of many overseas Chinese leaders is to help the Chinese enter the economic mainstream:

> Presently the young people, in reality, don't need you to motivate them [to assimilate], they are already assimilated into local society. We don't need to worry about that.
>
> (025//138)

This statement of fact joined together a conflicting view of how to deal with the issue of assimilation. The interviewee emphasised that '99.9 per cent' of the overseas

Chinese in the Netherlands are 'patriotic' and hope for China to grow strong. The idea was to strengthen Chinese ethnic business in order to be able to enter the 'mainstream' (025//139). The strategy for achieving liberation from the catering business was to make it prosper and form an advantageous starting point for

> assimilating with local society, entering Dutch mainstream society and ultimately achieve political participation.
>
> (025//139)

The next generation would have to compete with 'the foreigners' (i.e. Dutch people) for real.

One British interviewee (064//*passim*) noted that the second- and third-generation overseas Chinese sought to become absorbed into mainstream society through Chinatown Lions Clubs and Associations of British and Chinese University Students (abacus), which joined the young Chinese together and at the same time sought to include British members. The declared rationale of some ethnic Chinese organisations is to seek assimilation for their members.

The collective effort to strengthen ethnic Chinese business as the basis for assimilation makes sense in a society where the overseas Chinese feel excluded or marginalised. Assimilation can best occur from a position of economic strength where the overseas Chinese enjoy respect from 'mainstream' society. This, ironically, prolongs and strengthens the manipulation of ethnic symbolism.

Conclusion

Construction of a European Chinese identity?

Identity

This book began with a quotation from a letter to the editor from a Chinese teenager in Sweden. Her Chinese identity has little to do with the matters of the overseas Chinese communities in Europe, for she experiences an adolescent's existentialist problem of belonging both here and there, of having a sense of being rooted somewhere other than her class mates. She may grow up to find most of the Chinatown symbols of minor importance, she may become a Swedish woman with a personal interest in and special knowledge of China, or she may move to China in search of her roots. She may find a career in overseas Chinese associations and the ethnic economy; or she may find herself in opposition to them. From her perspective there are many options that can be realised. Her future is not defined by the existence of Chinese identity or an overseas Chinese community, and it is only partly influenced by the ethnic origin of her parents.

Chinese identity may be both an existential choice and a matter for creative invention: being Chinese is what you make of it. It is also an imposition on the individual by society. Social expectations and stereotypes force upon the individual patterns of perception and behaviour that are sometimes hard to escape. The individual is thus forced to relate to ethnicity as a social condition. Ethnic identity may, depending on the context, deprive the individual of opportunities, or it may provide him or her with exploitable assets, and it may in some cases be irrelevant for his or her opportunities.

It is how society constructs ethnic identity that ultimately determines the situation of the individual. To put it in more precise terms: what counts is how different groups of people use ethnicity to create divisions between each other, depriving each other of rights and assets and bestowing rights and assets on each other. In this process of 'boundary management', many political, economic and social factors assume ethnic significance, and ethnic and cultural symbols assume political, economic and social value. For example, selling Chinese cuisine as an ethnic and cultural symbol became a profitable economic activity; it was facilitated by labour market exclusion of the Chinese from mainstream employment, and it was able to absorb new waves of migrants flexibly; its niche character allowed it to exploit ethnic symbols. The construction of identity is universally in the hands of people who pursue their interests as groups and individuals. Ethnic symbols are only symbols because somebody uses them as such. A skilful ethnic leader may manipulate symbols to achieve aims, as in the case of the Antwerp Chinatown; or a local council or an investment company may find a Chinatown an attractive development proposition.

The instances of identity-building addressed in this book take many forms. Migration, history, sub-ethnic identities, citizenship and residence, multicultural policies of European states, patriotic policies of Chinese governments, Chinese ethnic associations, ethnic businesses, and Chinatowns all merge to form the substance of Chinese ethnic identity. Each of these is shaped by people who pursue their own interests, or claim status and rights by using the Chinese ethnic label. Overseas Chinese identity as discussed in this book is thus a product of many diverse influences that determine the *agency* of different groups and individuals.

Although particular cultural, social, economic and political issues can explain ethnic behaviour to a certain degree in specific contexts (like in the case of chain migration from Hong Kong's New Territories to Britain or from French Indochina to France), it is obvious that they cannot provide general explanations of the formation of Chinese identity in Europe. It is not labour market exclusion, ethnic economic niches, transnational institutions or multicultural policies in their own right that shape overseas Chinese communities. The crucial element is the way in which members of the Chinese communities collectively use ethnic labels and ethnic symbols to shape social reality, and how individuals seek to influence these processes to further their own interests. This explains the diversity of overseas Chinese communities across Europe, as well as important similarities among them.

European borders do create difference between Chinese communities, for each European country provides different resources to be used in identity-construction by overseas Chinese, and dissimilar immigration histories add to the diversity. Efforts by the European Union to deal with immigrant communities pull in another direction, providing some community leaders with shared visions and a pan-European circuit for their ambitions. Policies promoted by the governments in the Chinese Mainland and in Taiwan (even though they are divided by the cross-Strait schism) also help homogenise the use of ethnic labels, for they promote national icons and points of reference that do not recognise the borders in Europe; they even strengthen the focus on Europe as an entity, because they promote pan-European overseas Chinese organisations and the formulation of pan-European agendas among the overseas Chinese.

The commercialisation of the ethnic label in Chinese catering (and in some parts of Europe in the formation of Chinatowns) is an important element in identity-building. The use of ethnic icons within a successful business setting gives strength to economic, political and cultural rallying along ethnic lines. Inclusion of ethnic elements may give an edge in city planning and investment projects, leading to collaboration between overseas Chinese entrepreneurs, local government and large corporations. Local city regeneration projects centred on Chinatowns have gained financial support from the European Commission, thereby adding to the pan-European inclination among overseas Chinese community leaders. A large business sector delivering goods and services for Chinese catering operates across European borders in order to profit from scale of operation within the single market.

The transborder pull of Europe, of course, does not engender one pan-European overseas Chinese identity. However, it contributes a range of resources that the overseas Chinese can claim by asserting ethnic labels.

Although Europe does not provide a very strong infrastructure for multicultural politics (as issues on nationality, immigration and citizenship are, in general, a matter for national governments), groups in European countries promoting anti-racist activism, race relations agendas, and cultural diversity increasingly see themselves in European and global contexts. Chinese working in such contexts, while asserting a Chinese ethnicity, include it within wider issues of ethnic exclusion and racist prejudice.

For the individual, Chinese ethnic identity may position itself as an asset to be used or as a burden difficult to avoid. Assimilation with the 'host' culture appears as an option for many overseas Chinese; for some Chinese parents in Europe, helping their children to overcome linguistic, educational and cultural barriers is a greater priority than the maintenance of their 'Chineseness'. Some do assimilate; for them, participating in community activities or using ethnic symbols is of minor importance. Being of Chinese origin for them is an existential condition of little importance in their lives.

Some who have assimilated find, in common with many other Europeans, an interest in exploring their origins. The knowledge that their past sets them off from their friends and peers encourages them to seek their roots. For them, learning a Chinese language and about China becomes a hobby, and sometimes a path into a career, where the use of ethnic identity becomes an important aspect of their lives. Others who have assimilated may find themselves socially disadvantaged and seek to improve their situation by asserting their ethnic origin. The line between those who are and those who are not members of overseas Chinese communities is not fixed.

The example of one particular overseas Chinese association may serve as an example of the variability of ethnicity. The association in question was the overall Cantonese-based organisation in one medium-sized British city. It had a long history of internal disagreements, due both to personality clashes and differences of origin (in the New Territories and Hong Kong Island); city council provisions of support and funds did not alleviate these tensions, but did give them new dimensions. A lottery money grant for community development further exacerbated the divisions, and liaison officers employed by the city council became the target of resentment from all groups involved. Mainland Mandarin-speaking immigrants arriving in the 1990s began to form a new community of highly educated residents and began to make claims on the city council. They used the local Chinese Student and Scholar Association and money and logistic support from the education section of the Chinese consulate to organise Chinese festivals, cooperating with the local overseas Chinese association. The local overseas Chinese association was so divided that it could no longer arrange such events on its own. The cooperation between the two bodies was regarded positively by the city council that subsequently provided financial support. New appointees to local authority liaison posts went to highly qualified Mandarin-speaking new immigrants. As the Chinese Student and Scholar Association increasingly became an unsuitable organisation for the many new long-term residents who had found work in the region, some of them joined the leadership of the original association. Due to the lack of a common Chinese language (the old members spoke Cantonese and the new Mandarin), the working language of the association became English. Is, in this instance, the cost of shared assertion of Chinese identity the abandonment of Chinese language as a shared medium of communication?

The constellation of issues differs between localities and situations – one case cannot provide more than an example of how overseas Chinese groups, Chinese and local government officials and others use the Chinese label. How does this case fit into the wider perspective? Although the general trend is that Cantonese loses and Mandarin gains importance within Chinese communities, the above example says little about general developments. It does reflect the efforts of the Chinese overseas affairs and consular officials to unite all overseas Chinese under one banner (a policy Chinese officials pursue worldwide). From that perspective, using English is only a temporary anomaly.

European Chinese?

This book has introduced the conditions of overseas Chinese across Europe and sought to identify the issues that unite and separate them.

The Chinese are not better or more united Europeans than other European residents. Some pan-European overseas Chinese association leaders do have visions and cooperation that span Europe. Europe has some policies towards migrant groups aimed at ethnic inclusiveness across borders, but these policies tend to unite migrants across ethnic differences. Chinese authorities hope that the Chinese can unite across Europe, but their efforts mainly affect a small group of association leaders.

The points that unite the overseas Chinese within the individual European nation states and in the local communities are – on balance – of greater significance for them in their daily lives. Divisions and tensions in overseas Chinese societies provide good evidence that they share identity: they invest in ethnic symbols and disagree about their use. If conflict is a measure of the intensity of overseas Chinese ethnic identity, the local and national arenas are more important than the European ones.

Europe does not provide most overseas Chinese with any resources to compete for; it is too distant and abstract. But on the personal level, the story may be somewhat different. Among our interviews, migration *within* Europe was not uncommon. From Britain to the Netherlands and Germany, from the Netherlands to Italy, from Germany to Belgium and from the Netherlands to Austria. We heard of migration from Hungary to Italy and Spain, and from Italy to France. We were told about family members spread across Europe. Family links, of course, are not *ethnic* bonds; family visits and communication do not in themselves shape ethnic communities. These family bonds undoubtedly help some overseas Chinese to a better understanding of conditions in other parts of Europe on a personal level, but they have nothing to do with Europe or ethnic identity.

It is possible to travel through Europe mainly speaking Chinese with local people, be it Cantonese, Mandarin or Teochiu. It is possible to find speakers of these forms of Chinese in all major cities, and one would only need to know a few words in European languages to buy tickets and the like. One's travel through Europe could be booked through a Chinese travel agency. In many cities one could stay in Chinese hotels. All meals could be Chinese. In large cities, there are frequent Chinese cultural events and local daily media in Chinese. For Chinese travelling in Europe the ability to talk to locals in Chinese seems to be an advantage – an Italian and Norwegian meeting during a journey, for example, would normally both need to resort to a foreign language to communicate.

The Chinese presence in large parts of Europe and their visible role in catering and other service sectors, of course, do not mean that they are ethnically unified as European Chinese, although it may in some cases be easier to find common rapport between a Chinese in Kiruna and in Marseilles than between a Swedish and a French person from those cities. The real test, of course, is what happens if an overseas Chinese moves between European places. The availability of an 'overseas Chinese' infrastructure does help the Chinese migrant, as it would anywhere in the world. An ethnic Dane migrating to Austria, Italy or the Czech Republic would find no or only an insignificant compatriot community to rely on.

The question about a European Chinese identity, therefore, should be seen in the context of how the political, economic and social environment helps shape the ways in which the overseas Chinese use their ethnic identity. Europe as a political entity plays a minor role.

Approaches

Who are the overseas Chinese in Europe? This book deals with a question that cannot be answered in any simple way. The criteria by which one can classify and summarise overseas Chinese and understand them as a group, be it in Europe or in individual European countries, all seem inadequate.

Fredrik Barth's understanding of 'ethnic boundaries' does help us towards an understanding of how overseas Chinese communities perpetuate themselves and undergo dynamic changes in European countries. The origins, political inclination, and social characteristics of the overseas Chinese differ widely both within European states and across Europe, and yet in public contexts they are regarded as a community. We have seen how overseas Chinese leaders promote an idea of a shared community, and we have seen how sub-ethnic divisions reinforce such an idea. We have also seen how the reference to an authentic Chinese 'home' culture on public ritual occasions like Chinese New Year Festivals and public speeches asserts Chinese ethnic distinctiveness, and how ethnic symbols are actively used in the catering industry and in Chinatowns. The Barthian boundary management, however, goes further than the explicit use of ethnic markers in contexts where different ethnic groups meet. Boundary management is an important element of individuals' pursuit of social status, economic profit and political influence. The *agency* of those involved in ethnic boundary management is entrenched in the economy, social structures and politics. They construct Chinese identity to further their interests. The use of Chinese lanterns, dragons, yin-yang symbols and other decorations in the catering industry is an example of *business branding* where the economic benefit is immediately visible. Arches, signboards with Chinese characters, and festivals in Chinatowns support this economic utility. In addition, catering is a flexible sector that enables the upkeep of migrant labour that is otherwise marginalised.

Chinatowns are also a major asset for local authorities in European countries, often included in initiatives to regenerate derelict areas, and also considered part of the tourism industry. Social services for overseas Chinese residents form part of local governments' activities, either inspired by national race relations policies, or in order to solve local problems. Chinese language schools for overseas Chinese children in many places receive some aid from local authorities. The interaction between local authorities and overseas Chinese community leaders creates the conditions for political assertion of ethnic difference. The interaction is more often than not channelled through civil society organisations: migrant, native-place and similar associations are established by the overseas Chinese, while community centres, health clinics and other institutions are established by local governments to cater for overseas Chinese (often with Chinese community leaders as board members and advisors). For those who engage in Chinatown and community politics, upholding and interpreting ethnic difference is essential. Political status and influence is premised upon the assertion of Chinese separateness within the wider society.

The 'home' governments seek support for their political and economic interests by appointing overseas Chinese leaders to symbolic political posts, and by promoting economic links with overseas Chinese communities. These links are premised upon the assertion of ethnic identity. For community leaders the honours bestowed by 'home' authorities give status and influence that reinforce their role vis-à-vis local authorities in the 'host' countries.

The ethnic boundary is thus a fundamental condition of migrant society, around which economic and political structures which are crucial for the distribution of resources and refer to ethnic difference as a criterion have been erected. Ideas, cultural images, myths, symbols, moral judgements and so on revolve around the utility-maximising behaviour of the participants. In some contexts, of course, people of Chinese origin may free themselves from participation; this is increasingly the case for second- and third-generation Chinese in Europe. In other contexts, where the institutions of ethnicity impose themselves with greater force in the form of racist separation, it may be impossible to extricate oneself from the Chinese ethnic category.

Beyond the ethnic boundary as a factor shaping the political economy of overseas Chinese community, Chinese ethnicity is the product of a long history, involving the establishment of the Chinese nation state, the migration of Chinese to different parts of the world, the history of Chinese migration to Europe, and the diverse sub-ethnic origins of the Chinese communities in Europe. These work both to integrate the Chinese as one group and to divide them. Ideas of the Chinese nation, the assertion of cultural Han unity, a shared written language and a common history, and the claim to a morally distinct civilisation different from Western civilisations serve to unify the overseas Chinese across all other divisions.

The dividing factors, in particular the cross-Strait political division among overseas Chinese, tend to reinforce the idea of Chinese identity, for both those who see the Republic of China (in Taiwan) and those who regard the People's Republic of China (in the Mainland) as the real China contend for the same ethnic and national symbols. The political disagreement engages both sides in similar processes of imagining a homogenous Chinese culture. Dialects provide focal points for asserting difference. Yet dialect speakers are drawn towards Mandarin as a national language; they assert linguistic difference within the framework of a shared language. Historically, the dominance of Cantonese among overseas Chinese in some areas and Hong Kong's role as a separate polity with a distinct culture allowed Cantonese speakers to dissociate themselves somewhat from other Chinese; this was very much helped by the Cultural Revolution and the Cold War. Reform and opening on the Mainland and Hong Kong's retrocession have forced Hong Kong migrants to see themselves as an, albeit culturally and politically distinct, part of the larger Chinese nation.

Dialect and regional divisions among the overseas Chinese often originate in strong historical animosities, as evidenced by the case of migrants from Taishan and from Southern Zhejiang. Their competition is focused on the same ethnic resources, and claims to be culturally and socially distinct are phrased in similar ways. Why do they persist in Europe? Sub-ethnic distinctions are politically useful for community leaders. The assertion of local ties with 'homelands' in China allows overseas Chinese community leaders to gain recognition and status, and it allows them to establish native-place associations as springboards for influence in other ethnic associations in the Chinese community. For the Chinese authorities in the Mainland, such local links were essential for gaining access to 'old' overseas Chinese who supported the Nationalists on Taiwan. Localism, therefore, is not only a colourful variation of the national ideal, it is instrumental for forging the national integration.

It is, in my view, not useful to reduce Chinese identity to a practical utility, or the claim that Chinese culture is a shallow emblem used for business purposes. It is interesting to observe how the political economy of the ethnic boundary creates ingenious expressions of ethnic culture. The diversity and richness of overseas Chinese communities, the many historical origins, the histories of migration, the use of ethnic symbols to achieve political aims, and the many fascinating life stories of overseas Chinese indicate that a reductionist rejection of Chinese ethnicity would not be appropriate.

Notes

Preface

1 References to the interviews are in three different formats in order to make attribution impossible. References in interviews to specific places, persons and organisations have, where not essential in the context, been anonymised. It is still possible for people with intimate knowledge of the community to guess the identity of some of the interviewees, but this is unavoidable in research like this.

2 The title of the research project was *European Chinese, Chinese Europeans: Strategies and Identities*; grant number: L324253003.

Introduction

1 Cited in *Renmin Ribao (Haiwaiban)*, 13.01.1999, p. 3.

2 In contrast, there is a vast literature on the overseas Chinese globally, mainly concerned with their communities in Southeast Asia and the New World, see Pan (1990; 1998), McKeown (1999) and Weggel (1996). Heitmann (1999) has compiled a bibliography of relevant of works organised by region and annotated with key words.

1 European Chinese identity in the 1990s

1 Dikötter (1996); see also Dikötter (1997), Chow (1997) and Osterhammel (1997, 117–119).

2 The term 'imagined community' is borrowed from Benedict Anderson (1983), who used it to explain the genesis of nationalism in Europe, which eventually shaped the nation states.

3 Huang Sande's account is supported by research by Zhou Yumin and Shao Yong (1993, 447–9); and by Cai Shaoqing (1987, 299–312).

4 Their virtual disappearance is according to Ernest Gellner (1983) due to the homogenising effect of nationalism that did not tolerate ethnic difference within its bounds. Where such distinctions still exist in Europe, any primeval credentials they may possess are easily eclipsed by struggles over political power, social status and economic resources, for example in Ulster, between northern and southern Italy, and between Germany's 'old' and 'new' federal states.

5 The issue of such diversity as a structuring factor in the organisation of overseas Chinese communities was first synthesised by Lawrence Crissman (1967). Bryna Goodman (1995) has examined the role of native place as a focus of identification

among migrants in Chinese history. Mak Lau-Fong explores how dialect groups became sub-ethnic Chinese communities in Malaya (Mai Liufang 1985).

6 This is based on a small number of interviews with Belgian overseas Chinese. There does not exist any sufficient study of language use among overseas Chinese in Europe to make statements beyond scattered observations.

7 On sub-ethnic groups, see Liu and Faure (1996).

8 On the reborn significance of the native place in China's recent internal migration, see Solinger (1997), Tomba (1998), Xiang (1998), and Ma and Xiang (1998).

9 Informal conversation, 1996.

10 The Chinese consulates issue passports for and attest statements on Chinese citizens who are not properly registered in their place of residence in Europe. Normally, the consulates demand formal statements from specially recognised overseas Chinese associations in support of the claims of such citizens. Passports and official statements issued by the official representation of the state of origin have been indispensable aspects of the procedure in most amnesties for illegal immigrants in Italy, France, Spain and Portugal. This gives great influence to presidents of officially assigned Chinese associations, an influence that local officials in the sending areas are keen to make use of when illegal immigrants hailing from their area seek to normalise their status in their country of residence.

11 Den kinesiske Forening, Danmai Huaren Xiehui.

12 Fuzhou tongxianghui.

13 Chaozhou tongxianghui.

14 Details of how the legal requirements are administrated can be found in a circular from the Danish Ministry of Justice, 'Cirkulære om dansk indfødsret ved naturalisation (til politimestre og politidirektøren i København)', *Ministerialtidende*, 1997 hæfte 38 (3. Oktober 1997) nr. 132. Detailed instructions to the local police authorities (which handle the applications) indicate that applicants must have sufficient oral skills in Danish to make themselves understood. The decision to bestow Danish nationality on named foreigners is made by passing a law in parliament once every year. Foreigners between 18 and 23 years who have been resident continuously in Denmark for at least ten years can be naturalised by an administrative decision.

15 Certificates of naturalisation are granted in accordance with the British Nationality Act 1981 which came into force on 1 January 1983. An application can normally be submitted on the completion of the fourth year of residence, so that the naturalisation takes effect from the completed fifth year of residence.

16 Measures proposed in early 2002 would, if they were formally introduced, require that applicants for naturalisation must pass a test of their ability to speak English and must swear an oath of allegiance.

17 The origin was in the United Nations' *Universal Declaration of Human Rights* in 1948. Group and minority rights, however, did not gain importance before the 1960s, and terms like 'affirmative action', 'minority rights', 'plural' or 'pluralistic society' and 'culturally differentiated societies' only gradually entered political debates in Europe during the 1970s and 1980s. The main efforts initially aimed to deal with racism and religious intolerance and were gradually extended to the treatment of immigrant groups.

18 This theme has particularly been developed in a volume edited by Joppke (1998) and with special reference to France and Germany in a book by Kastoryano (1996).

19 See Ogden (1993) for a general discussion and Live (1998a, 111) for a description of the consequences for the Chinese in France. This *republican* ethos was not only directed against immigrant groups, as demonstrated in the neglect of France's native minority languages like Breton and local identities like the Corsican.

20 See *Bericht der Beauftragten der Bundesregierung für Ausländerfragen über die Lage der Ausländer in der Bundesrepublik Deutschland* (December 1997). Draft.

21 'Norme urgenti in materia di asilo politico di ingresso e soggiorno dei cittadini extracomunitari e di regolarizzazzione dei cittadini extracomunitari ed apolidi già presenti nel territorio dello stato'. The Martelli Law consists of law no. 416 of 30 December 1989 and law no. 39 of 28 February 1990, amending law no. 416. The coordinated text of the two laws is published in *Norme in materia di asilo politico di ingresso e soggiorno dei cittadini extracomunitari*. Roma: Libreria dello stato, 1990, pp. 7–42.

22 Law no. 376 of 16 June 1996, 'Disposizioni urgenti in materia di politica dell'immigrazione e per la regolamentazione dell'ingresso e soggiorno nel territorio nazionale dei cittadini dei Paesi non appartenendi all'Unione europea'. *Gazzetta Ufficiale della Repubblica Italiana (Serie Generale)*. 137:156 (17 July 1996), pp. 10–15.

23 On the the two first amnesties, see Foot (1995, 146–8).

24 The labour market perspective of immigration policy in Italy has been subject to a detailed quantitative study of labour supply and demand by sector and region in Frey (1992). The main argument against the labour market approach in immigration legislation was its assumption that amnesties would do away with the irregular labour market. Even the official Martelli Conference that produced its findings in June 1990 acknowledged that the law had not been able to reduce irregular labour relations, and that amnesties were unable to solve the problem.

25 Although Article 10 of the Martelli Law of 1990 provided for an amnesty for illegal immigrants who wished to work independently (this involved knowledge of Italian and other hard preconditions, which Chinese 'irregular' immigrants could normally not fulfil), the 'Dini Decree' of 1995 did not allow clandestine immigrants in Italy to register for an amnesty in any other capacity than 'dependent workers' (Ceccagno and Omodeo 1997). However, this rule seems to have been lifted in the latter part of the 1990s.

26 This dependency was in many ways similar to the dependency the labour voucher system in the UK imposed in the 1960s and 1970s.

27 Bauböck (1999, 143) makes the point that 'ethnic diversity is perpetuated through discrimination as well as through political mobilisation'.

28 The document was seen on http://europa.eu.int/search97cgi/ on 7 December 1998.

29 The Forum was suspended due to financial irregularities exposed during an audit by the EU authorities.

30 There is considerable difficulty in defining 'racist' movements and parties in Europe. Many agree that they do exist, carried by xenophobic sentiments, right-wing ideologies and populist programmes sweeping up protest votes in elections; yet due to the illegality of racist propaganda and symbolism, they cover their tracks, presenting their concerns indirectly. Also, the scope for interpretation of what constitutes racism is wide. On these and related problems, see Fennema (1997) and Thränhardt (1995).

31 That includes all levels of government and civil society concerned with the overseas Chinese as a group.

32 See http://www.rosettaproject.org under Nung–Vietnam.

33 I.e. Xinjiang Autonomous Region.

34 Symbolised in a Committee for Tibet, Mongolia and East Turkestan, established in 1994 (Besson 1998, 188).

35 See *Islamische Zeitung*, 23 Aug 1998, cited from http://www.unternehmen.com/IZ/ (4 December 1998).

2 Chinese migration to Europe

1 Angel Island was the immigration station in San Francisco that for Chinese immigrants gained a symbolic status similar to that of Ellis Island for European immigrants arriving in New York.

2 Waishengren, meaning people from outside Guangdong.

3 In 1901–2, for example, 120 Chinese students studied German literature, philosophy, politics and theology at the Friederich-Wilhelm-Universität in Berlin; in 1923, the number of Chinese at universities and colleges in Berlin is estimated to have been around 1,000; and in 1937, around 500 Chinese students remained in Berlin in spite of the political situation in Germany and the call to return to China to help in the fight against the Japanese invasion (Meng 1996, 30, 32 and 36).

4 The 'education fee' (peiyangfei) was rescinded in the mid-1990s as a part of the reform of the graduate labour market and university finances.

5 In Cantonese: Tang, Hau, Man, Pang, and Liu.

6 In Cantonese: Man.

7 They were called 'indigenous villagers' (yuan jumin) in the official terminology.

8 On this issue, see for example *Hong Kong Standard* 27.04.94, p. 3; 09.05.1994, p. 1;16.05.1994, p. 3; 25.05.1994, p. 4; *South China Morning Post* 04.07.1993, p. 3. On the involvement of British overseas Chinese in the petitioning, see *Jingji Ribao* (HK) 09.04.1994, p. A8.

9 *Ming Po* 29.03.1994, p. A4.

10 *Joint Declaration of the Government of the United Kingdom of Great Britain and Northern Ireland and the Government of the People's Republic of China on the Question of Hong Kong.* The draft text of the document was approved by the two Governments on 26 September 1984.

11 *The Basic Law of the Hong Kong Special Administrative Region of the People's Republic of China.* Adopted on 4 April 1990 by the National People's Congress.

12 See *Zhonghua Renmin Gongheguo Quanquo Renmin Daibiao Dahui Changwu Weiyuanhui Gongbao*, No. 4 , 20 May 1996, pp. 97–101; in particular formulations on p. 100.

13 One of our interviews was with an interviewee who had to excuse himself several times during the interview to address a banquet held in an adjacent room in honour of a visiting Cambodian minister.

14 I.e. visa as dependent workers.

15 Chinese ambassadors and consuls have clear instructions from Beijing to extend consular protection to and intervene on behalf of citizens of the People's Republic only, and not ethnic Chinese as such. This principle also extends to repatriating illegal immigrants.

16 I.e. Italians.

17 Other interviewees in a similar fashion refused to discuss illegal immigration, like in the answer of a Belgian overseas Chinese to a question on human trafficking from Zhejiang: 'I am not sure about this. I've heard that it exists, but I have no knowledge of it' (033//090). Or 'The Italian police permits that they do (black work), we don't know the concrete circumstances, we are not clear about it, but in the heart we understand what it is all about' (052//032).

18 Pairault (1995).

19 Campani, Carchedi and Tassinari (1994).

20 This is a common procedure. During the recent amnesty in Italy, the Chinese embassy also issued certificates, passports and other documentation, based on statements by specially authorised overseas Chinese organisations on the identity, present situation and conduct of illegal immigrants (–/080/029).

21 Zhong-Fa Youyi Huzu Hui, the Sino-French Association for Friendship and Mutual Help.

3   Chinatown, Europe

1 Lit. 'street of the Chinese', Tangren is a term originally used by the Cantonese to distinguish themselves from other people. The etymology is 'people of the Tang dynasty', signifying the descendants of the Chinese who arrived in South China during and after the Tang dynasty. It may, therefore, refer both to 'Cantonese' and 'Chinese'.

2 Lit. 'China-city'.

3 For example, it is the Chinese name of the large hotel, restaurant, gallery and convention centre Chinagora in Paris, and it is the inscription on the Chinatown arch in Liverpool.

4 Lit. 'Chinese port'.

5 In the mid-1990s, before Hong Kong's retrocession and before the Asian financial crisis, there was strong and sustained investment from Southeast Asia and Hong Kong in Europe, allegedly mainly from overseas Chinese. On top of that, both private investors and state corporations in the Chinese Mainland made significant investments in Europe throughout the 1990s. For large investors to obtain residence permits was normally not a problem. It is true that most Chinatowns could not absorb more activities, but it is also doubtful whether such capital investments were seeking a Chinatown milieu.

6 Quoted from the *Inspraakkrant Oosterdokseiland* (Public Hearing Paper on Oosterdokseiland), issued early Summer 2000, as seen on http://www.amsterdam.nl/nieuws actueel (30/06/2000).

7 Shunde and Nanhai are both part of the former 'three counties' (sanyi) area of Guangdong (Shunde, Nanhai and Panyu). As Panyu county has long been a rural jurisdiction under Guangzhou City, and Shunde and Nanhai both were counties under Foshan City from the 1950s until the early 1990s, when they were made county-level cities directly subordinated the province, the concept 'three counties' lost currency, and was replaced by a collective reference to 'Nan-Shun', i.e. Nanhai-Shunde.

8 A 'dancing dragon' (wulong) forms part of processions at Chinese festivals, normally consisting of a large, carved wooden dragon-head and a body and tail of 20–30 metres, carried by a band of dancing people.

9 Like in many other European Chinatowns, the volunteers carrying out dragon and lion dances are European amateurs in local martial arts clubs.

10 He thinks that Antwerp is well situated for tourists 'doing' Belgium by visiting Antwerp during primary stays in the Netherlands or Germany.

11 This view was echoed by Costa-Lascoux and Live (1995, 32).

12 One interviewee said: 'You do not need to build a Chinatown (Tangrenjie), Prato has already developed into one' (052//029). The way he expressed himself indicates that the use of the term 'Chinatown' in connection with these settlements in Italy feels awkward.

13 Lit. 'I engraved a signboard' (wo kele yige pai).

14 *Siyu Chinese Times*, no. 78, Oct. 1995, p. 24–5; no. 79, Nov. 1995, p. 25; and no. 82, March 1996, p. 22–3.

15 *Siyu Chinese Times*, no. 78., Oct. 1995, p. 24.

4 Formation of sub-ethnic identities

1 I use the name Siyi to refer to the region unless the distinction is relevant.

2 See Liu Nanwei (1994, 201–30); Ministry of Civil Affairs (1995, 52–4); and Chen Chao and Wang Xiguang (1986, 119–25) for details of the evolution of jurisdiction in the area.

3 According to incomplete statistics compiled in 1985, 16,000 of the 785,000 overseas Chinese from Taishan lived in Europe. The proportion is not likely to be different in other parts of the Siyi; in that case, the number would be around 35,000. See Taishan County Overseas Affairs Office (1992, 63).

4 The Hong Kong dollar's value approximated the value of the yuan. Individual donations also included donations from personal foundations.

5 See Wuyi University 1993, 8.

6 The earliest county was Xinhui, from which the three or four other counties were carved when their population of settlers grew in the early Ming Dynasty.

7 *Ouzhou Shibao – Nouvelles d'Europe* 10 Sept. 1997.

8   A large proportion of county magistrates appointed to Chixi were natives of counties with a large Hakka population.

9   For extended descriptions, see *Local History of Kaiping County* (Anonymous 1933, 171–81).

10 Dyer Ball in *Things Chinese*, quoted from Comber (1959, 29).

11 For descriptions of the coolie trade, see Campbell (1923), Pan (1990, 43–57) and Sinn (1995a, 1995b).

12 Mei (1979, 475–6) indicates that the leading merchants in America's Chinatowns were from the Sanyi region.

13 See Hua Linshan and Isabelle Thireau (1996) and Madeleine Hsu (2000) for a thorough discussion of the lineages of Taishan.

14 See Elizabeth Sinn (1995a, 1995b) for a general overview of the migrations through Hong Kong (the main port for migrants from the Siyi); and June Mei (1979) on the early (1850–82) migration of Siyinese to California. The absolute majority of Siyi migrants were labourers induced or abducted by crimps to become objects of the coolie trade.

15 Telephone conversation 16.05.1997.

16 In Mandarin Zhigongtang; in English often referred to as the Chinese Freemasons.

17 *Siyi Zonghuiguan bashi zhou nian jinian tekan. Yijiulingliu nian zhi yijiubaliu nian* (In Commemoration of 80 Years of the See Yip Association of England, 1906–1986), [Liverpool]: [1986], pp. 28–31 (bilingual; quoted from the English translation).

18 Both the Chinese and English versions state '18th'. However, from the context it is obvious that it must be '19th'.

19 *Siyi Zonghuiguan bashi zhou nian jinian tekan. Yijiulingliu nian zhi yijiubaliu nian* (In Commemoration of 80 Years of the See Yip Association of England, 1906–1986), [Liverpool]: [1986], pp. 77–82, lists the educational and occupational achievements of more than 60 second-generation Siyinese.

20 In Mandarin: Lundun Wuyi Tongxianghui.

21 Interview reference withheld for the sake of anonymity.

22 *The China Yearbook, 1935* (the Chinese title is *Zhonghua Nianjian*) does not include this information.

23 Zou Taofen (1936, 26) even claims that the Qingtian migrants in Europe had peaked at between 30,000 and 40,000 during the preceding decade.

24 These methods are not only used by people from Qingtian.

25 Inferred from a brief conversation in Brussels with an overseas Chinese affairs representative of the Taibei government, June 1996.

26 A working document of the Taibei government's Overseas Affairs Commission regards the situation of overseas Chinese organisations in France as one of 'dissolution'. The structure of the older organisations is corroding, and 'they cannot bring forth leaders of renown, and, of course, cannot condense the forces of the overseas Chinese organisations. Within the couple of years [of their existence], the new organisations have not been able to replace the social impact of the old organisations'. Such an interpretation, of course, suggests that the emergence of a Qingtian association in France in 1994 is merely attributable to local realignments among overseas Chinese organisations in France.

27 Association des Chinois résidant en France (Lü Fa Huaqiao Julebu); the name in French means 'Association of Chinese Living in France', whereas the Chinese name means 'Club of Overseas Chinese in France'.

28 Huayi, i.e. Southeast Asian descendants of Chinese.

29 Conversation with the person in question, Paris 1996.

30 Telephone conversation with Ma Zhuomin (Barcelona), 22.09.97.

31 He uses the Shanghainese word 'amulin', which means somebody who is naive or easily misled.

5   **Ethnic politics**

1   *Sic.* The interviewee used the term 'Ougongti' (European Communities) rather than 'Oumeng' (European Union).
2   For long periods of the twentieth century the existence of ethnic organisations was prohibited in France and Spain.
3   His concern was about being identified as boastful by other leaders. We have anonymised the information here, and so keep our promise of silence.
4   Several interviewees indicated that there were no membership registers, or that any there had been were never updated or used; membership fees are in many cases of no importance.
5   For an analysis of this see Liang (2001).
6   See pp 30–2 above.
7   Zhuyin Zimu is a special set of phonetic symbols, by which one syllable is represented with one or two symbols; it is popularly referred to as 'Bo-po-mo-fo'. Zhuyin Zimu was mainly used in Taiwan, while Hanyu Pinyin was preferred in the Mainland.
8   The Hong Kong government was an important source of support, as were the Taiwanese authorities. The Mainland adopted a very passive role in terms of text books, teacher training, and finance, but gradually built up supporting institutions in China, like the Chinese Language Institute which is affiliated Jinan University in Guangzhou.
9   These stereotypes incidentally differ radically from those used in China: the Chinatown festivals in Britain, France, Belgium and the Netherlands largely use symbolism extracted from Cantonese popular festivals, developing it further within the local context overseas, while the current popular festive trends in China, based on Canto-pop and Western influences (like the massive public use of Santa Claus) are largely ignored.

6   **European Chinese and Chinese patriotism**

1   The Hope Programme (xiwang gongcheng) aims a collecting support among overseas Chinese for the education of children in poor rural areas.
2   The interviewee used the terms 'tuanjie, liyong, fenhua, wajie'. 'Unite and exploit' refer to different ways of dealing with forces friendly to the CCP, and 'divide and disintegrate' with opposition forces (like Taiwan-leaning organisations and exile dissident groups).
3   The overseas Chinese policy between 1949 and 1970 has been examined in detail by FitzGerald (1972) and Zhuang Guotu (1993).
4   The origin of the CCP's overseas Chinese work was in the participation in the Institute for the Overseas Chinese Movement, jointly established by the CCP and the Nationalists in 1926. It was not until after the Long March that it was formalised under the auspices of the Overseas Work Committee, established in 1937. In 1940, it was *de facto* vested in the Overseas Chinese Federation for National Salvation in Yan'an (see Yu Lehua 1994, 354–5). It was, perhaps for these historical reasons, always considered an issue of the united front.
5   Frequent statements in the media and popular literature indicate a much larger contribution to the Chinese economy from the overseas Chinese; such statements normally include investments originating in Hong Kong, Macau and Taiwan. However, the overseas Chinese do not include Chinese in Hong Kong, Macau and Taiwan.
6   The resumption of overseas Chinese affairs policy in the late 1970s was publicly heralded in a leading article and a transcript of a speech by Liao Chengzhi in *Renmin Ribao* on 04.01.1978. This reflected the themes of a meeting held in December 1977, following a remark by Deng Xiaoping to visiting overseas Chinese in September 1977 that 'overseas Chinese affairs work will get onto the agenda'. In those pre-reform days,

Marshall Li Xiannian's intervention was necessary to break Hua Guofeng's initial opposition (Xinhua News Agency 03.01.1978, in Anonymous 1978). It is important to consider that the revival of overseas Chinese affairs policy predated the start of the Deng reforms by more than one year.

7 The following description is largely based on Mao Qixiong and Lin Xiaodong (1993).

8 Official rules in the PRC between the 1950s and early 1990s indicated how work appointments should reflect people's educational levels. During the Cultural Revolution, it was a common punishment to appoint people to jobs 'below' the standard their educational level entitled them to.

9 Several Chinese government reports we have seen and personal accounts by overseas Chinese suggest that improper and illegal practices aimed at obtaining donations and investment or at involving overseas Chinese in corrupt schemes were not uncommon.

10 An account by Flower and Leonard (1998) about the building of a local temple in Sichuan gives an interesting perspective on how local interests and Party ideology interact. In this case not overseas Chinese policy, but development of tourism was the logic used by locals to further their interests.

11 The Chinese term for patriotism (aiguo) is ambiguous, as it is felt by many to imply both 'love for the country' and 'love for the state'.

12 Both institutions were the symbolic embodiment of the People's Republic's political legitimacy, for they represented the broad, popular coalition of 'progressive forces' that under the leadership of the CCP established the People's Republic and instituted the 'New Democracy' that Mao Zedong had outlined in the 1940s.

13 Later posted on the http://www.ocac.gov.tw web site of the Overseas Chinese Affairs Commission

14 When the Mainland dissident Wei Jingsheng visited Taiwan in 2001, making strong polemic statements against China's unification with reference to the Mainland's political system, he caused great unease and consternation in Taiwan. Even those who promote Taiwanese independence in some form seemed to be taken aback, feeling that Wei did not further their cause.

7 Chinese business, ethnic business

1 *Huaqiao jingji gaikuang* (Outline of Overseas Chinese Economy), published on http:// www.gcbn.net (as seen in September 1999), provides a rough country-by-country overview of the economic situation among overseas Chinese.

2 Emmanuel Ma Mung (1993, 1) on France, citing Roger Waldinger's work on the USA.

3 By the early 2000s, the restaurant had changed decoration and food style, now serving Chinese dishes. Had the market changed, or had the 'ethnic' inclination of the entrepreneur finally gained dominance over his economic calculus? We shall never know for sure. However, this particular puzzle does not need to exercise us any more.

4 The number of Italian amnesties to illegal Chinese immigrants was 4,498 in 1987 and 9,747 in 1990. The number of Chinese with residence permits rose from some few hundred in 1975 to 22,875 in 1993 (Carchedi, 1994, 51).

5 The embassy apparently made no public statement, and initially sought to dissuade the overseas Chinese from making a demonstration in Hamburg. However, we infer from several interviews that the embassy later tacitly supported the demonstrators.

Bibliography

Adolino, Jessica R. (1998), *Ethnic Minorities, Electoral Politics and Political Integration in Britain*. London: Pinter.

Anderson, Benedict (1983), *Imagined Communities*. London: Verso.

Anonymous (1933), *Kaiping Xianzhi* (Local History of Kaiping County). [Reprint edition: Guangdong Sheng Kaiping Xian zhi. In the series *Zhongguo Fangzhi Congshu*, no. 6, Taibei: Chengwen Chubanshe, 1966].

Anonymous (1978), *Bixu zhongshi qiaowu gongzuo* (We Must Emphasise Overseas Chinese Affairs Work). Hong Kong: Sanlian Shudian Xianggang fendian.

Archaimbault, Charles (1987), 'Boeren en landlopers: Migranten uit Oost-China'. In Gregor Benton and Hans Vermeulen (eds), *De Chinezen*. Muiderberg: Dick Coutinho, pp. 22–6.

Barth, Fredrik (ed.) (1969), *Ethnic Groups and Boundaries*. Oslo: Universitets Forlaget.

Bauböck, Rainer (1999), 'Liberal Justifications for Ethnic Group Rights'. In Christian Joppke and Steven Lukes (eds), *Multicultural Questions*. Oxford: Oxford University Press.

Benton, Gregor and Edmund Terence Gomez (2001), *Chinatown and Transnationalism. Ethnic Chinese in Europe and Southeast Asia*. Canberra ACT: Centre for the Study of the Chinese Southern Diaspora, Division of Pacific and Asian History, Research School of Pacific and Asian Studies, Australian National University.

Benton, Gregor and Frank N. Pieke (eds) (1998), *The Chinese in Europe*. Basingstoke, Hampshire: Macmillan.

Benton, Gregor and Hans Vermeulen (eds) (1987), *De Chinezen*. Muiderberg: Dick Coutinho.

Besson, Frédérique-Jeanne (1998), 'Les Ouïgours hors du Turkestan oriental: de l'exil à la formation d'une diaspora', *Cahiers d'études sur la Méditerranée orientale et le monde turco-iranien*, no. 25 (January–June), pp. 161–92.

Blotevogel, Hans Heinrich, Ursula Müller-ter Jung and Gerald Wood (1993), 'From Itinerant Worker to Immigrant? The Geography of Guestworkers in Germany'. In Russell King (ed.), *Mass Migration in Europe. The Legacy and the Future*. London: Belhaven Press.

Bortolotti, Franco (ed.) (1993) *La città della Piana*. In the series *Ires Toscana quaderni*, no. 15–16 (September–December). Firenze: Ires Toscana.

Bortolotti, Franco and Tassinari, Alberto (1992) *Immigrati a Firenze. Il caso della collettività cinese*. In the series *Ires Toscana quaderni*, no. 8 (July–August). Firenze: Ires Toscana.

Bourdieu, Pierre (1977), *Outline of a Theory of Practice*. Cambridge: Cambridge University Press.

Brass, Paul R. (1991), *Ethnicity and Nationalism: Theory and Comparison*. London: Sage Publications.

Brubaker, Rogers (1992), *Citizenship and Nationhood in France and Germany*. Cambridge, MA: Harvard University Press.

Cai Shaoqing (1987), *Zhongguo jindai huidang shi yanjiu* (Research on Chinese Lodges and Societies in Modern History). Beijing: Zhonghua Shuju.

Campbell, Persia Crawford (1923), *Chinese Coolie Emigration to Countries within the British Empire* (Reprint edition: London: Frank Cass, 1971).

Campani, Giovanna, Francesco Carchedi and Alberto Tassinari (eds) (1994), *L'immigrazione silenziosa. Le comunità cinesi in Italia*. Torino: Edizioni della Fondazione Giovanni Agnelli.

Carchedi, Francesco (1994), 'La presenza cinese in Italia. Direzionalità dei flussi, dimensioni del fenomeno e caratteristiche strutturali'. In Giovanna Campani, Francesco Carchedi and Alberto Tassinari (eds), *L'immigrazione silenziosa. Le comunità cinesi in Italia*. Torino: Edizioni della Fondazione Giovanni Agnelli, pp. 41–74.

Ceccagno, Antonella (ed.) (1997), *Il caso delle comunità cinesi. Comunicazione interculturale ed istituzioni*. Roma: Armando srl.

Ceccagno, Antonella (1998), *Cinesi d'Italia. Storie in bilico tra due culture*. Roma: Manifestolibri srl.

Ceccagno, Antonella, and Maria Omodeo (1997), 'Gli effetti del Decreto Legge 489/95 sui cinesi di Prato'. In Antonella Ceccagno (ed.), *Il caso delle comunità cinesi. Comunicazione interculturale ed istituzioni*. Roma: Armando srl, pp. 59–68.

Chen Chao and Wang Xiguang (1986), *Zhongguo xianshi zhengqu ziliao shouce* (Handbook on Administrative Divisions of Counties and Cities in China). Beijing: Ditu Chubanshe.

Chen Murong (ed.) (1990), *Qingtian Xianzhi* (Local History of Qingtian County), Hangzhou: Zhejiang Renmin Chubanshe.

Chen Sanjing (1986), *Huagong yu Ouzhan* (Chinese Workers and the European War). In the series *Zhongyang Yanjiuyuan Jindaishi Yanjiusuo zhuankan*, no. 52. Taibei: Zhongyang Yanjiuyuan Jindaishi Yanjiusuo.

Chen Sanjing (1996), *Lü Ou jiaoyu yundong* (The Education Movement in Europe). In the series *Zhongyang Yanjiuyuan Jindaishi Yanjiusuo shiliao congshu*, no. 27. Taibei: Zhongyang Yanjiuyuan Jindaishi Yanjiusuo.

Chen Tianjun, Huang Renfu and Huang Zhongji (comp.) (1985), *Taishan Xian qiaoxiang zhi* (History of Taishan County, Native Place of Overseas Chinese). Taishan: Zhonggong Taishan Xianwei Xuanchuanbu.

Clegg, Jenny (1994), *Fu Manchu and the 'Yellow Peril': The Making of a Racist Myth*. Stoke-on-Trent: Trentham Books.

Chiu, Stephen W. K. and Ho-fung Hung (1997), *The Colonial State and Rural Protests in Hong Kong*. Hong Kong: Hong Kong Institute of Asia-Pacific Studies, Chinese University of Hong Kong (*Occasional Paper* no. 59).

Chow, Kai-wing (1997), 'Imagining Boundaries of Blood. Zhang Binglin and the Invention of the Han "Race" in Modern China'. In Frank Dikötter (ed.), *The Construction of Racial Identities in China and Japan*. London: Hurst, pp. 34–52.

Cohen, Abner (ed.) (1974), *Urban Ethnicity*. London: Tavistock.

Cohen, Myron L. (1994), 'Being Chinese: The Peripheralization of Traditional Identity'. In Tu Wei-Ming (ed.), *The Living Tree. The Changing Meaning of Being Chinese Today*. Stanford: Stanford University Press, pp. 88–108.

Colombo, Massimo, Corrado Marcetti, Maria Omodeo, and Nicola Solimano (1995), *Wenzhou–Firenze. Identità, imprese e modalità di insediamento dei cinesi in Toscana*. Firenze: Angelo Pontecorboli Editore.

Comber, Leon F. (1959), *Chinese Secret Societies in Malaysia: A Survey of the Triad Society from 1800 to 1900*. New York: J. J. Augustin.

Costa-Lascoux, Jacqueline and Live Yu-sion (1995), *Paris-XIIIe, lumières d'Asie*. Paris: Éditions Autrement.

Crissmann, Lawrence W. (1967), 'The Segmentary Structure of Urban Overseas Chinese Communities'. *Man* vol. 2, no. 2, pp. 185–204.

Dikötter, Frank (1992), *The Discourse of Race in Modern China*. London: Hurst.

Dikötter, Frank (1996), 'Culture, "Race" and Nation: The Formation of National Identity in Twentieth-Century China'. *Journal of International Affairs* vol. 49, no. 2 (Winter), pp. 590–605.

Dikötter, Frank (1997), 'Racial Discourse in China. Continuities and Permutations'. In Frank Dikötter (ed.), *The Construction of Racial Identities in China and Japan*. London: Hurst, pp. 12–33.

Duara, Prasenjit (1997), 'Nationalists Among Transnationals: Overseas Chinese and the Idea of China, 1900–1911' In Aihwa Ong and Donald M. Nonini (eds), *Ungrounded Empires: The Cultural Politics of Modern Chinese Transnationalism*. London: Routledge, pp. 39–58.

Duara, Praesentjit (1998), 'Transnationalism in the Era of Nation-States: China, 1900–1945'. *Development and Change*, (October), 29: 4, pp. 647–70.

Favell, Adrian (1998), 'Multicultural Race Relations in Britain: Problems of Interpretation and Explanation'. In Christian Joppke (ed.), *Challenge to the Nation-State. Immigration in Western Europe and the United States*. Oxford: Oxford University Press, pp. 319–49.

Fennema, Meindert (1997), 'Some Conceptual Issues and Problems in the Comparison of Anti-Immigrant Parties in Western Europe'. *Party Politics*, vol. 3, no. 4, pp. 473–92.

FitzGerald, Stephen (1972), *China and the Overseas Chinese. A Study of Peking's Changing Policy, 1949–1970*. Cambridge: Cambridge University Press.

Flower, John and Pamela Leonard (1998), 'Defining Cultural Life in the Chinese Countryside. The Case of the Chuan Tzu Temple'. In Edouard B. Vermeer, Frank N. Pieke and Woei Lien Chong (eds), *Cooperative and Collective in China's Rural Development*. Armonk, N.Y: M.E. Sharpe.

Foot, John (1995), 'The Logic of Contradiction: Migration Control in Italy and France, 1980–93' In Robert Miles and Dietrich Thränhardt (eds), *Migration and European Integration. The Dynamics of Inclusion and Exclusion*. London: Pinter Publishers, pp. 132–58.

Frey, Luigi (ed.) (1992), *Aspetti economici dell'immigrazione i Italia*. Milano: Franco Angeli.

Fukuyama, Francis (1995), *Trust: The Social Virtues and the Creation of Prosperity*. London: Hamish Hamilton.

Gellner, Ernest (1983), *Nations and Nationalism. New Perspectives on the Past*. Oxford: Blackwell Publishers.

Giese, Karsten (1998), 'Patterns of Migration from Zhejiang to Germany'. In Gregor Benton and Frank N. Pieke (eds), *The Chinese in Europe*. Basingstoke: Macmillan, pp. 199–214.

Goodman, Bryna (1995), *Native Place, City, and Nation. Regional Networks and Identities in Shanghai, 1853–1937*. Berkeley: University of California Press.

Guiraudon, Virginie (1998), 'Citizenship for Non-Citizens: France, Germany, and the Netherlands'. In Christian Joppke (ed.), *Challenge to the Nation-State. Immigration in Western Europe and the United States*. Oxford: Oxford University Press, pp. 272–318.

Hamilton, Gary G. (1977), 'Ethnicity and Regionalism: Some Factors Influencing Chinese Identities in Southeast Asia'. *Ethnicity* no. 4, pp. 337–51.

Hassoun, Jean-Pierre (1992), 'Pratiques religieuses et entreprises chinoises à Paris. Un paysage favorable'. *Revue Européenne des Migrations Internationales*, vol. 8, no. 3, pp. 139–153.

Hassoun, Jean-Pierre (1993), 'Des patrons "chinois" à Paris. Ressources linguistiques, sociales et symboliques'. *Revue française de sociologie*, vol. 34, no. 1, pp. 97–123.

He Fulai (1893), *Xinning Xianzhi* (Local History of Xinning). (Reprint edition: n.l.: n.p., 1968 in three volumes).

Heitmann, Barbara (1999), ' Die VR China und ihre Nachbarn: 11. Die Auslandschinesen. Kurzbibliographie'. *China aktuell*, (Februar), vol. 28, no. 2, pp. 160–70.

Honig, Emily (1992), *Creating Chinese Ethnicity. Subei People in Shanghai, 1850–1980*. New Haven: Yale University Press.

House of Commons (1985), *Second Report from the Home Affairs Committee. Session 1984–5. Chinese Community in Britain*. London: Her Majesty's Stationery Office.

Hsu, Madeleine Y., 'Migration and Native Place: Qiaokan and the Imagined Community of Taishan County, Guangdong, 1993–1993'. *The Journal of Asian Studies*, vol. 59, no. 2 (May 2000), pp. 307–31.

Hua Linshan and Isabelle Thireau (1996), *Enquête sociologique sur la Chine 1911–1949*. Paris: Presses Universitaires de France.

Huang Daqiang *et al.* (1993), *Zhongguo xingzheng guanli da cidian* (Dictionary of Administration in China). Beijing: Zhongguo Wuzi Chubanshe.

Huang Sande (1936), *Hongmen geming shi* (Revolutionary History of the Hongmen), n.l.: n.p.

Huntington, Samuel P. (1996), *The Clash of Civilizations and the Remaking of World Order*. New York: Simon and Schuster.

Hyde, Francis E. (1956), *Blue Funnel. A History of Alfred Holt and Company of Liverpool From 1865 to 1914*. Liverpool: Liverpool University Press.

Hylland Eriksen, Thomas (1993), *Ethnicity and Nationalism. Anthropological Perspectives*. London: Pluto Press.

Jiang Jing (1984), 'Qingtian huaqiao zai Ouzhou de chuangye – ji Yidali qiaoling Hu Xizhen xiansheng' (The European Enterprise of a Qingtianese Overseas Chinese. In Memory of the Italian Overseas Chinese Leader Mr Hu Xizhen). In Wu Ze (ed.), *Huaqiao shi yanjiu lunji* (A Collection of Research Articles on Overseas Chinese History) Vol. I. Shanghai: Huadong Shifan Daxue Chubanshe, pp. 386–94.

Joppke, Christian (1998) (ed.), *Challenge to the Nation State. Immigration in Western Europe and the United States*. Oxford: Oxford University Press.

Kastoryano, Riva (1996), *La France, l'Allemagne et leurs immigrés: négocier l'identité*. Paris: Armand Colin.

Kastoryano, Riva (1999), *Transnational Participation and Citizenship. Immigrants in the European Union*. Aalborg: Center for International Studies, Aalborg University. *Discussion papers* no. 9.

Kastoryano, Riva, 'Turkish Transnational Nationalism: How the "Turks v Abroad" Redefine Nationalism'. In Flemming Christiansen and Ulf Hedetoft (eds), *The Politics of Multiple Belonging. Ethnicity and Nationalism in Europe and East Asia*. (Forthcoming)

Li Minghuan (1998a), 'Transnational Links among the Chinese in Europe: A Study on European-wide Chinese Voluntary Associations'. In Gregor Benton and Frank N. Pieke (eds), *The Chinese in Europe*. Basingstoke: Macmillan, pp. 21–41.

Li Minghuan (1998b), *Ouzhou huaqiao huaren gaikuang diaocha baogao* (Report of an Investigation of the Conditions of Overseas Chinese in Europe). Amsterdam: n. p.

Li Minghuan (1989), 'Amusitedan tangrenjie de lishi bianqian' (The Historical Evolution of Amsterdam's Chinatown). *Huaqiao huaren lishi yanjiu*. No. 4, pp. 31–39.

Liang Xiujing (2001), 'Exploring the Identity of Overseas Chinese Community Leaders in Europe' (PhD thesis presented to the Faculty of Humanities, Aalborg University February 2001).

Liang Xiujing and Flemming Christiansen (1998), 'Chinese Pan-European Organisations', in Lynn Pan (ed.), *The Encyclopedia of the Chinese Overseas*. Richmond, Surrey: Curzon Press; Singapore: Chinese Heritage Center.

Liu Nanwei (ed.) (1994), *Zhonghua Renmin Gongheguo diming cidian. Guangdong Sheng* (Topographic Dictionary of the People's Republic of China. Guangdong Province). Beijing: Shangwu Yinshuguan.

Liu, Tao Tao and David Faure (1996), 'Introduction: What Does the Chinese Person Identify With?' In Tao Tao Liu and David Faure (eds), *Unity and Diversity. Local Cultures and Identities in China*. Hong Kong: Hong Kong University Press.

Live, Yu-sion (1994), *Chinois de France. Un siècle de présences de 1900 à nos jours*. Paris: Éditions Mémoire Collective.

Live, Yu-sion (1998a), 'The Chinese Community in France: Immigration, Economic Activity, Cultural Organisation and Representations'. In Gregor Benton and Frank N. Pieke (eds), *The Chinese in Europe*. Basingstoke: Macmillan.

Live, Yu-sion (1998b), 'France'. In Lynn Pan (ed.), *The Encyclopedia of the Chinese Overseas*. Richmond, Surrey: Curzon Press; Singapore: Chinese Heritage Centre, pp. 311–12.

Luo Xianglin (1933), *Kejia yanjiu daolun* (An Introduction to the Study of the Hakkas). Xingning: n.p. (Reprint edition: Taibei: Nantian Shuju, 1992).

Ma Mung, Emmanuel (1991), 'Logiques du travail clandestin des Chinois'. In Solange Montagné-Villette (ed.), *Espaces et travail clandestins*. Paris: Masson, pp. 99–106.

Ma Mung, Emmanuel (1993), 'The Chinese Entrepreneurship in France'. Paper presented at the International Symposium on Ethnic Chinese Economy, Shantou University, Nov. 27–Dec. 2, 1993.

Mai Liufang (1985), *Fangyanqun rentong. Zaoqi Xin-Ma ren de fenlei faze* (Dialect Group Identity. A Study of Chinese Subethnic Groups in Early Malaya). In the series *Zhongyang Yanjiuyuan Minzuxue Yanjiusuo zhunakan yizhong*, no. 14. Taibei: Zhongyang Yanjiusuo Minzuxue Yanjiusuo.

Mao Qixiong and Lin Xiaodong (eds) (1993), *Zhongguo qiaowu zhengce gaishu* (Outline of China's Overseas Chinese Policy). Beijing: Zhongguo Qiaowu Chubanshe.

Marsden, Anna (1997), 'Le comunità cinesi viste dalla stampa: informazione e stereotipi'. In Antonella Ceccagno (ed.), *Il caso delle comunità cinesi. Comunicazione interculturale ed istituzioni*. Roma: Armando srl.

May, J. P. (1978), 'The Chinese in Britain, 1860–1914'. In Colin Smith (ed.), *Immigrants and Minorities in British Society*. London: George Allen and Unwin.

McKeown, Adam (1999), 'Conceptualizing Chinese Diaporas, 1842–1949'. *The Journal of Asian Studies*, vol. 58, no. 2 (May), pp. 303–37.

Mei, June (1979), 'Socioeconomic Origins of Emigration. Guangdong to California, 1850–1882'. *Modern China*, vol. 5, no. 4 (October), pp. 463–501.

Meng Hong (1996), *Chinesen in Berlin*. Berlin: Die Ausländerbeauftragten des Senats von Berlin.

Ministry of Civil Affairs (1995), *Zhonghua Renmin Gongheguo xingzheng quyu diance 1995* (Outline of Administrative Areas in the People's Republic of China, 1995). Beijing: Zhongguo Ditu Chubanshe.

Ministry of Public Security of the People's Republic of China (1993), *Zhonghua Renmin Gongheguo quanguo fen xian shi renkou tongji ziliao, 1992 niandu* (National Population Statistics of Counties and Cities in the People's Republic of China, 1992). Beijing: Qunzhong Chubanshe.

Office of Population Censuses and Surveys and General Register Office for Scotland (1993), *1991 Census. Ethnic Group and Country of Birth. Great Britain.* 2 vols. London: Her Majesty's Stationery Office.

Ogden, Phillip (1993), 'The Legacy of Migration: Some Evidence from France'. In Russel King (ed.), *Mass Migration in Europe. The Legacy and the Future.* London: Belhaven Press.

Original Compilation Group of the History of Taishan County (1985), *Taishan Xian qiaoxiang zhi* (The History of the Overseas Chinese Home Communities in Taishan). Taishan: Zhonggong Taishan Xianwei Xuanchuanbu.

Osterhammel, Jürgen (1997), *Shanghai, 30. Mai 1925. Die chinesische Revolution.* München: Deutscher Taschenbuch Verlag.

Pairault, Thierry (1995), *L'intégration silencieuse. La petite entreprise chinoise en France.* Paris: L'Harmattan.

Pan, Lynn (1990), *Sons of the Yellow Emperor. The Story of the Overseas Chinese.* London: Mandarin.

Pan, Lynn (ed.) (1998), *The Encyclopaedia of the Chinese Overseas.* Richmond, Surrey: Curzon Press; Singapore: The Chinese Heritage Center.

Pugliese, Enrico (1991), 'La portata del fenomeno e il mercato del lavoro'. In Maria Immacolata Macioti and Enrico Pugliese, *Gli immigrati in Italia.* Roma–Bari: Gius. Laterza & Figli, pp. 5–89.

Purcell, Victor (1951), *The Chinese in Southeast Asia.* London: Oxford University Press.

Redding, Gordon (1990), *The Spirit of Chinese Capitalism.* Berlin: de Gruyter.

Segre, Anna (1991), 'L'immigration extra-communautaire dans le Piemont et en Italie: Au-delà du travail clandestin'. In Solange Montagné-Villette (ed.), *Espaces et travail clandestins.* Paris: Masson, pp. 93–8.

Shi Cheng (1987), 'Qingtian huaqiao tedian chutan' (On the Characteristics of Overseas Chinese from Qingtian). *Huaqiao Lishi*, no. 1, pp. 38–45.

Sinn, Elizabeth (1995a), 'Emigration from Hong Kong before 1941: General Trends'. In Ronald Skeldon (ed.), *Emigration from Hong Kong.* Hong Kong: The Chinese University Press, pp. 11–34.

Sinn, Elizabeth (1995b), 'Emigration from Hong Kong before 1941: Organization and Impact'. In Ronald Skeldon (ed.), *Emigration from Hong Kong.* Hong Kong: The Chinese University Press, pp. 35–50.

So, Pamela (1997), 'Wo zenyang yishile wo de yuyan' (How I Lost My Language). *Brushstrokes – Juyanji* (Liverpool), no. 6 (June), p. 23.

Solinger, Dorothy L. (1997), 'Migrant Petty Entrepreneurs and a Dual Labour Market?' In Thomas Scharping (ed.), *Floating Population and Migration in China. The Impact of Economic Reforms. (Mitteilungen des Instituts für Asienkunde*, no. 284), Hamburg: Institut für Asienkunde, pp. 98–118.

Soysal, Yasemin (1994), *Limits of Citizenship. Migrants and Postnational Membership in Europe.* Chicago: University of Chicago Press.

Soysal, Yasemin (1996), *Changing Parameters of Citizenship and Claims-Making: Organized Islam in European Public Spheres*, in the series: *European Forum. EUI Working Paper EUF* No. 96/4. Badia Fiesolana, San Domenico: European University Institute, Florence.

Summerskill, Michael (1982), *China on the Western Front. Britain's Chinese Work Force in the First World War.* London: Michael Summerskill.

Taishan County Overseas Affairs Office (1992), *Taishan Xian huaqiao zhi* (Chronicle of Taishan's Overseas Chinese), n. p.

Teixera, Ana (1998), 'Entrepreneurship of the Chinese Community in Portugal'. In Gregor Benton and Frank N. Pieke, *The Chinese in Europe*. Basingstoke: Macmillan.

Thränhardt, Dietrich (1995), 'The Political Uses of Xenophobia in England, France and Germany'. *Party Politics*, vol. 1, no. 3, pp. 323–45.

Thunø, Mette (1997), 'Chinese Migration to Denmark: Catering and Ethnicity' (PhD dissertation, Copenhagen).

Thunø, Mette (1998), 'Chinese in Denmark'. In Gregor Benton and Frank N. Pieke (eds), *The Chinese in Europe*. Basingstoke: Macmillan, pp. 168–96.

Thunø, Mette (1999), 'Moving Stones from China to Europe: The Dynamics of Emigration from Zhejiang to Europe'. In Frank N. Pieke and Hein Mallee (eds), *Internal and International Migration: Chinese Perspectives*. Richmond, Surrey: Curzon Press, pp. 158–80.

Tilly, Charles (1996), 'Citizenship, Identity and Social History'. In Charles Tilly (ed.), *Citizenship, Identity and Social History* (International Review of Social History Supplement 3). Cambridge: Cambridge University Press.

Tomba, Luigi (1998), 'Exporting the "Wenzhou Model" to Beijing and Florence: Labour and Economic Organization in Two Migrant Communities'. In Hein Mallee and Frank N. Pieke (eds), *Internal and International Migration: Chinese Perspectives*. Richmond, Surrey: Curzon Press, pp. 280–94.

Tung, William L. (1968), *The Political Institutions of Modern China*. The Hague: Martinus Nijhoff.

Venturini, Alessandra and Damiano Bonini (1993), 'Politiche del lavoro per gli stranieri extracomunitari'. In Elena Granaglia and Marco Magnaghi (eds), *Immigrazione: Quali politiche pubbliche?* Milano: Franco Angeli srl, pp. 61–95.

Vermander, Benoît (1999), 'The Law and the Wheel. The Sudden Emergence of the Falungong: Prophets of "Spiritual Civilisation"', *China Perspectives* 24 (July–August), pp. 14–21.

Viroli, Maurizio (1995), *For Love of Country: An Essay on Patriotism and Nationalism*. Oxford: Clarendon Press.

Wakeman Jr., Frederic (1966), *Strangers at the Gate. Social Disorder in South China 1939–1861*. Berkeley: University of California Press.

Watson, James L. (1975), *Emigration and the Chinese Lineage. The Mans in Hong Kong and London*. Berkeley: University of California Press.

White, Paul, Hilary Winchester and Michelle Guillon (1987), 'South-East Asian Refugees in Paris: The Evolution of a Minority Community'. *Ethnic and Racial Studies*, vol. 10, no. 1 (January), pp. 48–61.

Wong, Bernard P. (1982), *Chinatown. Economic Adaptation and Ethnic Identity of the Chinese*. New York: Holt, Rinehart and Winston.

Wong, Maria Lin (1989), *Chinese Liverpudlians. A History of the Chinese Community in Liverpool*. Liverpool: Liver Press.

Wong, Siu-lun (1985), 'The Chinese Family Firm: A Model?' *The British Journal of Sociology*, vol. 36, no. 1, pp. 58–72.

Wu Daorong (comp.) (1920), *Chixi Xianzhi* (Local History of Chixi County) (Reprint edition: Guangdong Sheng Chixi Xian zhi. In the series *Zhongguo Fangzhi Congshu*, no. 56, Taibei: Chengwen Chubanshe, 1967).

Wubben, H. J. J. (1986), *'Chineezen en ander Aziatisch ongedierte' – Lotgevallen van Chinese immigranten in Nederland, 1911–1940*. Zutphen: De Walburg Pers.

Wuyi University (1993), *Wuyi Daxue 1993.11.28 qingdian zhuankan* (Wuyi University. Commemorial Print for the [Occasion of the School Anniversary] Ceremony on 28 November 1993). Jiangmen: Wuyi Daxue, 16 pp.

Xiang Biao (1998), 'Zhejiang Village in Beijing: Creating a Visible Non-State Space Through Migration and Marketized Networks'. In Frank N. Pieke and Hein Mallee (eds), *Internal and International Migration: Chinese Perspectives*. Richmond, Surrey: Curzon Press.

You Hailong (1996), *Yingguo huaqiao shouce*. London: Xingdao Zhongguo Shiye (Yingguo) Youxian Gongsi.

Yu Lehua (ed.) (1994), *Huaqiao shi gaiyao* (Outline History of the Overseas Chinese). Beijing: Zhongguo Huaqiao Chubanshe.

Yu Mingren (1996), 'Qingtian yuan zhuer' (The Maidens of Qingtian). *Qingtian Huikan* (Taibei), no. 68, pp. 29, 31.

Yuan Guoen (1991), *Longbao quanshu. Lü Ou ju Fa zuixin shiyong zhinan* (Longbao Reference Book. The Newest Practical Guide for Residents in Europe and France). Paris: Longbao Chubanshe.

Zhang Danian (ed.) (1996), *Wuyi huaqiao wenxian xuanbian* (Selected Documents of Overseas Chinese of the Cities of Wuyi). Hong Kong: Yinshui Shushi.

Zheng Dehua and Cheng Luxi (1991), *Taishan qiaoxiang yu Xinning Tielu* (The Home Community of Taishan's Overseas Chinese and the Xinning Railway). Guangzhou: Zhongshan Daxue Chubanshe.

Zhou Yumin and Shao Yong (1993), *Zhongguo banghui shi* (History of Chinese Fraternities and Lodges). Shanghai: Shanghai Renmin Chubanshe.

Zhuang Guotu (1993), 'Xin Zhongguo zhengfu dui haiwai huaqiao zhengce de bianhua (1949–1965 nian)' (Changes in the policy of New China towards the overseas Chinese). In Editorial Board of Historical Research on Overseas Chinese, *Zhongguo huaqiao lishi xuehui changli shizhou nian jinian lunwenji* (Collection of Articles on the Occasion of the Tenth Anniversary of the Overseas Chinese History Association of China). Beijing: Dongfang Chubanshe, pp. 308–23.

Zou Taofen (1936), 'Zai Fa de Qingtianren' (The Qingtianese in France). In Zou Taofen, *Pingzong jiyu xuanji* (Selected Epistles From My Peregrinations). Shanghai: Taofen Chubanshe, pp. 25–9. (Third edition 1947.)

Index

Adolino, J.R. 26
All-China Returned Overseas Chinese Association 129
Amsterdam Chinatown, atmosphere of 68; investment in 70, 71; location of 71; and meeting needs of the elderly 70, 72; planning/development of 69–71; and property-owning considerations 70–1; reasons for 71–2; as tourist attraction/shopping area 68–9; value of 69, *see also* Chinatowns
Anderson, B. 11, 180
Angel Island 37, 182(1n)
Antwerp Chinatown, and building an arch 74–5; development of 73; ethnic background to 75; and exploitation of cultural symbols 74; and performance of dragon dance 73–6, 184(8n, 9n); and rivalry with Amsterdam 75; and tourism 75–6, 184(10n), *see also* Chinatowns
Archaimbault, C. 102, 104
arches 27, 74; building 79–82; linked to prestige 79; location of 79; London/Manchester 80–2; support from Hong Kong elites/overseas Chinese 81; symbolic aspects of 79
assimilation 21; different systems for 22; and dispersal of immigrants 22; identity 3, 4, 175; lack of 4; and naturalisation 22, 181(14n, 15n, 16n); policies for 21–2
Association des Chinois résidents en France 106, 185(27n)
Association for Overseas Chinese History (Jiangmen) 89
Association of People from Taishan 89–90
Association of Qingtian Compatriots in Europe 100–1

associations, and change in meaning/function over time 96–7, 123; and Chinese values 117; and clique-formations 118; creation/development of 75, 82–4, 118, 186(2n); cross-border operations 123; and discourse of altruism 117–18; diversity of 114–18; effect of European unification on 124–5; EU links with 24–30, 123; leaders of 117–23; and membership registers 121, 186(4n); neighbourhood 73; professional/business 115; proliferation of 118, 122; Qingtian 100–1; as representation/non-representation of Chinese 116–18; Siyi 96–100; as symbols/institutions 125–6, 186(9n); types of 114–15; and variability of ethnicity 175–6; voluntary 82–3
Associations of British and Chinese University Students (abacus) 172

Baoan 93
Barth, F. 14, 177
Bauböck, R. 182
Benton, G., and Gomez, E.T. 149; and Pieke, F.N. 2, 170; and Vermeulen, H. 5
Berlincioni, M. 168
Besson, F.-J. 34–5, 36, 182
Blotevogel, H.H. *et al.* 27
Bologna 137–8
Bortolotti, F. 151
Bourdieu, P. 15
Brass, P.R. 14
Britain, ambiguity of system in 25–6; bifurcation of policy in 26; and problems of full participation 26; provision of services in 26–7; rules for

Italy, amnesty for non-European workers in 28, 29, 182(25n); business enterprises in 151–4, 168, 187(4n); Chinatowns in 77, 184(12n); concern for ethnic groups in 28; immigration legislation in 28–9, 182(21n, 22n,); labour market perspective in 28–9, 182(24n); local/central policy in 29–30; registering of enterprises in 29

Jiang Jing 102
Jiangmen City 88–9
Joppke, C. 181

Kastoryano, R. 30–1, 181

labour market, in France 154–5; in Italy 28–9, 152–4, 182(24n); in Mainland China 130, 187(8n); recruitment into 40–1
languages 177; and change over time 18; and creation of speech communities 18; crisis in 124, 125, 186(7n); encouragement of 138; Hakka 16–17; and lack of text books/support material 124, 186(8n); learning of 56–7; Mandarin/Cantonese 16–17, 18, 124, 180(5n); multi-lingual aspects 17–18; ranking between 17; Siyi speech links 89; use of local dialects 17
leadership 179; community 84, 117–18; elite aspects 119; features of 120; founders 120; honorary 120; interlocking 83, 84, 122; intermediary role 138; legitimacy/status 121–3, 124; multiple functions 118–21
Lee Teng-hui 168
Li Minghuan 123, 125
Li Xiannian 186(6n)
Liang Xiujing 117, 122, 125, 186; and Christiansen, F. 124
Lions Clubs 115, 172
Liu Nanwei 90, 184
Liu, T.T. and Faure, D. 13, 181
Live, Y. 45, 181
Liverpool Chinatown 77, 84, 85, 96–7, 98, 99, *see also* Chinatowns
London Chinatown 77, 80, 97, 99, 165, *see also* Chinatowns
Luo Xianglin 90

Ma Mung, E. 154, 157, 187
Ma Zhuomin 108–10, 111–12
McKeown, A. 180

Mai Liufang 181
Mainland policies 174, 179; and academic/scientist co-operation 134; changes in 129; and co-optation 138–9; dealing with new migrants 137–8; and decline in central control 133; and education 130; effect of protest movements on 134; and employment 130, 187(8n); and giving of status 132–3; and 'great cause of national unification' 134–5; institutional frameworks 128–9; and investment 131, 132, 187(9n); and local interests/Party ideology 132–3, 187(10n); and notion of 'Greater China' 135–7; and patriotism 133–4, 145–6, 187(11n); political/economic interaction 132–3; and protection of graves 133; and restoration of confidence 129–31; and restoration of property 130–1; revival of interest 129, 186(6n); and sharing in common struggle 129–30; significance of 129; towards Taiwan 139–44
Manchester Chinatown 77, 80–2, 84, 98–9, *see also* Chinatowns
Mao Quixiong and Lin Xiadong 186
Mao Zedong 135, 187(12n)
Marsden, A. 63
Martelli's Law (Italy, 1990) 28, 29, 182(25n)
May, J.P. 97
Mei, J. 90, 185
Mekong association 118
Meng Hong 183
Migrants' Forum 30–1, 182(29n)
migrants/migration 5; business purposes 42–4; case studies 49–64; chain 39, 48, 103, 153, 174; early European 92–3; illegal/Zhou Yiping case 59–64, 183(15n, 16n, 20n); institutionalisation/commercialisation of 39–40; Mainland policies for 137–8; mentality/global reality 95–6; myths concerning 37–40; New Territories to Britain 49–56; and recruitment of labour 40–1; as resettlement of refugees/political asylum 41–2; Southeast Asia to France 56–9; structuring influence of European states on 24–30; for study 44–7; and value of ancestral origin 19, 181(8n); waves/patterns of 40–9; within Europe 176